CRITICS PRAISE ANN RULE'S *NEW YORK TIMES* BESTSELLERS

THE END OF THE DREAM AND OTHER TRUE CASES
Ann Rule's Crime Files: Vol. 5

"In the hands of a master true crime writer like Ann Rule, their stories take on a poignancy that goes far beyond mere cops-'n'-robbers stuff. Without resorting to psychobabble, Rule tells us—through exhaustively detailed interviews with lovers, friends, and families—what led three such talented men to such tragic ends." —*Seattle Times-Post Intelligencer*

"Ann Rule's true-life crime stories read better than most fiction murder plots." —*St. Petersburg Times*

BITTER HARVEST

"True crime queen Rule continues her reign at the top of the genre with another tension-filled, page-turning chronology and analysis of a psychopath in action. . . . It is Rule's expert attention to detail that makes this Medea-incarnate story so compelling. . . . Through exhaustive research, Rule slowly reveals the widening chinks in Green's psychic armor as she fails in her first marriage, then in various attempts to become a practicing physician, and then in her emotionless marriage with her second husband. By the time readers reach the end of Rule's gripping saga of sin and murder most foul, they will understand at least partly the roots of Green's madness." —*Publishers Weekly* (starred review)

The sensational #1 bestseller!
DEAD BY SUNSET

"A cast of characters like this would provide fascinating material for any capable reporter. . . . Ann Rule is more than capable. The author . . . admirably recounts this labyrinthine tale . . . [and] brings to her work the passion, the prodigious research and the narrative skill necessary to create suspense."
—*The New York Times Book Review*

IN THE NAME OF LOVE AND OTHER TRUE CASES
Ann Rule's Crime Files: Vol. 4

"Arresting, that's what it is. . . . Ann Rule keeps finding true crime stories that somehow fell through the national press cracks, and retelling them in red-hot-off-the-police-blotter style."
—New York *Daily News*

A FEVER IN THE HEART AND OTHER TRUE CASES
Ann Rule's Crime Files: Vol. 3

"Like a fine police reporter, she digs and digs and recounts the stories behind the stories of obsession, betrayal and murder. In this field, Rule rules."
—New York *Daily News*

YOU BELONG TO ME AND OTHER TRUE CASES
Ann Rule's Crime Files: Vol. 2

"Ann Rule . . . dissects the dark heart of a killer with surgical precision. Nobody does it better."
—Edna Buchanan, *Miami Herald*

A ROSE FOR HER GRAVE
AND OTHER TRUE CASES
Ann Rule's Crime Files: Vol. 1

"Ann Rule . . . has a great knack for horrific detail."
—New York *Daily News*

Ann Rule's #1 *New York Times*
bestselling novel
POSSESSION

"A gripping, powerful and terrifying novel. . . . The author spares the beholder nothing at all." —James Dickey

"*Possession* kept me writhing in its grip from beginning to end." —John Saul

EVERYTHING SHE EVER WANTED

"Yet another true crime triumph for Ann Rule. . . . A magnificently constructed book." —*Washington Post Book World*

"Ms. Rule . . . now turns her devastatingly accurate insight to the twisted mind of a modern-day Southern belle. A measure of how well she succeeds is the feeling that came over me after reading just a few paragraphs about Pat Allanson. I wanted to reach into the book and strangle her."
—*The New York Times Book Review*

IF YOU REALLY LOVED ME

"Meticulous reporting . . . the characters are fascinating."
—*People*

Books by Ann Rule

Bitter Harvest
Dead by Sunset
Everything She Ever Wanted
If You Really Loved Me
The Stranger Beside Me
Possession
Small Sacrifices

A Rage to Kill and Other True Cases
  Ann Rule's Crime Files: Vol. 6
The End of the Dream and Other True Cases
  Ann Rule's Crime Files: Vol. 5
In the Name of Love and Other True Cases
  Ann Rule's Crime Files: Vol. 4
A Fever in the Heart and Other True Cases
  Ann Rule's Crime Files: Vol. 3
You Belong to Me and Other True Cases
  Ann Rule's Crime Files: Vol. 2
A Rose for Her Grave and Other True Cases
  Ann Rule's Crime Files: Vol. 1

For orders other than by individual consumers, Pocket Books grants a discount on the purchase of 10 or more copies of single titles for special markets or premium use. For further details, please write to the Vice President of Special Markets, Pocket Books, 1230 Avenue of the Americas, 9th Floor, New York, NY 10020-1586.

For information on how individual consumers can place orders, please write to Mail Order Department, Simon & Schuster Inc., 100 Front Street, Riverside, NJ 08075.

ANN RULE

A RAGE TO KILL

AND OTHER TRUE CASES

ANN RULE'S CRIME FILES: Vol. 6

POCKET STAR BOOKS

New York   London   Toronto   Sydney   Tokyo   Singapore

The sale of this book without its cover is unauthorized. If you purchased this book without a cover, you should be aware that it was reported to the publisher as "unsold and destroyed." Neither the author nor the publisher has received payment for the sale of this "stripped book."

The names of some individuals in this book have been changed. Such names are indicated by an asterisk (*) the first time each appears in the narrative.

An *Original* Publication of POCKET BOOKS

A Pocket Star Book published by
POCKET BOOKS, a division of Simon & Schuster Inc.
1230 Avenue of the Americas, New York, NY 10020

Copyright © 1999 by Ann Rule

All rights reserved, including the right to reproduce
this book or portions thereof in any form whatsoever.
For information address Pocket Books, 1230 Avenue
of the Americas, New York, NY 10020

ISBN: 0-671-02534-1

First Pocket Books printing August 1999

10 9 8 7 6 5 4

POCKET STAR BOOKS and colophon are registered
trademarks of Simon & Schuster Inc.

Cover art by James Wang

Printed in the U.S.A.

To my friends, a thousand homicide detectives from at least a hundred different departments around America. For almost thirty years, I have watched them work under circumstances that most people could never imagine. When the rest of us are enjoying holidays, spending time with our families and sleeping, they are often out in the field, slogging through rain, mud, snow, and sometimes blood. They are coping with the devastation that violence can do to the human body. They come to know and care for the victims they never met in life, and they strive to find who took their lives away even if it means working twenty-four to thirty-six hours without sleep. They are skilled, dedicated, dogged, tough, perceptive, tender, inquisitive, compassionate, hard-nosed, meticulous, and sometimes even clairvoyant. We all hope we will never need their services, but if we should they will do their best to deliver justice. Yes, the homicide guys are sometimes full of black humor—but I have also seen most of them cry.

Dedication

To my friends, a thousand homicide detectives from at least a hundred different departments around America. For almost thirty years, I have watched them work under circumstances that most people could never imagine. When the rest of us are enjoying holidays, spending time with our families and sleeping, they are often out in the field, slogging through rain, mud, snow, and sometimes blood. They are coping with the devastation that violence can do to the human body. They come to know and care for the victims they never met in life, and they strive to find who took their lives away even if it means working twenty-four to thirty-six hours without sleep. They are skilled, dedicated, dogged, tough, perceptive, tender, inquisitive, compassionate, hard-nosed, meticulous, and sometimes even clairvoyant. We all hope we will never need their services, but if we should they will do their best to deliver justice. Yes, the homicide guys are sometimes full of black humor—but I have also seen most of them cry.

And, finally, a salute to Detective Sergeant Don Cameron, thirty years with the Seattle Police Department's Homicide Unit, on his retirement. A better

Dedication

homicide detective never served. And to Chuck Wright, who also retires in 1999 after three decades with the Washington State Department of Corrections. Chuck has helped rehabilitate the thousands of people who have been assigned to his caseload, and he has also worked tirelessly for victims' rights.

Acknowledgments

With ten different cases, you can imagine how many different police departments and prosecutors' offices I interviewed and how many people have helped me put this anthology of case files together. I want to thank the following detectives: Steve O'Leary, John Nordlund, Gene Ramirez, Ed Striedinger, Steve Kilburg, Rob Blanco, Don Redmond, Paul Barclift, Dwight Caron, K. C. Jones, Dick Nelson, Richard Schoener, Keith May, Ted Forrester, Ted Fonis, Dick Sanford, Don Cameron, Dick Reed, Benny DePalmo, Duane Homan, Billy Baughman, Roy Moran, Ivan Beeson, Wayne Dorman, Jerry Yates, Bill Karban, John Boren, George Helland, Bob Fox, Len Randall, Rolf Grunden, and Ken Schnorr.

Many of these men have retired; some have died. They all solved seemingly impossible cases.

I also thank journalists Carol Ostrom, Eric Lacitis, and Eric Sorensen. And my friends, researchers, and first readers: Gerry Brittingham Hay, Barbara Easton, Donna Anders, Mike Rule, and Leslie Rule Wagner.

To my work crew, who are finally planting flowers and building decks where there was once only mud: Don White, Dave Bailey, and Larry Ellington.

Acknowledgments

As always, I am grateful for my agents, Joan and Joe Foley, and my editors at Pocket Books and Simon & Schuster, Emily Heckman, Fred Hills, and Burton Beals (who continue to remind me ever so tactfully that I am not yet the only writer in the world who never makes a mistake).

And I thank my readers. First, I thank you for buying and reading my books. Second, I bless you for your letters. They make me smile, make me think, and give me new subjects for future books. You can reach me on the Internet at www.annrules.com (my Web page) and at P.O. Box 98846, Seattle, Washington 98198. Sometimes I can't answer my mail personally—but I know you would rather have a new book to read than a letter. I *do* answer all truly urgent mail. If you would like a copy of my sporadic—but free—newsletter, send me your address at one of the above locations.

Contents

Contents

Truth will come to light; murder cannot be hid long.
—SHAKESPEARE

Other sins only speak; murder shrieks out.
—JOHN WEBSTER

Murder will out.
—CERVANTES

Foreword

It is difficult for me to keep a semblance of order in my office since my shelves are jammed with files, photographs, tapes and videos, notes on long legal tablets, yellowing newspaper clippings, and magazines full of the hundreds of articles I have written about criminal cases. Many of these cases are indelibly stamped on my memory, coming back to play across my mind at unexpected moments. And, surprisingly, I had almost forgotten some of them until I started to poke through my archives. I never remember names, anyway; rather, I tend to recall the *circumstances* of a particular crime in minute detail, as if I researched it only yesterday.

The cases in this book, my sixth volume of crime files, come from many different phases of my career. Some are drawn from current headlines, and others go back to the years when I visited one police department or another along the West Coast, asking detectives to tell me about their most memorable cases. In those days, I was raising four children on my own and I often wrote two articles a week to be sure we had grocery money. Along the way, I learned a great deal about criminal behavior, *and* about how good detectives solve cases.

Many of you have asked me to write a book filled with these shorter cases. *A Rage to Kill* is my answer to your request. There were various reasons why I didn't go on to write a complete book about these stories. A few were short, violent vignettes that made headlines for only a day or two. Others are from police files marked "Closed: Exceptional"—which means that the guilty person is *known* by detectives but, due to lack of physical evidence, has never been arrested. Sometimes, it was simply because the timing was wrong; I was already occupied with writing another book.

I must admit that a couple of these earliest homicide puzzles occurred so early in my writing career that I was convinced no one would buy a book from a young mother who lived in a little town in the State of Washington. (These occurred well before the Ted Bundy saga that I told in *The Stranger Beside Me*.) Even so, I saved them because I knew someday I would want to retell them.

The first case is called "A Bus to Nowhere," an almost unbelievable tale of terror that reads as if it must have happened in an action movie. The newspapers that carried articles about this fatal bus ride are still quite clean and crisp; the story is current, and the wounds of the injured are still healing.

"The Killer Who Planted His Own Clues" may make you feel that there is no safe place to hide, and "The Lost Lady" is a mystery about a beautiful psychic heiress that has stumped investigators for more than two decades. "Profile of a Spree Killer" is an in-depth look at a particular and unusual species of mass murderer, and "Ruby, Don't Take Your Love to Town" will probably make you cry.

Other cases in this volume are: "That Was No Lady," "As Close as a Brother," "To an Athlete Dying Young," "Born to Kill?" and "The Killer Who Talked Too Much."

These ten cases demonstrate how wide the range of human emotions that can lead to homicidal rage really is.

Because I have been fortunate enough to meet so many of my readers, I know that you wonder as I do about why seemingly normal people commit horrendous crimes. We also ponder the vagaries of fate that place people with apparently safe lives in the paths of killers. Sometimes their killers were complete strangers, and sometimes they were close friends or relatives. In many instances, I have been able to isolate the probable cause of homicidal violence. And then there are times when I simply cannot.

Going back through my work is a little like reading an old diary. I cannot help but think, "Had *she* lived, she would be forty-five now; she was only a young bride when she died," or "That case could have been solved so easily with the forensic technology of the nineties." Today, I wince to see that I described a fifty-two-year-old woman as "elderly" and a forty-year-old victim as "middle-aged." Our perspective certainly changes as we ourselves mature!

Some of these cases did not have proper endings when I wrote them. Now they do. One is still a mystery. Too many of them were not the final cruel handiwork of a particular killer, and I have, sadly, had to revise them to add new crimes. The men and women convicted in these murder cases ranged from brilliant and manipulative to downright clumsy and stupid. The one trait they had in common was *a rage to kill.*

A Bus to Nowhere

This is a case that might well have come out of a bad dream. It demonstrates how little control humans have over their own destinies, and how disaster sometimes comes while we are involved in the most mundane pursuits. Along with a million other people, I watched it unfold on my television screen. But don't jump to conclusions; this is not a review of the Columbine High School massacre in Littleton, Colorado, although the motivation behind the two incidents are, perhaps, almost identical. Rage and resentment hidden beneath a bland façade can explode in ways we might never imagine, and sometimes that kind of hatred can smolder for a very long time, even for decades.

On the day after Thanksgiving, 1998, I was cleaning my kitchen, which, for me, was playing hookey from writing. Like many moms with big families, I had spent all the day before cooking and this seemed a good time to try to create some kind of order in my kitchen drawers and cabinets. This was my idea of a holiday, polishing silver, lining cupboards and washing dishes while I watched daytime television.

But I was snapped out of my reverie when I heard the announcer cut into Oprah *with a news bulletin; his voice had a nonprofessional edge to it that gave away what was clearly his own shock. I looked up at my little kitchen TV set to see an image there that made no sense at all. I recognized a familiar bridge, but everything else was a jumble of crushed metal, emergency vehicles, victims with bloody clothing, and sobbing bystanders. For the next three hours, I watched, transfixed with horror.*

We all tend to think that really bad things are not going to happen in the town where we live—that we are somehow protected by the law of averages, fate, and even angels. The classic quote from bystanders who cluster around a murder or a multiple fatality accident is always, "Things like that don't happen in our town." Television reporters seem to love that quote, no matter how predictable it has become. But sometimes, terrible things do happen right down the street from where we live. The tragedy that occurred in Seattle on the day after Thanksgiving, 1998, was like that, and the reasons behind it made for an unfathomable puzzle at first.

I set out to try to find some answers. What I eventually discovered was shocking. More than any case I've written about to date, this one demonstrates that there are people who live and breathe and move among us who live in a completely alien world. In Seattle, on the day after a holiday that traditionally signifies warmth and love, one of those people brought untold pain to perfect strangers. I had to know who he was, what he looked like, and, most important, what drove him to do what he did. You couldn't really tell who he was from the statements of almost forty eyewitnesses; he might have been a dozen different men.

And no one knew who really lived behind his handsome, pleasant facade.

The Thanksgiving holiday, 1998, was no different from any other holiday, although Thursday, the day itself, was fairly quiet. Most residents of the western half of Washington State were grateful that the week's tumultuous weather had tempered just a little, and that there was power to roast their turkeys, since a storm packing 70-mile-an-hour winds had swept in on Monday and knocked power out in 200,000 homes. Ten inches of snow fell in the Cascade Mountains and the first gully-washing rains of what would prove to be a winter of record rainfall had begun. Thanksgiving Day itself was mostly cloudy, a little rainy, but the gale-force winds had diminished to only breezes. Friday was the same. That was fortunate for anyone living along Puget Sound or Elliott Bay; high tides of over twelve feet were expected and 70-mile-an-hour winds would have taken out a lot of docks and bulkheads and carried away boats and buoys. That had happened often enough over the Thanksgiving holidays of the past.

There are no holidays in a homicide unit; there are only detectives who have the day off, detectives who are on call, and detectives who are on duty. When something catastrophic happens, the whole police force is, of course, available. Those in the first category in the Seattle Police Department's Homicide Unit can breathe easy on a holiday, but the next two are either listening for their pagers to beep or working on open cases. Holidays tend to breed homicides; people who manage to avoid each other—and are wise to do so—the rest of the year are thrown together, with sometimes fatal results. They drink too much, get too little sleep, are worn out by travel, and generally tend to behave badly if they have a propensity for badness in the first place.

Detectives Steve O'Leary, John Nordlund, and Gene Ramirez were only on call on November 27, and thankful for that. They figured they were through the worst of the weekend by Friday. Steve O'Leary and his wife were having a delayed holiday dinner with her grandmother at a restaurant called Claire's Pantry in the north end of Seattle that afternoon. Between his turkey and his pumpkin pie, O'Leary happened to glance up at the television set placed there in deference to football fanatics. "When I saw what I saw," he recalled, "I wondered why they hadn't called me. A moment later, my pager sounded. And that was the beginning of it."

Traditionally, in every city in America, the day after Thanksgiving is the kick-off of the Christmas shopping season. Die-hard shoppers have barely digested their turkey dinners before they are up and headed to the malls and downtown. That was true in Seattle on November 27, too; most of the shoppers drove private cars, but hundreds of them took advantage of the Metro Transit park-and-ride lots located on the borders of the city. They rode the bus—no parking hassles that way.

Forty-four-year-old Mark McLaughlin was well into

his twentieth year as a bus driver for the Metro King County bus system, and he was a familiar and cheerful presence on the Number 359 daytime route from Shoreline in the far north end of Seattle to the downtown area. Mark was a big man with broad shoulders, a deep chest and a comfortable belly. He was six feet, two inches tall, and weighed over 250 pounds, and his partially white beard made him look a little older than he really was. Many of his regular passengers felt that he was a good friend and they looked forward to his kidding, just as his fellow drivers and the mechanics at the bus barn did. He could wrestle the huge articulated buses with an ease a smaller man might envy. McLaughlin loved his job, and he was a complete professional in a career that required a driver to be not only skilled behind the wheel, but adept at dealing with the problems, complaints and eccentricities of the passengers who hopped on board and took a seat behind him.

Driving a transit bus has never been an easy job in Seattle. Three decades or more ago, the buses got their power from overhead electric wires. They were half trolley/half bus, and their connecting rods were forever detaching and swinging free. Drivers had to stop, get out, risk getting a shock as they struggled to get their rig back on track. Later, Metro went to regular buses, but when the transit company purchased sixty-feet-long, forty-thousand-pound, articulated buses, everyone eyed them with suspicion. These buses had an accordion-like midsection that connected one ordinary-size bus to another. Articulated buses could carry twice as many passengers, and slide around corners like a Slinky toy. At first the concept didn't seem natural—or even safe. But some of the drivers, including Mark McLaughlin, were willing to give them a try. Before long, the behemoth buses were taken for granted.

Mark McLaughlin lived away from the city in Lynnwood, halfway between Seattle and Everett. He was divorced and had custody of his two sons, who were sixteen and thirteen. His seventy-eight-year-old mother, Rose, lived nearby, and he had brothers and a sister close by, too. After Mark graduated from Ingraham High School in 1972, he married his first wife, a local girl. He enlisted in the Army and trained to be a medic.

When his Army stint was over in 1979, he went to work for Metro. His first, young marriage ended and so did his second marriage, but he didn't give up on the possibility of finding someone who would be right for him. He raised his boys, drove the big buses, and hoped for a happier future. He found it in what had become his world—on the bus. Sometime in 1990, Mark was driving through the suburb of Bothell when he met a young woman who was a regular passenger. She was pretty and petite with long blond hair and she always got on with two small children, a baby carrier and a jumble of bags that held diapers, bottles and other baby paraphernalia. Mark always got out of the driver's seat and helped the young mother get settled. The sight of her struggling with her babies and their gear touched his big heart.

Her name was Elise Crawford. When the bus was nearly empty during off-peak hours, Elise and Mark talked. He learned that she was alone and he told her his second marriage had ended. After months, he asked her out and she said yes. Inevitably, perhaps, they fell in love. They became engaged and joined their families, moving into a modest three-bedroom house in Lynnwood. Mark welcomed Elise's children; he was such a natural father that he had been awarded custody of his second wife's son by her earlier marriage. Now, Mark and Elise had four children—his two, her two.

Mark and Elise had wedding plans for the spring of 1999. They were going to marry at his mother Rose's home, and his sister Debra was helping Elise with the plans. It wouldn't cost a ton of money, but they would have spring flowers, bridesmaids in pastel dresses, and a great buffet. Mark and Elise had each known lonely days, and this marriage was going to be forever.

When he wasn't driving a bus, Mark McLaughlin was an avid fan of the Seattle Sonics and Seahawks. He loved the outdoor opportunities in the Northwest, and he was a hiker and an amateur photographer. Elise worked as a nurse at Virginia Mason Hospital, and she took a second job clerking at a J.C. Penney store on the weekends. Mark was driving extra shifts, and it seemed only fair that she help, too. With four kids and a wedding coming up, they needed extra money. Their big dream was to buy their own home together, someplace with bedrooms enough for everyone. There was no reason to think they wouldn't be able to realize that dream.

Where they lived didn't really matter to Elise. After being alone with her small children, often being afraid of sounds in the night, she felt so safe with Mark. He was a big bear of a man who looked after everybody. "He was a wonderful man," Elise recalled of their happiest days. "We had just started to make it. I was never afraid of anything with him here."

As a nurse, Elise worried sometimes about Mark's weight and urged him to cut back on his appetite. But he seemed healthy, and he had boundless endurance.

and Elise had a perfect day on Thanksgiving; nt to his mother's house for a turkey dinner along w he rest of their relatives. One of Mark's favorite cousins drove down from Vancouver, B.C., for the weekend. He and Mark planned to take the kids on a hike on Saturday, but first Mark had a shift to drive for Metro. He started at 11:30 on Friday morning, driving Number 359. He would be home in plenty of time to eat leftovers and watch a few of the games during the football marathon that weekend.

Mark worked out of Metro's North Base located at Interstate 5 and 165th; he'd been there since it opened in 1990. It was close to his home, and daytime runs were usually pretty easy when it came to trouble from passengers, even though his route was one of three in the Metro system with the most incidents involving violence. You could never guarantee that there wouldn't be a drunk or some druggies on the bus, but there were certainly fewer than during late night runs. Drivers all over the city had had their problems with "gang bangers" and other riders who seemed to have more potential for trouble than the average passenger. On some routes, it seemed that the transit drivers had to spend more energy maintaining order on the bus than they did driving. County-wide, Metro was averaging about ten incidents a day. Some were only minor altercations among or between passengers, some were over fare disputes, and, in rare instances, the drivers themselves were assaulted. But, considering that 217,000 people rode the bus every day, the average wasn't bad.

A lot of the hassles were over fares, so Metro's policies dictated that drivers were to *request* that a fare be paid, but to back off if a passenger was combative. Keeping the peace was the most important thing.

Mark McLaughlin's easy manner and ready grin helped him defuse potential trouble most of the time. When he had to stand up and be heard, he was fully capable of doing that. But the day after Thanksgiving was a happy day. It was his last day of work before a week off.

Even the weather seemed to be a good omen. Suddenly, where there had been rain, wind, clouds, snow and sleet, the skies parted in the early afternoon and the sun burst forth. It was November, but it seemed almost like April. For an hour or two, it was shirt-sleeves weather, and neighborhoods along McLaughlin's route were alive with people taking advantage of a beneficent warm wind, and nowhere more than in Fremont.

The Fremont neighborhood is located in the center of the north end of Seattle. It was once a staid middle-class enclave, but it reinvented itself and became innovative, funky, colorful and much to be desired by those with open minds. Brazenly calling itself the "Center of the Universe," Fremont has shops with items found nowhere else. The statuary here ranges from someone's inherited life-size rendition of Lenin to the Fremont Troll. The Troll is a creation of artist Steve Badanes, a hulking monster three times larger than any human, who holds a hapless life-size Volkswagen bug in one mighty claw. Hunkering down under the north end of the towering Aurora Bridge, The Fremont Troll, fearsome as he looks, is also considered lucky and tourists and locals alike often meet at the cement monster.

At three on Friday afternoon, several young people left their small apartments to hang out near the Troll under the bridge, which runs parallel and close to the soaring Aurora Bridge, both spans crossing the Lake

Washington Ship Canal which cuts the landscape between Lake Washington, Salmon Bay, and Shilshole Bay. The young people below the overpasses could hear the rumble and *thunkety-thunkety* sound of tires overhead from the small and large bridges, but the noise was so familiar they unconsciously lifted the level of their voices, laughing and talking without really being aware of the traffic above.

Mark McLaughlin headed south toward the center of Seattle on Aurora Avenue North. Along the way, he would pick up some thirty-three passengers, as diverse in age and errand as any busload of people could be. The only thing that they had in common, really, was that they happened to be on the same bus at the same time. Some of them were going downtown to start their Christmas shopping, some were going to work, some to visit friends, and some were headed home. A few recovering addicts were headed for a rehab center. Although all schools and most offices in the Seattle area were closed that Friday after Thanksgiving, the bus would surely be at least half full by the time they reached the Aurora Bridge.

Jerome Barquet, forty-seven, got on the bus at Aurora Village sometime between two and three and chose a seat just in front of the bendable midsection on the right side. He peered out the window as they picked up other passengers and turned back onto the main thoroughfare, Aurora Avenue. Bill Brimeyer, twenty-three, sat about four seats in front of Barquet. Gary Warfield, also forty-seven, sat down close to Barquet in the fourth row of seats, and immediately began reading the textbook he carried. He was studying for a final exam, and needed to cram as much information as he could before his test.

Lacy Olsen was thirteen; she got on at Aurora Village with her friend, Brandy Boling, sixteen. They sat near the articulated divider in the middle of the double bus and began to talk and giggle as teenagers will. Brodie Kelly also boarded Number 359 at Aurora Village. He sat in the first section of the coach, but near the accordion divider. He had his earphones plugged in and was listening to his portable CD player.

Alberto Chavez and his cousin got on the bus at 145th and Aurora and took a seat close to the midsection of the double coach. Alberto looked out the window as they headed south. Barbara Thomas hopped on near the drivers' license bureau at North 132nd.

Jennifer Lee was sixteen, and a high school junior. She worked in the afternoons at a retirement home in downtown Seattle. She enjoyed her job and she was a breath of fresh air for the seniors who lived in the complex. She bounced down the aisles, oblivious to the driver and the other passengers. Regina King, twenty-eight, caught the bus at North 130th. She worked at a theater and she had already done some heavy-duty shopping that day. Her arms were loaded with packages. She found an empty seat, arranged her shopping bags on her lap and fell asleep, lulled by the sunshine through the windows and the hum of the engine.

Shawn Miller and his sister, Leanna, took seats in rows two and three near the front door on the right side. They didn't notice the man who sat in the first seat facing the driver until Leanna looked around, studying her fellow passengers. The man looked to her to be in his thirties, and he wore a dark jacket. It was his sunglasses that caught her attention. They had some kind of "shade" coming down on the side so that his eyes were completely hidden. She wondered if he was coming from an optometrist's office and if the sun was bothering him. He sat silently, staring at the bus driver.

Francisco Carrasco, thirty-one, had been visiting with friends in the north end of the city, and he paid his fare at 80th and Aurora. "I sat on the second seat behind the back stairs in the 'trailer' part of the bus on the driver's side."

Jeremy Hauglee was nineteen, and he headed as he usually did toward the rear of the bus, sat down and immediately put on his earphones. Soon he was lost in his own world.

Judy Laubach, forty, worked in the financial division at the downtown flagship Nordstrom's store. She had a flexible work schedule that allowed her to go in as early as nine A.M. or as late as noon, depending on her workload. It was very rare for her to head downtown so late, but on this afternoon she had debated going in at all. Finally, knowing she had some work to catch up on, she left home shortly before three, catching Number 359 near the Presbyterian church at Green Lake. She sat on the right side just behind the handicapped section—in the first seats that faced forward. Deep in thought, Judy was only peripherally aware of the man who got on the bus a few stops before the Aurora Bridge.

Herman Liebelt, sixty-nine, caught the bus, as always, near Green Lake. He had finished his weekly three-mile walk around the scenic city lake, had gone to visit an old friend, and was headed to the Urban Bakery for a cup of coffee before heading home to a senior citizens housing building downtown. Liebelt was alone in the world except for some stepchildren in California, but he wasn't a lonely man at all; he believed in getting out of his apartment and talking to people. When the weather was good, he loved to sit on a bench at Green Lake and discuss life and the world with strangers who paused to chat. He never lacked for someone to talk to; people seemed to be naturally drawn to him.

P. K. Koo was seventy-six, and spoke virtually no English. He took his seat three back from the front on the opposite side from Mark McLaughlin. He watched what was going on around him, and saw a number of people get on at various bus stops. Idly, he noted the tall white man who got on three or four stops before the big bridge.

Aurora Avenue North used to be one of the major thoroughfares in Seattle, but with the advent of the Interstate 5 freeway, it is now only a surprisingly narrow street lined mostly with businesses that saw their good years in the fifties and sixties. Passing decades-old landmarks like the trumpeting elephant sign and the Twin Tee Pees, the number 359 runs through neighborhoods, past motels and restaurants, the Washelli cemetery, the sweeping park with a walking track that surrounds Green Lake, and past the zoo at Woodland Park before it heads into downtown.

At Woodland Park, Mark McLaughlin detoured off Aurora to pause at bus stops along Stone Way North. And then at North 38th, he wrenched the wheel hard and headed up onto the southbound ramp that led back onto Aurora over the long bridge that crosses the Lake Washington Ship Canal. At its highest point, the Aurora Bridge arches 175 feet above the water.

It was a few minutes after three P.M.

Shortly after the long bus lumbered up the ramp, something happened, something that seemed almost surreal to those passengers who were alert to what was going on around them. They watched it happen almost without comprehension, the way the eye fixes on a magnified blow-up of some everyday item which, enlarged, *looks* foreign. It takes a few moments to recognize what one is actually seeing. The passengers could not compute what *they* were seeing.

There wasn't even time for panic or for anyone to stop what they watched. And, like many eyewitnesses, later they could not agree on the precise details of what they saw. The *only* thing they would be in consensus about was that a man got up, and walked silently up to the bus driver. Before they could wonder why he was getting up, since there was no stop on the bridge, many passengers heard a series of loud noises—"pops," "bangs," "firecrackers."

Some who were familiar with guns knew they were hearing gunfire; some were puzzled. And, then, within a matter of seconds, the 20-ton bus began to veer left.

Later, some of the thirty-three passengers on that bus would try to make some sense out of what had happened to them.

"Moments after I got on," Judy Laubach recalled, "I remember a gentleman getting up and walking past me. He had on a blue, horizontally striped shirt, and he walked up past the people sitting in the front of the bus. I didn't see the gun, but I heard two gunshots—BOOM! BOOM!—and I said to myself, 'He just shot the bus driver!' The bus went across the center lanes. I recall a couple of bumps and the bus came to a stop. I remember praying. I heard some gurgling—something—I don't know if it was me or a body next to me or what. Then I remember sirens and a rescuer coming to help. I remember looking up at a rescuer and some glass was falling in my face, and I remember him telling me to look down so the glass wouldn't get in my eyes. The next thing I remember I was in an ambulance, and the bumpy ride to the hospital."

Judy Laubach wasn't sure if she'd stayed inside the bus before it came to a stop, or if she'd been thrown out.

P. K. Koo tried to find the words to describe what had happened. Koo, whose English was so spotty that he needed an interpreter, said he had had a clear view of the gunman. "He said nothing at all. The man didn't do anything," Koo recalled as he tried to explain that there had been no fight, no argument, no incident on the bus. "He just got up and went to the driver. I heard two shots. He was about forty, tall, slim—a good-looking man. He had a jacket on and some sunglasses."

Henry Luna had been reading the manual that had come with his cellular phone. He heard the "pop-pops," followed by a second burst of sound. "People started yelling 'Gun! Gun!' I got down on my knees. I didn't even know the bus had been in a wreck until some people pulled me out . . ."

Francisco Carrasco didn't see the shooting. "I was talking with someone when I heard what sounded like a backfire," he said. "I remember the bus hitting something and I was thrown into the rear stairwell. I covered my head with my arms and grabbed hold of a bar, but when I looked, the whole right side of the bus was gone. If I would have been thrown another foot or two, I would have been gone, too. Diesel fuel was spilling all over me, soaking my clothes and head. I thought it was going to explode so I walked off the bus where the doors in the right side were missing. I remember the ground I got out on was asphalt. I walked across the street, dragging my left leg. There were people who tried to help."

When Regina King woke up, it was to screams and the sense that the bus had crashed against something. She heard no gunshots and no disturbances.

Thirteen-year-old Lacy Olsen saw it happen. She heard the "pops," and saw two bright flashes spit from the gun in the man's hand, and then scarlet blood that erupted, staining Mark McLaughlin's uniform shirt. Try as she might, she could not remember the man who'd held the gun in his hand. But she knew she had seen the gun, and the muzzle flash. "It happened really quick. I thought the man with the gun was sitting down."

Lacy couldn't remember anyone shouting or any angry words. But after the gunshots, the bus took off like a roller coaster. First there was a big bump as it hit something on the bridge, and then there was an awful sense of free-fall as the bus left the bridge. Lacy didn't know what was down below and she wasn't even sure that they weren't still bouncing in the air over the bridge itself.

Bill Brimeyer had seen what happened. "I saw a white male wearing a black leather jacket, a fedora and dark sunglasses standing on the right side of the bus driver. I didn't hear any argument or conversation. I just observed him shoot the bus driver—maybe two or three times. The bus swerved left. The last thing I remember is the bus falling. After the fall, I climbed out of the window and yelled for people to call nine-one-one."

And the bus *had* fallen, although some of the shocked

passengers thought it had only struck something. The sixty-foot long, double-coached, twenty-ton bus had been a juggernaut without its driver at the wheel; it had careened into the concrete and steel bridge and crumbled it as it plowed through, and then, with its load of passengers, Number 359 had plunged over fifty feet.

Leanna Miller had noticed the man with the sunglasses stand up and move toward the driver just as they started over the Aurora Bridge. "I heard two or three gunshots—it was a 'popping' sound, and the man looked like he was trying to take control of the steering wheel. The driver was fighting with the man, and the bus swerved from the far right lane through the railing on the other side, and we went over. I ended up on the floor and everyone was on top of me, and the bus was all torn up. I tried to help people out of the bus."

Jerome Barquet lived to tell about what he had seen, too. "At about the Aurora Bridge, I observed an unknown male dressed in dark clothing approach the driver as if he was going to ask him a question. I saw him shoot the driver in the back three times. I didn't see the gun or the shooter's face. The bus driver slumped over the steering wheel, and the suspect tried to grab the steering wheel. The bus veered left across the northbound lanes of Aurora Avenue North and ran off the east side of the bridge."

Jeremy Hauglee heard a loud popping sound even while wearing earphones. "I thought it was a rock and then this other guy stood up to see what it was. Then I got down real fast because it was like gunshots. I had thoughts of dying, and then the next thing you know, the bus goes over the side. I remember being at the bottom of the bridge, hoping my body would move and be able to run. I'd heard the gunshots and I thought the dude still had the gun."

Barbara Thomas heard "three pops like firecrackers. I looked up and saw a big guy, six-two and about two hundred forty pounds, wide shoulders. He was wearing a loose shirt with a blue and gray checked pattern. After three pops, the bus started to turn to the left and hit the railing. . . . It all happened in about thirty seconds."

So many of the passengers remembered that everything had been normal, quiet, like every other day—*until* they saw the dark-haired man get up from his seat and walk over to Mark McLaughlin.

Brodie Kelly "saw a white man go forward and stand next to the driver. He was middle-aged with dark hair. He shot the driver two times. I saw the powder fly out from the gun. The bus then went off the side of the bridge. I heard people yelling to get off the bus. I crawled off the bus through an exit window. I left my Jansport pack on the bus—with about twenty CDs in it, a small purple notebook and a book, *Kiss of the Spider-woman*."

Jennifer Lee, sixteen, heard two gunshots. She rode the bus down, fully conscious the whole time. She saw people hurt and bleeding all around her after the crash and followed the instructions of a man who helped her through an emergency exit on the right side.

Gary Warfield's attention was snapped away from his textbook when he heard two pops. He looked up and didn't see anyone near the driver, but realized to his horror that the bus was out of control and they were going through the guardrail. "I thought we were goners," he would remember. "I never lost consciousness—I landed flat on my back under a seat." He tried to move and managed to crawl to a seat and sit there until a firefighter found him.

All around him, people screamed and moaned. A few were staggering blindly toward where the right side of the bus had once been, but where now there was only a wall of daylight.

Below the north ramp to the Aurora Bridge, people ran from their apartments at the sound that seemed like a hundred garbage cans smashed together. Several of the residents who had been loitering next to the giant Troll beneath the bridge realized that they had escaped being crushed by just a few feet. Where there had been lawn and flower gardens, now there was, incredibly, a bus. They huddled next to the Troll as debris rained down from above.

Sasha Babic, who was once a diplomat in Yugoslavia, was sitting at his kitchen table when his wife called that she had seen a bus falling from the sky. He looked out the window and saw that it was true. A bus, all crumpled metal and gaping holes, rested on the front lawn of his building, its two sections angled like a boomerang. It was as if the hand of God Himself had set the bus down. Another six inches forward and the front of it would have sliced through the apartment house. Another foot or two backward and it would have crushed the people under the bridge.

It had come through the evergreen trees, wheels down.

Babic ran to put on some shoes and called to his wife that he was going to try to help.

It was so quiet. Eerily quiet, except for some groans of metal settling. Dust rose from the wreckage; the scene looked like something out of a war at the world's end.

Kurt and Cat Malvana didn't hear the crash. Both are profoundly deaf, but Kurt was looking out the window and had seen something that didn't equate with what he knew to be true of the world; he saw the rear section of a bus dropping from somewhere up above. And then he was shocked to see a human being flying out a window of that bus.

Through it all, concrete, glass, metal, and fir branches fell like a waterfall over the houses and the apartment complex where eighteen people lived. A tenant in a second-floor apartment had been getting ready to take a shower when he heard a tremendous crash. He ran into his living room to see that his front door was gone, ripped away with half of his porch. His goldfish still swam calmly in an aquarium only inches away from the gaping hole. Only a few minutes earlier, another tenant had walked out the door where the front of the bus now sat.

Bob Heller, whose apartment house was two buildings down from the crash site, was talking on the phone when he heard the sound of "a whole bunch of dumpsters crashing.

"I went outside to see what happened," he said. "When I came down the alley, and around the corner, I saw the bus. I saw people crawling out of the side windows of the bus—it had just come to rest there. I turned around to someone behind me and yelled, 'Call nine-one-one!'

"I went to the front of the bus because I could see people's bodies still inside. The folding doors of the bus were so close to the apartment building and adjacent to a tree."

Looking for some way to help, Heller scanned the

accident site and saw a man who looked to be in his late thirties lying on his back. He wore a tan jacket, and Heller saw that he had blood on his forehead and was unconscious—if not dead. But he checked his pulse; there was a faint beat. Heller moved on to help people who were still trapped inside the bus. He found a torn section of the accordion joining panel, and saw that many victims were still trapped under the floor panels which had been thrown around like giant plates. He helped the people pinned under them, and talked with others who were wandering around the wrecked bus, dazed. "I checked them for injuries, asked them their names, and then suggested that they just sit down until the paramedics could come and help them."

It was close to 3:30 P.M. when David Leighton, a young Coastguardsman, was in his red pickup truck, driving his uncle, Jim Dietz, east along North 36th Street just where it ran beneath the Aurora Bridge. They came up a little incline and ran into what seemed to be fog. People were walking back and forth in the cloudy air. Leighton slowed down because of the congestion. And then they saw the still-quivering hulk of the battered bus in the yard of an apartment house. What they thought was fog was really concrete dust from the ravaged bridge rail. David said to his uncle, "My God, that *just* happened. We have to help."

He pulled over and the two men leapt out. People had begun to pour out of their houses all up and down the block, the horrified looks on their faces mirroring Leighton's and Dietz's. There were no emergency vehicles, no police cars, not even the sound of a siren at this point. David called out, "I know CPR. How may I help?"

There was no response at all. It seemed that everyone still on board the savaged bus was dead. David Leighton moved quickly, checking people who lay on the ground outside the bus before he moved through the gaping hole where the right side of the coach had been. He was checking for pulses and for signs of breathing.

"The first person I came to was lying outside the bus and had severely broken legs," he said. "He was unconscious, but someone was tending to him. I asked if he was breathing and he said, "Yes."

Sasha Babic was there, too, trying to help. The front door of the bus was open, and two men lay tangled at the bottom of a pile of bodies on the bus steps. One appeared to be in his sixties and the other in his thirties. The younger man looked dead, but he made a choking sound as hands reached to free him. The older man's head was jammed between the bus door and the frame. Babic and other bystanders used all their strength to free him.

A woman was caught inside the door too, and she was conscious. From deep inside, they heard a man's voice soothing her, "It's O.K., sweetheart. Everything will be O.K."

One of the teenagers from the bus wandered over to a curb and sat down, his CD playing as if the world hadn't just crashed around him.

In the distance, the forlorn keening of sirens began to sound. The first call to 911 had been clocked at 3:13 P.M. The first rescue units would arrive three minutes later.

For the moment, neighbors and passersby did what they could. Everyone on the bus *wasn't* dead, although many of them were terribly injured. They had all plummeted five stories from the bridge overhead, without seat belts, bouncing around like BBs in a tin can, and yet almost miraculously, many of them were alive.

David Leighton and several of the people who had rushed to help smelled the pungent odor of diesel fuel. It had poured out of the bus's tanks and saturated the ground and bushes, as well as many of the passengers. A spark or a lit cigarette could send the whole thing up in flames, and Leighton suggested that those not actively involved in the rescue effort move away from the bus.

He moved to the front of the bus and saw the man trapped on the bottom step; he was barely breathing and he was coughing up blood. The young Coastguardsman turned his head so he wouldn't choke. "Then I and another man slowly picked up the three individuals on top of him—trying to keep their necks as straight as possible—and we put them on the ground. Then someone yelled there were more people *inside* the bus. I crawled through the front window. I came across an older gentleman who was in shock, and looking for his shoe. I told him to stay seated. I noticed another man, a thin, younger man lying on the floor of the bus with severely broken legs. He was barely breathing. Another volunteer said he would stay beside him until help arrived."

Leighton climbed out of the bus and met the first police officer on the scene. He pointed out the three people whom he felt were the most seriously injured. Even a policeman, trained for disaster, was shocked by the horror he found; the bus was awash in blood, and so was the ground outside.

Seattle Patrol Officer David Henry had been in Patrol Unit 205, with a trainee aboard: Student Officer George Aben. He'd heard a radio broadcast that a Metro bus had driven off the Aurora Bridge. Disbelieving, he wheeled his patrol car around and headed there, arriving three minutes later. He grabbed his microphone and told Radio that there were "mass casualties," with a large amount of diesel fuel on the ground. Using the public address system in his car, he cleared unnecessary civilian bystanders from the scene.

Throughout the neighborhood where the bus had fallen, people were in shock. Those passengers who were somewhat mobile were trying to help others who whimpered in pain or who didn't move at all. The bus seats were tumbled and bent, and the floor seemed to be gone. There was no way of knowing how many passengers might have fallen out of the bus as it came off the bridge, and no way of knowing how many might now be trapped beneath it.

Patrol Officer Sjon Stevens wasn't far behind the first patrol officers on the scene. Domestic Violence Detectives Monty Moss and Mike Magan happened to be driving nearby when a call for help came over the police radio. Not one of them could have possibly envisioned how serious the emergency was. Their first thoughts had been, "A driver's been shot, he lost control of the bus, and it hit the curb, or a tree, or another car. . . ."

But none of them expected to find that an entire articulated bus, half-full of passengers, had gone over the bridge and dropped straight down. And no one knew yet that the bus had actually clipped the three-story apartment house on the way down.

Someone yelled that there were people on the roof who were injured. There weren't *people* on the roof. There was only one, Mark McLaughlin. He had crashed through the windshield of his bus as it went over through the cement bridge rail, and he had landed on the apartment house roof. While Leighton ran to a nearby house to try to find a ladder, Officer Henry somehow managed to shinny up a drainpipe to the roof. He clambered his way to the driver of the bus and saw that he was terribly wounded with what looked like gunshot wounds to the upper right arm, chest, and abdomen.

Suddenly, there were other policemen on the roof, too, and they helped David Henry pull the driver up and rolled him onto his right side so he wouldn't drown in his own blood. The gunshot wounds were, at this point, unexplainable. Henry had responded to a bus accident, and now he found the man in the Metro uniform near death—and not just from the accident. As they worked frantically over the big man, they saw that his eyes had become fixed and dilated. Henry could no longer get a pulse, and he began CPR while another officer began forcing air into the bus driver's lungs with an ambu-bag.

Helicopters from Seattle's television stations had already begun to circle the crash site, sending images of the disaster into homes across Washington State. The newscasters' voices were low and worried. This was no ordinary news story.

A helicopter moved in—too close. For ten seconds, the image of Mark McLaughlin appeared, showing emergency workers hunched over him as they desperately administered CPR to try to bring him back. The newsman back at the studio said urgently, "No, no—pull back. PULL BACK!" and the picture on the screen changed to a wider shot of the crippled bus.

People watching at home knew they had intruded far too much into someone else's life. Perhaps in someone else's death. It was too early for any next of kin to be notified, and there was always the chance that someone who loved the injured man on the roof might be watching.

David Henry yelled down for a fire department ladder truck to move in and bring a backboard up. If the driver was going to have any chance at all to live, Henry knew they had to get him to the hospital immediately. Carefully, they strapped the man whose name they didn't even know yet to the backboard and lowered him off the roof.

But it was too late. Despite all their efforts, Mark McLaughlin would be the first person in the bus crash to be declared dead.

Seattle is known for its outstanding fire department, both for its pioneer Medic One program with highly trained paramedics and for its arson unit, Marshal Five. Now its paramedics were called upon to use their skill in "triage"; this wasn't a test situation where "victims" are made up to look injured with fake blood, cuts and bruises. It was a real disaster that not one of them could have ever imagined. *Triage* is a French word that means to winnow out or to sort. It is an essential response to catastrophes where many, many people are badly injured. Most lay persons became familiar with the concept of triage after the horrific bombing in Oklahoma City in 1995.

Rescue workers, physicians and paramedics are trained to quickly evaluate the conditions of those injured, to separate the living from the dead, the critically injured from those who can wait a bit for treatment. There were some beneath the Aurora bridge whom no amount of first aid would help, some who looked terrible, but who were only bruised and battered, and far too many who needed treatment immediately.

Seattle firefighter/paramedic Andre McGann faced an

awesome task; his instinct and experience made him want to start helping the first person he saw, but his job that day was to separate the living from the dead, and the critical from the other injured.

Wearing a bright orange vest that read "TRIAGE," McGann carried rolls of the thin colored ribbons like surveyors use, and a roll of adhesive tape as he went to work, marking human beings.

Was the patient breathing and did he have a steady, moderate pulse? Was his blood pressure within normal limits? Was he able to talk intelligibly?

McGann moved rapidly among the crash victims. Those in the worst shape got a red ribbon around the upper arm; they were to be transported by ambulance to a hospital ER at once. The walking wounded got green tags, and those who were in serious condition—but who could speak—got yellow ribbons. The dead got black ribbons. Later wrist bands would be put on with words that started with letters of the alphabet, followed by "Doe": "Apple Doe," "Blackberry Doe," "Cadillac Doe . . ."

Carol Ostrom, a *Seattle Times* reporter, would ask Andre McGann later to relive those first minutes after he arrived at the unbelievable scene. The most difficult task was examining those injured who were not visibly breathing. McGann recalled grimly, "You give them one shot—tip their heads back."

If he could detect one murmur of breath, he quickly slipped on a red ribbon. If they didn't breathe at all, he tagged them black, and resolutely moved on to someone who might have a chance to live.

McGann, himself the survivor of a pedestrian–car accident when he was seven, had lived though twenty-seven fractures and critical internal injuries. Being a paramedic was his destiny. He was doing the job he'd wanted to do for most of his life. He had only about five seconds with each patient, and he wanted to save as many victims of the bus crash as he possibly could. Like all Seattle Fire Department paramedics, he was conditioned to treat one or two patients at a time. He had almost three dozen in front of him. The name of the game was percentages, not individuals. It was agonizing for him to have to walk away from any patients that he might have saved had there been more time and more help.

At Seattle's prime emergency care hospital, Harborview Medical Center, the man who *was* Medic One and who had supervised the training of class after class of paramedics, kept in touch by radio. Dr. Mike Copass called the shots. It was he who would decide which patients would go to particular hospitals; no one could do a better job than Copass at assessing the capability of a hospital to treat so many injured. He talked to a medical command officer at the scene, and calmly gave hospital destinations. The worst trauma cases were loaded into ambulances headed for Harborview where they would be treated by crews who were adept at dealing with knifings, gunshot wounds, and accident victims. That was what they specialized in.

Gradually, the rescue scene took on a kind of organized turmoil. MaGann's tapes and ribbons marked those who needed help at once, and there were sixty-five rescuers, ten off-duty firefighters, five paramedic units, and twenty-seven aid vehicles on hand.

It was impossible at this point to account for everyone who had been on the bus; they couldn't even know how *many* people had been on the bus.

Lacy Olsen had wandered across the street. The thirteen-year-old girl remembered that the boards of the bus floor had "come up, and I was under them. People were yelling and screaming and crying, and I guess I kind of pushed [the boards] out of my way. I looked around and saw that the bus was basically split in half and I jumped out a window. I couldn't find Brandy. My eyes were blurry and I felt shaky, and I went across the street. There was a lady on the ground, and I was talking to her. Another lady came over—she lived around there—and she asked me if I was O.K. I said 'I think so,' but my ear was bleeding and my back was sore. It was hard for me to walk. I asked 'My friend? My friend?' and they said she was across the street. She was all cut up, and I just couldn't stand to see that."

Sixteen-year-old Brandy Boling had suffered severe abdominal wounds, a lacerated liver and kidney, but she was conscious and lucid. When Byron Juliano, who was employed by the U.S. West phone company, came upon the scene, he asked her what he could do to help. She replied, "Call my father," and she gave Juliano her dad's cell phone number.

Robert Boling answered his phone to hear a man's voice attempting to be reassuring, "Your daughter was in a bus that just went off the Aurora Bridge," Juliano said, "but she's O.K. She was on the bus, but she's O.K."

"She's *where?*" Boling gasped. "She's *what?*"

Both Brandy and Lacy would survive. They were taken to different hospitals and were both admitted in critical condition. Lacy had a severe back injury.

Judy Laubach, who wished she had never decided to go to work that day, was admitted in very serious condition with a flailed chest, a fractured scapula, a ruptured left lung, and a broken back. Like everyone else on the bus who had survived, she was covered with cuts and scrapes. Still, she felt lucky.

Francisco Carrasco had crawled out an emergency exit with his cousin Jose Navarrette, nineteen. They had wandered to another bus stop, waited, and then gotten on the Number 6 bus headed downtown. The two cousins went to a relative's house, unaware that they were in deep shock. Only then were they taken to the hospital, where they were both admitted.

Leanna Miller, who had tried to help others get out of the bus, was injured herself and was soon loaded into an ambulance. Her brother Shawn remembered, "I held on tight and I wasn't thrown from my seat—but Leanna couldn't hold on and she was thrown out of hers."

Laethan Wene, twenty-four, who had been on the way to a writers' conference, had escaped with minor injuries. So had Jerome Barquet, whose hand and arm were painfully, but not critically, injured.

Craig Ayers, thirty-seven, had severe abdominal wounds, Henry Luna had a fractured right leg and head cuts, Regina King had right leg and rib injuries, William Holt, forty-two, had a fractured femur and chest injuries. Catherine Tortes, thirty-nine, had a fractured spine, a broken leg and pelvic fractures. Amy Carter, eighteen, had a fractured femur and a broken pelvis.

Their cries for help had mingled together, as had the blood that flowed from their wounds. Fourteen of the most seriously injured passengers were taken to Harborview Medical Center, including Jian Suie, forty-two, with left shoulder and back injuries, and Charles Moreno, thirty-two, with crushing injuries to his arm and leg. Herman Liebelt, who at sixty-nine had still loved to walk three miles around Green Lake and discuss philosophy, was grievously injured with back, head, and pelvic injuries.

It didn't seem to matter where they had been sitting; their lives became dependent on chance the moment the bus they rode soared off the bridge. Those with young bones had done a little better than older riders, but all of them had come very close to death.

One of the first detectives arrived at fifteen minutes after three. Someone grabbed his arm and said, "My sister saw it! Some guy shot the driver. He was a white guy, wearing a brown jacket!" And then more voices called to him to go to the front of the bus. It was Sasha Babic, David Leighton, Jim Dietz, and off-duty firefighter Dave Birmingham, who were struggling to help the people caught on the coach's steps by the folding bus door that wouldn't open. The old man with the white beard had his head caught in the door and he was unconscious. The young woman trapped there was conscious but said she could feel nothing below her waist. The men exerted all their strength and the door finally gave.

The rescuers asked the detective to check on a white male who was lying with the lower half of his body underneath the bus. This was the man who had been on the bottom of the pile-up near the folding front door.

The man, who wore a brown vest, was unconscious. The officer saw that he had an injury to his right temple area, although there was so much blood that it was difficult for him to see how bad it was. The man was quickly loaded into an ambulance and carried away. At Harborview Medical Center, the man was found to be in far too critical condition for anyone to ask his name. ER physicians working over him realized that, along with his other critical injuries he, too, had been shot. In the head.

Once the scene was being taken care of by professionals, David Leighton, the young Coastguardsman, and his Uncle Jim weren't sure what to do. Leighton asked a police officer if he wanted a statement, but it was instantly clear there wasn't time for that—yet. Nephew and uncle, they were covered with wet blood, and they had begun to tremble ever so slightly from the shock of it all. They walked back to Leighton's red pickup and drove slowly away from the bus crash. Like so many others, they knew they probably wouldn't sleep that night.

The Puget Sound Blood Center sent out a call for donors to help the thirty-three injured people who had gone down with the bus. "[The shortage] could be pretty serious by Saturday morning," Candy Tretter, the manager of the Center said. "Types O and A, both positive and negative, are needed the most—as well as Type B positive."

A thousand people showed up to donate blood.

There was so much to be done. The Seattle AIS (Accident Investigation Section) was already on the scene, and their preliminary analysis matched the statements gasped out by victims who could talk, and those of witnesses who lived beneath the bridge. They could see that the huge bus had been headed south as it came up the ramp onto the bridge and that it had suddenly swerved over the center line while it was still over dry land. It had clipped a small van. Incredibly, that van driver had survived without serious injury. Seconds later, the front of the bus had taken out the cement and iron bridge rails and, like an action scene from a Dirty Harry movie, it had catapulted off the bridge, taking part of the apartment house roof and porch with it.

The AIS detectives were amazed that the bus had landed on its ruined tires after dropping over 50 feet. It could have been upside down or twisted like a snake, and that would have been worse. They began their Total Station recreation of the accident. To do this, they would take all the measurements of the bus crash both on and below the bridge to a fraction of an inch. Like surveyors, they used tripods, optics—tools that must be perfectly still as they measured. With a reflector, they "shot" the scene with a beam that gave them accurate measurements. It would take them hours and hours, but they were patient and methodical. They would be able to recreate this scene at any time in the future.

Where there had been frenzy, there was now a degree of organization as the AIS investigators took control of the accident scene.

Sergeant Fred Jordan, supervising the Two-George Patrol Sector, was armed with a description of the man who had shot Mark McLaughlin when he drove to Harborview. Most of the eyewitnesses said he had worn dark clothing, and all of them said he was Caucasian, tall, and had dark hair. As Jordan entered the Emergency Room at Harborview, he was met by Security Officer Karen Jacobsen. She handed him a plastic bag holding a handgun. It was a small caliber, shiny, steel-colored Derringer five shot. There were also some unfired bullets in the bag.

Karen Jacobsen told Fred Jordan that the gun had

been found hanging out of the right front pocket of one of the patients who had arrived from the bus crash scene, a man who looked to be about forty.

She escorted Jordan into an ER treatment room where she pointed out a tall, dark-haired man who lay naked on a gurney. He had a tube in his mouth, but all efforts to resuscitate him had ceased. He was dead. "That's the man who had the Derringer," she said.

The man's clothing had been cut from his body so that he could be treated. Jordan took possession of the remnants of his clothing, and bagged them for evidence in brown paper sacks, carefully initialing the bags, and adding the date and time before he secured their tops. These would be turned over to the homicide detectives who would be investigating the bus crash. The dead man had a yellow band around his wrist with the temporary I.D. given him : the words "Whiskey Doe."

Who *was* Whiskey Doe?

What had happened had happened. Even as the dead and wounded were carried off to hospitals and the King County Medical Examiner's Office, the time had come to find out *why* such a catastrophe had taken place, and *who* was responsible. It was ten minutes to four in the afternoon when Seattle homicide detectives received the first word that a Metro bus had crashed near 36th North and Aurora. The word coming back from passengers who had been able to blurt out statements to police and paramedics was that their bus driver had been shot.

And now he was dead.

Assistant Chief Ed Joiner walked into the Homicide Unit and asked the detectives there to respond at once to the scene. Sergeant Ed Striedinger and Detectives Steve

Kilburg and Rob Blanco left the downtown offices and headed north. The homicide detectives, whose job it was to investigate all suspicious deaths, raced to the crash site just beneath the north end of the Aurora Bridge.

The Aurora Bridge was a familiar place for them; it was the traditional site of suicides in Seattle, and had been for decades. The bridge was so high in midspan that death for jumpers, who were sick and tired of the world, was almost assured. A few people had survived a midspan plunge, but not many. Even more suicides had been accomplished by leaping off the ends of the bridge where the depressed jumpers had landed on boats and buildings. And, more optimistically, over the years police officers had arrived in time to save scores of would-be jumpers by talking them out of ending their lives.

The first phalanx of homicide detectives arrived at the bridge at two minutes after four. And there they saw a scene of such chaos that even they could barely believe what had happened. They watched as the last of the injured were carried off from the scene. Later that night, the bus would be lifted so searchers could check beneath it. If anyone had been walking outside the apartment house at the moment of impact, they might well have been crushed. The cluster of neighbors who had stood around the Fremont Troll talking and smoking were still pinching themselves with gratitude that they were alive.

As bad as the crash already was, the detectives knew it might get worse as reports came in from the hospitals where the injured were being examined.

But, as bad as it was or might become, it could have been a great deal worse. If Mark McLaughlin had been shot and then lost control of the bus only four or five seconds later, the double coach would have gone off the bridge over water that was a hundred feet deep. Instead of the injured landing in the front yard of an apartment house, they would have ridden the bus down and down and down to the bottom of the ship canal. Those who were unconscious and even those who might have managed to clamber out of the bus would surely have drowned. And then there would have been no statements about what had happened. No witnesses. No evidence. No survivors.

It was a terrible thought. Thirty-three people fighting for air under a hundred feet of murky water. The investigators wondered if that was what the shooter had planned all along, and if he had somehow misjudged the bus's location on the bridge.

Detectives Steve O'Leary, John Nordlund, and Gene Ramirez were paged to respond to the Homicide offices that Friday afternoon. Although many Seattle police officers and detectives would work to find out the reasons behind the shooting, the bulk of the investigation would be done by these three men. They were sent directly to Harborview Hospital, so they could begin to sort out the mystery of the crash of metro Number 359.

Among the three of them, they had almost fifty years of experience in solving homicides; still, they had never had a case quite like the one they faced now.

Each of them had come to Homicide through a circuitous route. Steve O'Leary had wanted to be a chef. Seattle's grand old Olympic Hotel had the best chef's training program in the area and he had applied there. "They said they didn't have any openings, and asked me if I wanted to be a bellman. I said, 'What's that?' " But O'Leary needed a job because he was going to college, so he soon found out that bellmen carried thousands of pounds of luggage.

The Olympic's bellmen shared an office with the hotel's security officers, all of them off-duty cops. "I got to know a lot of these policemen," O'Leary remembered. "I started scuba diving with them, and one of my cop friends said, 'Why don't you go down and take the test?' "

It sounded interesting to O'Leary. He passed with a high score, and was hired by the Seattle Police Department December 1, 1979. He never became a chef, but being a cop suited him. He walked a beat on the waterfront and in Chinatown for five years, worked with the Swat Team and Special Patrol, and then was assigned as a detective to the Sex Crimes Unit.

One of the things that tugged at O'Leary's heart the most was seeing children so afraid of testifying against their abusers. He devised a way to give them a little bit of power. "I loaned them my badge while they were on the stand," he said. "I pinned it underneath their clothes and no one could see it. But those kids knew it was there, and it seemed to give them some comfort."

O'Leary came into Homicide in October 1989. It was an assignment that few detectives ever want to leave, and he was no different.

Gene Ramirez started out in Patrol, but he broke department policy that says every rookie must work five years in Patrol before he can become a detective. Detective Sergeant Don Cameron had a major case where he needed someone who was fluent in Spanish to serve as an interpreter. After three years on Patrol, Gene Ramirez was assigned temporarily to Homicide. Not only was he a remarkably good interpreter, he proved to be a natural homicide detective. "I'm still here," Ramirez says, smiling. "I've been here for sixteen years." The other detectives call him "Eugenio."

John Nordlund served in the Navy until 1966, and then became a clerk in the FBI in Seattle. Asked what he did there, he immediately says, "I can't tell you," but then he smiles. Like all FBI employees, he had signed a document swearing him to secrecy about the inner workings of the Federal Bureau of Investigation.

Nordlund wanted to work in law enforcement in a more active way, and the Seattle Police Department was hiring. Another FBI clerk had signed on and encouraged Nordlund to give it a try. Initially, it was a way to stay in Seattle. "I was raised in Ballard [the city's Scandinavian enclave]," he said, "and I'd already been around the world with the Navy; I wanted to stay home."

Although they'd worked hundreds of homicide cases, each of the three detectives had cases they would never forget. Steve O'Leary solved the gruesome axe murder of a widow, using, among other clues, a single fingerprint and a stolen banana to establish commonalities between that murder and another attempted axe murder. John Nordlund worked the Wah Mee Massacre, where thirteen people were gunned down in an after-hours gambling spot in Seattle's Chinatown. The investigators who did the crime scene quite literally waded up to their pant cuffs in the blood that flowed from the victims. Nordlund and Don Cameron found the two gunmen who had been quite willing to sacrifice more than a dozen lives in exchange for gambling money.

Gene Ramirez remembered a 1996 case where a young man was killed under the Alaskan Way Viaduct. Ramirez had a perfect case, a perfect witness—until they got into court and he learned his witness had been in jail at the time he said he'd seen a murder. Disappointed for a while, Ramirez found a better witness. His deceptively gentle questioning elicited the *real* eyewitness, a girlfriend who had seen it all.

The trio of homicide detectives were as different in personality as it was possible to be; O'Leary was garrulous and enthusiastic, Nordlund, deadpan and cynical— at least on the surface—and Ramirez, soft-spoken and thoughtful. Each one of them was a meticulous investigator who knew people, psychology and how to work a crime scene. Together, they were a dynamite team.

Now, they were starting at the bottom step of a case that was basically "Murder and Attempted Murder of Thirty-Four Victims." They would try to determine if the killer was still alive. They wondered if it was possible that the shooter was one of the people who had been admitted to six different hospitals: Harborview, University of Washington Medical Center, Swedish Medical Center (First Hill), Swedish Medical Center (Ballard), Providence Medical Center, Northwest Hospital and Virginia Mason Medical Center. If the killer had been so angry at someone or some *thing* that he had been willing to sacrifice a whole busload of strangers, there was no guarantee that he would stop there.

There was a real sense of urgency about finding out the reasons behind what had just happened. Had the shooter been after Mark McLaughlin *personally,* or had he only been a target for what he represented?

While Gene Ramirez went to the scene of the crash, John Nordlund and Steve O'Leary joined Sergeant Fred Jordan at Harborview where he was standing by the body of the victim known only as Whiskey Doe. They studied the corpse. The man looked to be in his late thirties or early forties, he was quite handsome and well-groomed and was over six feet tall. Now that the ER staff had wiped the blood away, they recognized a contact bullet wound to the right side of his head.

Jordan showed them the bag containing Whiskey Doe's clothes; he had worn a brown insulated vest, a long-sleeved purple shirt, blue jeans, a blue-black rubberized waist strap—the kind that people who wanted to lose weight wore—a black tank-top with a Nike logo on it, thong-style briefs with blue and black horizontal stripes, and a blue tie with circular red designs, which was attached to a red and white elastic strap with duct tape. There was an additional red and white strap. Except for the last two items, the clothing was fairly expensive and hardly unusual. The weight-loss strap was strange; the dead man was not at all overweight.

He had had $12.75 in bills and change, a Swiss army knife, a key chain with three keys attached, and a Metro bus transfer. He had carried a gun, yes, but the derringer's cylinder was still loaded with five bullets. He hadn't fired it.

Jane Jorgensen, an investigator for the King County Medical Examiner's Office, would take custody of Whiskey Doe's body. She would roll his fingerprints so they could be run through AFIS (Automated Fingerprint Identification System) to see if there would be a match. Almost anyone in America who has applied for a job, joined the service, or been arrested has fingerprints on file somewhere.

While the detectives were at the Medical Examiner's office, the body of the bus driver was brought in. They learned the identity of the first victim in the puzzling shooting: Mark Francis McLaughlin, who was born on June 13, 1954. His address was listed as a single family dwelling in Lynnwood. They listened to a cursory report on his injuries: "two gunshot wounds to the right side." It would take a complete autopsy to know the extent of the damage caused by those shots.

O'Leary, Nordlund and Ramirez headed out to some of the other hospitals where victims were being treated. They would begin with interviews with those passengers who were able to talk: Jeremy Hauglee, Lacy Olsen, and P. K. Koo all gave O'Leary halting versions of the nightmare they had survived only hours before.

At 7:30 that first night, ID Tech Joyce Monroe entered Whiskey Doe's thumbprints into the AFIS computers. It wasn't long before an answer came back: the man was identified as Steven Gary Coole, but, oddly, several birthdates came back: 5/14/57, 5/14/59, 5/15/57 and 5/15/59. Steven Coole had been arrested for shoplifting at the Green Lake Albertson's Grocery store. Along with that, he had been charged with public park code violations, false reporting, and "obstructing." He had been in jail in July 1994 for those offenses. There was another shoplifting arrest listed in 1991. There was no information on *what* he had been accused of shoplifting, and there were no current warrants out for Coole.

It was a start. They had gone from being completely in the dark about Coole's identity to the knowledge that he was probably from the Green Lake–North End area, and that he'd been arrested for some minor crimes. They still didn't know if Coole was a victim or a shooter. Most of the witnesses had recalled hearing *two* spates of shots. Either the shooter had shot *both* McLaughlin and the man known as Steve Coole, or Coole himself had been the shooter. If the latter was true, he might have been fatally injured as McLaughlin fought with him over control of the bus.

Efforts would be made now to contact all Seattle hospitals to see if there was a medical history on file anywhere for a Steven Coole, and that could lead to information on his next of kin. In the meantime, Coole wasn't the only passenger whose name would be run through the computers for prior criminal history. But nothing much beyond traffic tickets and some minor drug violations popped up. Somebody on that bus had carried a dark secret inside his head, and the three investigators still had no idea who it was.

Steve O'Leary headed out to talk with more of the injured at one hospital, while John Nordlund went to see others on the list. It was not an easy job. Many of the passengers spoke no English, a few were developmentally disabled, one or two had been drinking just before they got on the bus, and all were in shock and in pain; very few were in a state to provide clear and coherent statements.

At the very least, the two detectives figured they could eliminate possible suspects as they questioned one after another of the people who had been on the bus. They weren't naive enough after years in Homicide to believe they could spot a killer just by talking to him, but they relied on a certain sixth sense, too.

AFIS was demonstrating once again what a remarkable investigative tool it was. Before the whorls, loops and ridges of fingerprints could be matched by a computer, using fingerprints as a means of identifying someone was catch as catch can. The FBI kept single prints on record *only* for the most wanted criminals in America, and all ten prints were necessary to identify an *ordinary* criminal. But the AFIS system has virtually changed the forensic identification world. One lone fingerprint can elicit remarkable information. Now, an investigator for the Medical Examiner's office called Steve O'Leary at 9:30 that first night to say that AFIS had spit out another hit on the prints taken from the unknown man with the bullet hole in his head. But the new information only made the case more bizarre.

On November 16, less than two weeks earlier, a King County ID officer had run prints of a John Doe for the Lynnwood Police Department. "They came back to a Steve Gary Coole."

O'Leary was elated, but not for long. Lynnwood police had arrested Steve Coole, but they didn't really know who he was. He was only a most peculiar man who had been hanging around a local park. On November 9, 1998, at about 1:30 in the afternoon, a father had been waiting for his nine-year-old daughter to take a shower after a swim in the pool at the Recreation Pavilion in Montlake Terrace, Washington. Because it was a public facility, he stood guard outside the curtain where she showered. He was glad he had when he was startled to see a tall man walk up and boldly peer over his shoulder into the shower stall.

"Back off," the father had said forcefully. "My daughter's taking a shower in there."

The man, who was described as tall and slender with a mop of brown hair streaked with gray, did move away—but only for a moment. He kept coming back, and walking much too close to the shower area several times, initially ignoring the father's warnings. "On the third warning, he finally left," the father told the Lynnwood police. "But I remembered him and what he looked like."

One of the lifeguards had noticed the man too, and she wondered why he was hanging around the pool.

A week after the incident, the girl and her father were again at the Montlake Terrace pool when he saw the man who had acted so strangely before. He decided that he wasn't going to wait for trouble; he dialed 911. The officer who responded to the call spotted the suspect in the Jacuzzi, and waited for him to move into the locker room. There, he attempted to talk with him. He took the most basic initial approach, asking the tall man who he was and when his birthday was. But the stranger insisted he didn't have any identification on him. Finally, he agreed to give the officer his name.

"Stewart Coltrane*," he said, adding that his birthdate was May 15, 1957.

"Why were you hanging around the girls' showers last week?" the policemen asked. "You were making people nervous."

Coltrane was adamant that he had done nothing wrong. "I just wanted to use the shower," he said. "She was taking too long, and I was getting impatient. I just wanted to see if she was done yet."

But he had been so persistent that he had alarmed the little girl's father, and he didn't seem to understand that, at best, he had used bad judgment. He insisted that he'd been within his rights. The officer told Coltrane it would be best if he left the Rec Pavilion. He headed off down the street, while the investigating officer checked computer bases for Coltrane's name. He learned there *was* no Stewart Coltrane who'd been born on 5/15/57, and he quickly steered his patrol car in the direction the suspect had walked.

"I got nothing on that name and birthday you gave me," the officer said when he caught up with the tall man, and Coltrane quickly gave him three more birthdays: May 14, 1957, May 15, 1959, and May 14, 1959. He didn't seem to be developmentally disabled, but he didn't even know his own birthdate! None of the dates he gave drew any hits on the computers as matching up with the name Stewart Coltrane. The suspect had then explained that he was from New Jersey. Maybe that was why the Northwest computers had no record of him. The policeman nodded and ran the name and the four birthdates through New Jersey computers. They drew no hits either.

Coltrane refused to show any documentation that would prove his identity, nor would he give the names of anyone who might identify him. If he hadn't been hanging around kids in the shower, the officer would have let it go. But there was something a little ominous about the man. He wouldn't give his home address or phone number. He demanded to talk to an attorney, deliberately escalating the conversation into an incident. At length, when he still would not give any accurate information about himself, he was booked into the Lynnwood jail for "obstructing."

"Stewart Coltrane" was given a "cash only" bail of $1,000. He wasn't in jail long. Someone in New Jersey contacted a bail bondsman in Seattle who provided the $1,000 bail. Stewart Coltrane, the alias for Steve Coole, walked out of the Lynnwood Jail a free and unidentified man.

O'Leary and Nordlund found the latest information

confusing. If the dead man from the bus crash was both the shooter and the suspected child molester in Lynnwood, it made no sense. The M.O.s were completely different, and they both knew that the profiles for sex offenders and mass killers weren't the same.

Even so, the Seattle homicide detectives were getting closer to finding out who the dead man really was. They ran the name Stewart Coltrane and found an address on 15th N.E. Gene Ramirez, O'Leary and Nordlund headed out there at 10:30 Friday night. They found the Ponderay Apartments easily enough, a four-story, square building in the University District.

It wasn't difficult locating Coltrane's unit; he was listed as the manager of the apartment house there. *That* was a bit of a surprise. They knocked, not really expecting anyone to answer; they figured Coltrane was lying on a slab at the M.E.'s office.

But someone answered the door, a large man with glasses. His hair wasn't shot with gray and he was neither tall nor slender. "I'm Stewart Coltrane," he acknowledged. "How can I help you?"

Coltrane gave his birthdate, and it wasn't even close to the ones given by the man at the public pool in Lynnwood. He looked as puzzled as the investigators until John Nordlund mentioned the name "Coole." Coltrane nodded. He knew a man named Cool. *"Silas Cool,"* he said. "You must mean Silas Cool. He's one of the tenants here. I hardly know him, but let me take a look at his records."

Coltrane checked the rent ledger. "Cool moved into Apartment 209 on June 18, 1985. He pays rent of $475 a month."

"What's he like?" O'Leary asked.

"I couldn't tell you."

"He's lived here for more than thirteen years, and you don't know what he's like?"

"I never see him. He keeps to himself. I see him maybe two, three times a year, tops."

Ironically, the real Stewart Coltrane's career dealt with people who were mentally and emotionally disturbed and he considered himself fairly good at recognizing people who were on the edge. He had never seen anything that unusual about Silas Cool, save for the fact that he was a loner. Coltrane said Cool paid his rent on time, minded his own business, and always kept his windows covered. As far as he knew, nobody in the apartment house knew Cool any better than he did.

It was with a mixture of anticipation and apprehension that Coltrane and the three homicide detectives headed up the stairs to the south side of the building. They noted two small windows in the back of the unit as they stood outside the door to Apartment 209. They knocked, but no one answered. They hadn't really expected that anyone would. Then Coltrane slipped the master key into the lock and turned the knob.

Ramirez, Nordlund, and O'Leary entered a dark apartment that smelled of dead air, dust, dirty clothes, and a strange sweet-sour mediciney odor. Even when they switched on a light, it was still dim; the bulbs were only forty watt. But they could see that this was a very small one bedroom unit. A short entry hallway led to the living room. There was a combination dining-room/kitchen area adjoining that, and a door led back to a bedroom and bathroom. The place was unkempt and dreary, and it had only a few cheap pieces of furniture. It looked lonely, and had a flat, lifeless quality about it.

Nordlund, Ramirez and O'Leary were looking for answers to what seemed an unsolvable mystery. If Silas Cool *was* the second fatality of the bus crash, they would never be able to ask him what had happened. All they could do was hope that there were some clues in his drab apartment.

They didn't have to move far inside before they spotted something that gave them goosebumps. There on the cluttered divider between the entry hall and the dining area were stacks of Metro Transit schedules, far too many for an average bus rider to have kept. They towered more than a foot high, and had begun to tumble down onto the dining room floor. They were for many different bus routes, all over the City of Seattle, and for other cities, too. Here, too, were notes Cool had written to himself, reminders that if he missed a Number 6 bus, he could catch a Number 40 within minutes. It looked as if Silas Cool's life had revolved around buses.

A man's wallet lay on the divider, too, with a driver's license inside made out to Silas Garfield Cool, born on May 14, 1955. That was a familiar date; the suspect at the pool had apparently given his correct birthdate—but with the wrong year, and his apartment manager's name instead of his own. However, this driver's license had expired in 1987, *eleven years earlier.*

The whole apartment had that lifeless feeling, like a place out of a William Faulkner story. The picture on the license was of a very handsome young man, a man probably in his late twenties. He *looked* like a younger version of the man in the ER, but it was hard to be sure.

They walked through the apartment, aware of their own footsteps, half-holding their breaths against the stale odor. There was a jumble of papers on the dining room table. Among them, O'Leary found a card from an attorney in North Plainfield, New Jersey. On the back, someone had jotted down a man's name and a Bainbridge Island, Washington, address.

The living room was sparsely furnished, although it was cluttered with papers, clothes, bags and boxes. There was a single, uncomfortable-looking chair with an ottoman in the living room, and two black-and-white television sets. There was a bookcase, but there were no books or magazines, no newspapers—nothing to keep the man who lived in the apartment up with current events. On one of the bookcase shelves, Gene Ramirez located a gun holder for an AMT .38 caliber pistol, a holster for a derringer, and a cigar box that held nine live rounds for a .38 caliber weapon.

The detectives photographed the room and the items of interest with a digital camera, and moved on to the bedroom.

There was no bed; rather, they found a blow-up mattress of the sort that campers sometimes carry on hiking trips. It was leaning against the south wall of the bedroom. A jerry-rigged screen made of a blanket hanging on a wire covered the north bedroom wall. When they moved the air bed and pulled the blanket aside, they saw that the walls were covered with photographs of naked or half-naked women. They looked up at the ceiling and found that it, too, was covered with nude photographs. When the doors were closed, there were more naked women on the other two walls; most of the shots appeared to have been torn from *Penthouse, Playboy,* or similar men's magazines; they weren't overtly salacious, but more the kind of thing that a teenage boy might collect.

"When he went to bed," Nordlund said, "He had his own gallery of women to stare at anywhere he looked."

"Yeah," O'Leary said. "He could choose his date for the night."

In the corner of the bedroom, they found both Beta and VHS video recorders and a stack of pornographic video tapes. It looked as if Cool had been rerecording the Beta tapes onto the VHS machine. The man, who had apparently communicated with no one in the real world, had led a rich fantasy life behind the door to his apartment.

Thong underwear, like that the dead man tagged "Whiskey Doe" had worn, but in garish patterns of animal prints and exotic colors, was scattered in the bedroom. "I wonder if he posed in that mirror?" O'Leary mused.

All of Cool's windows were covered, some with aluminum foil and some with dark green plastic garbage bags so that no natural light could get in and, perhaps most particularly, to prevent anyone from looking into his world.

The mediciney smell was explained when the investigators checked the bathroom. They had seen a number of containers of drugstore items in the living room, but nothing like the proliferation of bottles, jars, boxes and vials of nonprescription vitamins, pain-killers, herbal remedies, sports rubs, patent medicines, skin tonic, mens' cologne, hair dressing, and lotions that littered the counters and the sink and were jammed into the bathroom cabinets. The sink was too full to use, and to accommodate the overflow of products, Cool had fashioned a box that fit in the shower and he'd piled more of the stuff in there. The containers in the medicine cabinet had been there so long that their bottoms had rusted to the shelves. Most of the tops were also rusted or dried shut. This looked more like the bathroom of a very old man than it did that of an athletic-looking man in his early forties.

They found two pellet guns, and several knives—both hunting knives and switchblades. The man who had lived here seemed prepared to protect his bleak lodgings.

The kitchen was pretty much what they expected; dirty dishes and accumulated boxes covered the counter tops and filled the sink. The refrigerator's contents looked as if no one had really made a home here. The crowded shelves had the remainders of take-out dinners from a supermarket deli—fast food, half-eaten and moldering. There were many tiny bottles of alcoholic beverages, the kind that airlines serve. The oven and stove were filthy, covered with baked-on grease.

Only the refrigerator gave a clue about the man who had lived here. He had left notes to himself, anchored with magnets, some of which must have made sense only to him.

Who *was* Silas Cool? Or, rather, who had he been? Where had he worked, and with whom had he spent his time? Did anyone else know about this musty, pornography-filled apartment where he had apparently lived for almost fourteen years?

Silas Cool was dead, quite probably by his own hand. Seeing the .38 caliber bullets and the gun box, the three detectives suspected that he had also killed Mark McLaughlin, and attempted to take a bus load of thirty-three strangers down into the depths of the Lake Washington Ship Canal with him.

* * *

It was very late. After a last check with the hospitals to query the condition of the survivors, John Nordlund, Steve O'Leary and Gene Ramirez signed out of Homicide for the night. Tomorrow, they would hope to find someone who had actually interacted with Silas Cool—someone who might explain what forces had driven him. The man had lived in Seattle for at least thirteen years. *Somebody* had to know him.

"It was strange," Steve O'Leary would recall. "Usually, we get lots of calls after something like this from people who have something to share with us. Not one person from his neighborhood ever called us about Silas Cool—not one clerk at the supermarket to say she had rung up his groceries, nobody who knew him from the Laundromat, no one who talked with him on the corner. No neighbors. No one who should have been at least tangentially close to him. It was almost as if he had existed in a vacuum. An invisible man."

By Saturday morning, the reality of the bus tragedy had begun to sink in. Miraculously, there had been no more deaths although many of the survivors were still in critical condition. When the bus was lifted by cranes, the worst fears of the rescue teams didn't come true; there was no one underneath. Those who had literally walked away from the bus to nowhere caught themselves wondering if it had all been a nightmare. But the headlines on the *Seattle Times* and the *Seattle Post-Intelligencer* blazed that it really *had* happened. Color photographs of the destroyed sections of the articulated bus took up half a page. It rested there so close to the apartment house, so close to the giant Troll who lived under the Aurora Bridge, the wreckage like two sides of a giant triangle, its accordioned midsection stretched and torn.

Still, it had landed on the ground amidst the last browning leaves of autumn and not in the deep water beneath the bridge. The ruined hulk would be lifted onto a truck and taken to the bus garage where it would be treated as a crime scene by Seattle detectives.

The postmortem examination on the body of Silas Cool was performed by King County Assistant Medical Examiner Dan Straathof shortly after 7 A.M. on Saturday. The body still wore the yellow identification band around the right wrist reading "Whiskey Doe." It was simply an accident that he had happened to get the "Whiskey" label from the paramedics. There were so many "Does" at the accident scene that they all had to get names that went with letters of the alphabet. There was no odor of alcohol about his body. The triage team who had moved swiftly through the accident scene locating victims and evaluating their condition and had placed a strip of white adhesive tape on his right chest that read "13." As it turned out, he had, indeed, been unlucky 13.

Silas Cool weighed 198 pounds and measured just under six feet—although earlier descriptions had listed him as several inches taller. His hair was brown with thick swatches of gray, he was clean-shaven with clipped sideburns, and his teeth were in good repair. His body was clean and well-kept. He looked for all the world like a normal man in his early forties, who was in good shape and good health, but who had been in a very bad accident.

Silas Cool had suffered numerous wounds, commensurate with that accident; the question was whether they had occurred before or after his fatal gunshot wound. His spinal column was fractured at the C-6 level due to a blunt force injury. Had he lived, he might well have been paralyzed to some extent. Other passengers had suffered similar injuries; it was what happened to a body if it fell from a great height.

Cool had bitten through his tongue, and his lungs and liver had hemorrhages from impact wounds. There were multiple abrasions and contusions. He had probably been brain-dead, but technically alive, as the bus fell to earth.

But Dr. Straathof determined that Silas Cool had not perished because he was in a bus that tore through a guardrail and plunged several stories to the ground. The fatal wound was the gunshot wound. That point of entry was just above his right ear. The skin around the wound had the familiar "stellate" tears that come with a contact gunshot as the skin itself is drawn momentarily into the gun barrel by the gases there, torn, and released. The bullet's path was one of massive destruction through the brain itself, exiting near the top of the head. Any signs of life thereafter would have been mostly reflexive as the body struggled to live. That would explain the agonal gasps noted by the rescuers who struggled to free him from the bottom of a pile of people who had been thrown onto the bus steps.

If there is a classic gunshot suicide pattern, Silas Cool's wound fit the criteria. It would probably be impossible to know just when Cool shot himself. But it would have to have been just after he shot Mark McLaughlin. He could not have done it after the bus crashed to the ground; he had been beneath a pile of passengers, his arms pinned.

In an attempt to answer at least *some* questions, a blood screen was done for alcohol, opiates, cocaine, amphetamines, PCP, marijuana, methadone, propoxaphene, benzodiazapene and barbiturates—in short, all the possible drug groups that might have an effect on the central nervous system. Every single test came back negative. The *only* thing that Silas Cool's blood tested positive for was caffeine. Cool might have collected tiny airplane bottles of liquor, but he had not drunk from them the day of the accident. There would be no easy explanations for the tragedy on the bus.

This man had been in the peak of physical condition when he died. He had no ailments. Despite the fast-food diet in his refrigerator, he still had only very minor streaks of atheroma (fatty deposits) on his coronary arteries. All things being equal, he probably would have lived to be a hundred.

The postmortem examination of bus driver Mark McLaughlin's body yielded some sadly ironic truths. He had been struck twice by .38 bullets. The wound that looked the most dangerous from the outside wasn't; that bullet had entered his right abdomen and passed through soft tissue behind his vital organs, ending benignly in his thigh. It was the bullet fired into his upper right arm that had killed him. And that was because it went completely through McLaughlin's arm, exited, and reentered his right chest. That wound track was through the seventh intercostal space, through his liver, through the transverse colon, and then, tragically, it had pierced the aorta—the major artery of the body. Seconds later, already hemorrhaging fatally, he had been catapulted through the bus windshield to the roof of the apartment house.

Mark McLaughlin had had no chance at all to live. Like the man who shot him, the bus driver was in good shape when he was shot, his arteries clear and healthy, his heart valves unmarked by anything more than minor fatty deposits. He had been somewhat overweight, but he was in excellent condition. He, too, would probably have lived to a ripe old age if he hadn't been the victim of Silas Cool's inscrutable rage.

At noon on Saturday, Gene Ramirez started searching over the Internet for any relatives Silas Cool might have had. He checked Plainfield, New Jersey. That was where the lawyer's card was from, and Cool had told the Lynnwood officer that he was from New Jersey. Ramirez found a listing for a couple named Cool living in Plainfield, and copied down the phone number of Daniel and Ena Cool. It was possible they were Silas Cool's parents, or perhaps his aunt and uncle. He gave the number to Kathy Taylor in the M.E.'s office for possible notification of next-of-kin. Twenty minutes later, she called Ramirez back. The Cools in Plainfield were, indeed, the parents of Silas Garfield Cool. She had told them that their son was dead, and it had, of course, been devastating for them. They were expecting a call from the homicide detectives who might explain to them what had happened to their son.

Steve O'Leary placed a call to Daniel Cool. This was one of the most difficult parts of being a homicide detective, but he had to find out as much as he could about Silas Cool. The elderly man was both upset and baffled when O'Leary told Daniel Cool that the detectives believed that his son had caused the bus crash. Cool said he had never known Silas to own any firearms. It was absolutely incomprehensible to him that Silas could have deliberately hurt anyone. That just wasn't like his boy.

"Where does Silas work?" O'Leary asked.

"He can't—couldn't—work," Cool replied. "He has had a serious back problem for many years."

Silas had played golf in high school, his father said, but somehow he had injured his back and it had plagued him ever since. But no, he hadn't seen a doctor about it in many years as far as the elder Cool knew.

As tactfully as he could, O'Leary asked if Silas had been under psychiatric care. His father said he never had, as far as he knew. "We knew he was a loner," Cool said, but they had never thought Silas had any real problems.

His father said that Silas had worked until about 1987 or 1988 for King County in Seattle in the King County Building and Land Use Department. He had an associate degree in civil engineering from Middlesex County College in New Jersey.

But then Silas's back had just become too painful for him to work full-time. He had wanted to move back to New Jersey, but his dad said he had talked him out of that. It was arranged for his parents to send him $650 a month until he found something that he could work at. O'Leary learned that Daniel Cool's sister, who was in her nineties, had also helped Silas out for two decades—ultimately sending him over $30,000 in Certificates of Deposit. Somehow, the years had stretched, and ten years later his parents were still sending Silas monthly checks.

Steve O'Leary let the old man go to try and deal with the loss of his only child. They would have more talks as the detective tried to form a more complete picture of what Silas Garfield Cool had been like.

The next phone call into Homicide was from the Medical Examiner's Office. Herman Liebelt, sixty-nine, had died of his injuries. Like Silas Cool, Liebelt had found his way to Seattle from the East Coast. Beyond that, they were so different. Liebelt, the one-time saxophone-playing bandleader, sailor in the Korean War, purchasing agent, had begun life in Amsterdam, N.Y. His last years were spent reading everything from popular fiction to deep philosophical works. He had lived on the shoe-string that many seniors do, but he'd been a happy man with friends and myriad interests. He had found joy in little things and in new friends, and now he was gone. His painful injuries were too severe for a man nearly seventy to survive.

In the early afternoon of Saturday, November 28, two men who worked at the Union Gospel Mission in Seattle arrived at the Homicide unit. Bill Wippel and Peter Davis said they had heard the name "Silas Cool" on the news. Finally, someone had recognized him and wanted to talk about how they had known him. They asked to see a picture of the man known as Silas Cool, and Nordlund and O'Leary showed them the booking photo taken in 1994 after a shoplifting arrest.

They recognized Cool. He was one of those who had come to the mission to eat a meal now and then. "He's eaten with us several times," Wippel said. "At least twice this past month. He never caused any trouble, was very neat and clean, and polite to our staff."

Still, Wippel and Davis had known Silas Cool only on a very surface level. He must have been hungry; simple arithmetic would substantiate that. His folks sent Cool $650 a month; his rent was $475. That left him $175 a month for food, utilities, clothing, and transportation.

They found no record of any Certificates of Deposits in Cool's name. He had spent it all, maybe on his scores of medications. "Those Union Gospel meals must have helped him out," O'Leary commented.

Records at the mission, which had helped thousands of homeless and down-on-their-luck people in Seattle for many years, showed that Silas Cool had filled out meal tickets on October 20 and November 20; he had attended chapel, but he had never spent a night in the mission.

"I remember him," Wippel said, "because the guy stood out in the crowd. He was clean-cut, handsome. He didn't look like a street person. He kept to himself, didn't talk to anyone. I do know I looked him in the eye and made contact with him, and he smiled. He gave no indication that he was a violent person."

The mission staff knew that the people who came to them for food and lodging often guarded their past from prying eyes, and they never pressed. Wippel and Davis knew nothing at all about Silas Cool's world outside the food lines, but he had always seemed as though he could have made a success of life. He *looked* like success.

In reality, Silas Cool, either unwilling or unable to work, had lived his life close to the bone. On Monday, the homicide investigators checked with the State Department of Public Assistance to see if Cool had received benefits of any kind, and they found he didn't get any Social Security payments for being disabled, or any state Labor and Industry benefits.

Steve O'Leary talked in more detail with Daniel Cool, Silas's father and, with his permission, took a tape-recorded statement.

Silas Cool's early life had been anything but average.

Daniel Cool's career as an accountant for a petroleum company had taken him all over the world. He had met and married Ena, four years younger than he and a native of South Africa. Silas was born in Palenbang, Sumatra, Indonesia, in 1954. They had moved to Pakistan when Silas was a very small boy. Finally, they had come back to the U.S., settling in North Plainfield, New Jersey, in 1960, when Silas was five years old. He was their only son, their only child. They were nearly old enough to be grandparents when he was born.

"What kind of child was Silas?" O'Leary asked.

"A very good child," Daniel Cool said, "Well-mannered, quiet. The neighbors used to comment and say, 'He's such a good boy,' but I guess all kids are good."

Silas had graduated from North Plainfield High School in Plainfield, New Jersey, in 1973. He had always earned respectable—if not spectacular—grades. If Silas had a passion, it was golf, although he had never played on a high school team. "He played at local clubs," Daniel said.

In his yearbook, Silas gave his plans as "playing golf at the farm." But his father was convinced that he had hurt his back severely during one of his mighty swings.

Girls? Daniel couldn't recall that Silas dated girls in high school. "My wife and I thought that was because of his 'scoliosis problem.' It made him on the shy side. I wish we could have caught that earlier . . ."

The only job Silas had had in New Jersey hadn't lasted long. He had worked as an usher in a theater. "He lost that one because they caught him leaning against the seats," his father told O'Leary. "But that was because of his back problems hurting him."

Silas moved to Seattle in 1979. "He just wanted to

explore the West Coast and he ended up in Seattle. He had a little Mustang then, and he drove out there—straight from New Jersey to Seattle."

Even though he had no friends in Seattle, Silas hadn't had trouble getting a job, not with his civil engineer training. "He had lots of different jobs—all different jobs. But he lost most of them because of his back problems," Daniel Cool recalled.

In about 1985, Silas had gone to work for the county. Cool didn't know why that had ended, but it had. He thought that Silas's back must have gotten really bad about the same time.

"He called us on March 25, 1989. He said he was going to move back home and we talked him out of that. His back was bad. He told me once in 1989 that his back was so bad he just wanted to swat people." And still, his father didn't want him to give up and move home, although his mother worried.

Cool recalled that Silas had made "a mistake" in applying for disability for his back, and never got any compensation from the government. So the family had started to support him. "I think we've probably given him at least $75,000 over the years," his father said. "Silas was just doing everything he could for his back pain. He had magnetic belts he put on, and massagers, and he lay down a lot. He told me one doctor said he just had to live with it. He came back here and we took him up to a hospital, and they didn't make us feel very confident. Since then, he just didn't go to any doctors."

Despite the chronic pain he seemed to be in, Silas didn't take any prescription medication, relying, his father said, on vitamins and health food supplements.

It seemed impossible to O'Leary that a man could be as

disengaged from the world as Silas Cool had been and not have someone notice. He pushed a little harder, "He *never* exhibited any behavior as a child that would concern you—or your wife? Never had any psychiatric care?"

Daniel Cool was adamant that Silas had never been under psychiatric care. Steve O'Leary got the impression that this would have been shameful for his family. No, his father insisted. Silas had been fine. *Fine.* "No—No counselors. No problems. I hear he was eating in soup kitchens out there?" his father said uncomfortably.

"Yes—to save money," O'Leary said.

This was difficult for the old man; he had tried his best to see that his son had enough to get by on.

"Did Silas ever seem depressed or angry?" O'Leary asked.

"No. Oh, one time we went out to dinner—when he was here a month ago—and he seemed a little irritated about the service. I think that was at the International House of Pancakes."

Silas had always come back once a year to see his parents on the East Coast. "We saw Silas last October," his father said, "when he came to see us for twelve days. We find it really hard to believe that he shot a bus driver. This would have been *totally* out of his character. I bought him a BB gun once, way back when he was a sophomore in high school. I don't know what ever happened to that, but he wasn't interested in guns. Never."

As O'Leary tried to find *something* that might account for the tragedy on the bus, he elicited only "normal" things in Silas Cool's childhood. His father remembered that he had been a Boy Scout, and had gone to Bible school. He had never been in the service. He was never interested in guns at all.

"In the last several months," O'Leary began, "can you think of anything different in his behavior?"

"He was slightly agitated—but more on his own, again, like he'd be lying on the bed with his back problem in the afternoon, and he'd take a little walk somewhere. He could only go so far, and then he'd have to lie down again. He had that 'twitching' in the neck. The back situation was what he mostly complained about."

As far as Daniel Cool knew, his son had no friends in Seattle. He never talked about anyone. No dating, no interaction with anyone at all. This had not, apparently, seemed strange to the old man. This was how Silas had always been.

"Did he talk about the buses?"

"Never mentioned them—except to say they had good bus service in Seattle."

"Any hobbies?"

"Oh, he used to have a bicycle. I don't know if that's still in the apartment. He used to do bike riding when he first went out there. He used to go to the library a lot. He swam for his back. He used to swim a lot. That's how he got in trouble on the sixteenth."

"Do you know why he gave the officer a false name?"

"He was just a little irritated with the arresting officer. And he didn't have any ID. And then he slurred his name so it sounded like 'Steve' instead of 'Silas.'" Daniel Cool said he had arranged for the bail bondsmen to get his son out of jail after the misunderstanding at the pool.

"And, until last Friday," O'Leary tried again, "he never exhibited any anger toward anyone, and he never expressed any interest in getting back at anyone?"

"Not at all," the old man sighed, utterly defeated by the catastrophe and loss that had come to him in his mid-eighties. "Boy, that's what surprises us. All of a sudden, flip your lid, and shoot a bus driver. . . . It's astounding to my wife and me. We can't figure that out. There's [got to be] a motive behind that. You go on a bus with a couple of guns? My wife and I can't understand that."

Nor could anyone else.

Steve O'Leary thought that it must have taken an incredible amount of sheer will for Silas Cool to keep a "lid" on his rage when he visited his parents. Or it may have taken a tremendous amount of denial for *them* not to see that the perfect, well-behaved son was losing his mind. It was probably a little of both.

But maybe Silas's asocial behavior wasn't strange to his parents. *They* had no close friends in New Jersey, or anywhere. Daniel's sister in Wisconsin was the closest person to him, outside of his wife, Ena. The Cools had never been mixers. They had one son. One cat. They had their own interests.

During the processing of the wrecked shell of Bus Number 359, a loose .38 pistol was found where it had apparently skidded along the floor. That gun was tested for fingerprints, and on November 30, a single print on the magazine proved to be that of Silas Cool. That was good physical evidence linking Cool to the gun, but now the gun had to be tied to Mark McLaughlin's murder.

The .38 was test-fired in the Washington State Patrol Crime Lab and the bullets were compared to those taken from McLaughlin's body. The lands and grooves that striated the metal were identical. A gun with Silas Cool's print on it, and an AMT .38 caliber pistol that came from the box in his living room, had been used to shoot Mark McLaughlin. It was all there.

Gradually, the picture of the man who had sent a busload of human beings over the Aurora Bridge was becoming three-dimensional. A county worker who had been Silas Cool's supervisor a decade earlier when he worked for the King County Building Department called the investigators. "He was a weird fellow," the man recalled, adding that Silas had had few social graces and didn't get along with his fellow workers. "He was a racist, too," the man said. That was totally against policy in King County. The supervisor said that Cool had been allowed to resign from his job, but in reality his presence in the department was so controversial that he had been forced out.

Pictures of Silas Cool had been posted at bus stops and stations to see if anyone recognized him. It remained hard to determine if Cool had had a particular beef with Mark McLaughlin or if his vengeful act had been directed at the world in general. A female Metro driver called the investigators to say that Cool's face was very familiar to her. He'd been on her bus a couple of times. "At the end of last winter, he got on my shuttle route near Green Lake," she said. "He immediately started complaining about the temperature inside the bus. He wanted no heat on. He actually walked up and down the aisle opening windows. He was complaining about germs in the air . . ."

Cool's behavior had been bizarre enough to frighten her, she said, and she was relieved when he got off after a few miles. "But I saw him again when I was driving downtown. He wanted to go to the University District and I told him I was the slowest bus to get there. That time, he was very well dressed."

Another Metro driver remembered Silas Cool, who had gotten on his bus in the downtown area. "He was unruly and obnoxious," the male driver said. "I've seen him on my bus three or four times this year."

It appeared that Silas Cool's obsession, passion, avocation, hobby—his whole life—had been spent riding the buses of Seattle. He had acted as if he owned them, and he was frequently abusive with the drivers.

Still another driver called John Nordlund. He knew Silas Cool, too. "He would just stare at me—a blank intimidating stare. And I would just stare back at him. He had a reduced fare permit, but I haven't seen him since last summer."

A second female driver notified the homicide detectives that she recognized Silas Cool. Her voice was a little shaky as she recalled how he had boarded her bus at the north end of Seattle only one week before the bus crash. "He got on my bus and immediately started harassing me. He made comments about my 'beautiful face and eyes,' and I had to forcefully tell him to be quiet and sit down." She said she hadn't reported him; he had seemed like just another person who was either drunk or mentally disturbed, and every bus driver in the city had to deal with those problems every day.

More and more calls came in from bus drivers. Silas Cool hadn't been a *big* problem but he had been a problem all over the city. A woman driver recalled that he'd been on her bus, which had a route that went east and then south of downtown—the opposite direction from Cool's apartment. "He got on the bus, sat in the middle, and he was checking out teenagers," she said. "I noticed him especially because it was dark out and he was wearing sunglasses. He scared me—enough so that I called my coordinator and reported it."

Nobody at North Plainfield High School had thought much about Silas Cool in the years since graduation. Apparently, he hadn't drawn much attention when he *was* in school. He had been sent an invitation to his class's twenty-fifth reunion, which was to be held on the weekend after Thanksgiving. Because Silas was one of the "lost" graduates, the invitation was sent to his parents. There was no response.

The welcoming cocktail party for The Class of 1973 was just warming up in New Jersey at six P.M. on Friday, November 27. In Seattle, it was, of course, three P.M., moments before the shots sounded on Bus Number 359.

By Saturday afternoon, the reunion in North Plainfield was buzzing with the news of one of their former classmates. They couldn't help but speculate that Silas Cool might have made some kind of statement meant to shock them. If that was the reason behind the shooting, it had worked. His name was on everyone's lips at the reunion. Silas Cool was not someone who stood out in anyone's memory. He wasn't memorable for anything *but* his name.

"Cool" was slang that seemed to get recycled every generation or so. But Silas Cool was not "cool" at all. He wasn't anything but average. He didn't drink or go to parties. He didn't date. "He was a very quiet kid," one male classmate said. "Not a troublemaker."

It was faint praise. When members of the Class of 1973 were approached by the media to give quotes, few of them had anything to offer more than speculation about why *somebody* would shoot a bus driver; few even remembered who Silas was, or if they did, they could not recall a single anecdote involving him.

His English teacher in tenth grade saw the story on the television news and said, "I found it very hard to sleep last night. People are obviously very different the rest of their lives than they were in tenth grade, but he was a really nice kid and he fit in." He said Silas had laughed at jokes, once someone made the effort to draw him in.

Silas's biology teacher remembered a loner, but one who showed no sign of problems. "He was what I would call a straight-arrow kid, typical student, clean-cut—but you never know what's going to happen in someone's lifetime that would make them do something like he did in Seattle. I'm flabbergasted." His journalism teacher said he had been "sweet and kind," but that he had never stood out from the crowd.

It was the same at Middlesex College in Edison, New Jersey. Silas had attended classes there from September 1975 to June 1978. He had gotten an A in statics, the study of forces in structures, but that was one of his few outstanding grades. His professor couldn't recall him. "No one remembers him specifically," Frank Rubino said, "but when they check back in their record books, everybody finds him . . ."

No one knew Silas Cool when he was a teenager, and no one knew him when he was forty-three. He seemed to have spent his whole life on the edges of other people's lives, a person of so little importance that few remembered him.

In his Seattle apartment, he was "S. Cool," the man whom his neighbors didn't know.

Seattle reporters flew to New Jersey to try to get an

inside look at Silas Cool's life there. Eric Sorensen of the *Seattle Times* managed to obtain an interview with Daniel and Ena Cool. He found them in their very small, one-floor home, decorated modestly with some of the things they had brought back from their travels. The pair of bronzed baby shoes were from Singapore and had a little plaque reading, "Silas Cool, May 14, 1955."

Ena Cool, seventy-seven, spoke with a South-African accent, still, as she echoed the bewilderment of her husband. "I can't believe Silas is dead," she said. "I can't believe he'd do something like that. He was here only a month ago, and he didn't give any indications he would do such a thing. You always think—if you're left alone, you're going to have your son around. But it's not happening that way."

Ena Cool said that she had been forty-three when Silas was born, and Daniel was forty-seven. As older parents, they accepted his quietness happily. "He was quiet, unassuming, a mind-his-own-business type. He never bothered anybody," Daniel said proudly.

Ena and Silas were always close. After he graduated from high school, she recalled that he had gone with her back to South Africa when her mother became ill. While he was there, he had trained as an architect for the engineering department of the City of Durban. She said he was very good at the kind of drawing architects and engineers use—all straight careful lines and angles.

After he drove his Mustang out to Seattle, his parents had never really been sure what Silas's life was like—apart from his back problems. They lived their lives 3,000 miles apart except for his yearly October visits. Although they believed he had scoliosis, he had never been treated for it in the traditional way—by wearing a full body cast to straighten out the curvature of the spine.

They didn't know about his jobs out west, except that he lost them often. Ena Cool remembered visiting her son in Seattle in 1991, but, oddly, she described an apartment at a different address than the one he had lived in since 1985. Either she was mistaken on the date, or her son had rented a clean, nicely decorated apartment on a temporary basis so that she would not be disappointed in him. She was positive the nice apartment was on Taylor Avenue N. Silas Cool could not have taken his mother into an apartment with photographs of naked women on the walls and stacks of pornographic videos. Where *had* he taken her during her visit seven years earlier?

His parents admitted that Silas had been easily angered during his last visit home. He had spent those twelve days in October with them, and he had been angry that they had to wait in line at the restaurant—the incident Daniel Cool related to Steve O'Leary. Silas had insisted that they leave the line and go to another restaurant, his parents said. Yes, he had been angry at the neighbor's dog for barking, and he had yelled at it. But what was neurotic about that, they asked? Anyone would have.

Although Silas's parents had sent him nearly $700 a month, plus gifts at Christmas and on his birthday, the airplane tickets to fly home in October, and his aunt had been very generous, he was frustrated because he didn't have any income that he'd earned himself. He felt that he was a burden on his parents, which, of course, he was. His mother sometimes thought that there must be *some* job that he could do with his hands, a job that wouldn't strain his back.

"He was just wasting his life, when you think about it," she said sadly, "But what can you do?"

Ena showed Eric Sorensen the last postcards that Silas had sent them. He called them "E and D" and the cards read like a normal, cheery, communiqué. He spoke of a PGA golf tournament that was to be held in a Seattle suburb, and of his walk to Albertson's grocery near Green Lake. He asked if their ancient cat was still growing fatter. He told them what he had eaten for supper, and about riding a bus. He sounded like the son they wanted so badly to believe in.

Toward the end of his life, his mother said she had urged Silas to move back home. His room was still there for him, a small room with barely space for a bed, a dresser, and a postage stamp of a desk. He had resisted that idea, because he needed to move around. "He said he could do more there [in Seattle]," Ena Cool said. "He could get around on buses and go where he wanted to go, whereas here [without a car], you're pretty stuck."

At length, Ena Cool said tentatively, "He seemed on the very withdrawn side [in October] if you know what I mean."

"It was the back pain," Daniel said quickly. "I think his nerves were in such a state . . ."

Indeed they were. Within six weeks, Silas's "nerves" were at the point of exploding. Clearly, the problems that had undoubtedly haunted him for years had started to unravel and the tightly controlled world inside his apartment and inside his own head were threatening to burst forth. It was only a matter of when and on which bus.

Not surprisingly, the bulk of the information that was coming into the Homicide unit was in response to the pictures of Silas Cool that were posted at bus stops. A woman recognized Cool, and said she had spoken to him on the bus earlier in the fall. He'd been complaining that the bus drivers were rude, that people were generally rude. He had shown her a small gun that he carried, and commented that things were getting so bad he was going to buy another gun.

And, apparently, he had.

The last person to talk to Silas Garfield Cool before he erupted on Bus Number 359 may have been Dorna Stone, who served free Thanksgiving Day meals at the University Temple United Methodist Church. She remembered a neatly dressed man carrying a backpack. He was tall and handsome and scarcely looked like a "street person." He came in and sat down at a table where she was talking with several other volunteers. As he enjoyed the holiday meal, he told them that he knew which churches served free meals.

He also told them about which dumpsters held the best food. It was an odd conversation to have with a man who looked like a middle-aged corporate executive who was dressed down on his day off in a plaid sports shirt and jeans. He struck Stone as a nice guy who didn't seem to be stressed or unhappy. He spent about fifteen minutes in the church basement eating his meal, and then stopped on his way out to ask for more food, which he took with him.

She was quite sure that that pleasant, good-looking man had been Silas Cool.

John Nordlund, Steve O'Leary, and Gene Ramirez continued to question survivors as their condition improved enough to warrant it. They found nothing new;

some had seen the man in dark clothing stride up to the bus driver and shoot him twice without exchanging so much as a word. Some had been sleeping, reading, or distracted, and realized they were in trouble only as the bus took flight.

Most of the survivors were doing well, but Charles Moreno, thirty-two, lost a leg and faced the loss of an arm. A private and shy man who was scrupulously honest even when he was having a rough time, he was a recovering alcoholic who was in his sixth year of sobriety when the accident occurred. A relative of Moreno's recalled one of Moreno's many good deeds. "One time, he found a blank money order, and we needed it, but he insisted on turning it into Safeway. It was for $160 and we fought over it, but he insisted . . ."

As the Christmas season, 1998, was in full bloom, the groundswells from the bus crash continued to blunt the lives of those who'd been on the bus, those in the apartment house it hit, and even those who had participated in the rescue attempt. Many of the victims would be in the hospital until months into the New Year, and Metro was making arrangements to assist them with funds and counseling. The apartment dwellers had to find new lodging while the damage, estimated at about $200,000, was repaired. Beyond the monetary loss and the physical pain, the psychological cost was immeasurable. There were those who grieved and those who woke in the night full of fear. That would never really go away.

And something else had risen its ugly head; one of the bus passengers had tested HIV positive. Now, the rescuers who had plunged into a literal sea of blood, some of them cutting themselves on the jagged edges of the torn bus, were warned that they should submit to tests that would show if they had contracted the deadly virus. And they couldn't be sure for six months. It was a concept that most lay people who run to rescue their fellow human beings never think of; where there is blood now there is always danger.

On December 8, fellow bus drivers, passengers, dignitaries and the Seattle public said good-bye to Mark McLaughlin, who had tried desperately to save his passengers by keeping his bus on the bridge. A procession of eighty buses drove slowly down Fourth Avenue toward the Key Arena, where five thousand people waited for a memorial service honoring both Mark McLaughlin and Herman Liebelt. Two Seattle police motorcycle officers led the procession and a tow truck pulled an empty bus emblazoned with McLaughlin's badge number: 2106. His photo and his uniform jacket hung behind the driver's seat, and thirty-two purple ribbons marked the seats where the surviving passengers had sat eleven days earlier. There were two black ribbons: one for McLaughlin and one for Liebelt.

But there was no ribbon at all for Silas Cool.

The buses rolled silently for an hour, blocking intersections, and seizing the street for that time in honor of the bus driver and the old man. No one minded. What had happened to them was something all drivers and many riders had feared. "We knew it was only a matter of time," one driver said. "You never know who's sitting next to you . . ."

No one can really know what went on in Silas Garfield Cool's head. He is not a villain in the traditional sense of the word because he was undoubtedly insane.

He was a quiet boy who never quite fit in—who became a quiet man who didn't fit in at all. His "bad back" was probably only an excuse for his inability to deal with the world. He had run as far as he could from his boyhood home, seeking a geographic solution to the thoughts that plagued him. But when he got to Seattle in 1979, Silas Cool found that he'd brought all his demons with him. He could not bring himself to admit that it was his mind that was so fragile that he could not work, but he could blame it on his painful spine. He may even have "felt" pain, and picked the term *scoliosis* to describe his ailment. He spent a tremendous amount of money on cure-alls, magnets, belts, and massagers but none of those could fix his mind, and so he still felt pain.

Silas Cool was about twenty-four years old when he drove his Mustang to the Northwest. Already, according to his supervisors at work, he could not get along with his peers. Already, he was scornful of African-Americans and Asians, perhaps convinced in his own mind that they were a danger to him. The undiagnosed illness that eventually destroyed him had begun to grow like the faintest cuttings of ivy in his thought patterns. As the years passed, the "ivy" wound itself around and around his brain processes. Because he kept himself entirely alone, there was no chance for anyone to help him. He got no psychiatric treatment and no pharmacological treatment.

For Cool, who was entranced, beset, consumed, haunted, obsessed, and possessed by buses, it *was* only a matter of time before someone or some thing triggered his fear and rage. The fact that the catastrophic shooting on the bus was virtually simultaneous with the homecoming reunion for the Class of 1973 cannot be ignored.

It is quite possible that Silas *did* resent being teased about his name, being called a "cool guy" a quarter of a century before. He may well have harbored a resentment that burgeoned along with his developing paranoia. He may have wanted to show those classmates who barely remembered him that he was the most famous of them all. Twenty-five years after the fact, his actions were not unlike those of the violent outsiders in the 1990s high school massacres.

It was only a matter of five seconds. If Bus Number 359 had fallen from the top of the Aurora Bridge, Silas Garfield Cool would have taken nearly three dozen people with him in a headline-grabbing suicide plunge. And he would have achieved a ghastly sort of celebrity. He may have planned for it to be that way. But bad timing and fate foiled those plans.

The Killer Who Planted
His Own Clues

Mystery writers like to say there is no such thing as a perfect murder, but they're wrong. There are probably thousands of perfect murders and they're not all committed by brilliant killers. If a victim isn't missed when he or she vanishes and no body is ever found, or if one is found and not identified, the killer is free and clear.

In this case, the victim was found quickly and identified at once, but her not-too-bright killer attempted to complicate the crime scene by setting up red herrings. He left all manner of false clues for the homicide detectives, but he was completely oblivious to the real clues that remained. Most murderers are caught because they leave infinitesimal pieces of themselves behind, unaware that forensic science and detectives' technical skill have evolved to a point that is almost uncanny.

But the killer in this case caught himself because he was bored and made a stupid decision. It was so stupid that the detectives who tracked him never considered that anyone who was trying to evade capture would make such a blatant mistake; they found that mistake in their routine checks, not in their prime crime scene investigation.

The shy spinster school teacher was an unlikely target for a murderer. "Spinster" is an outdated description for most single women, bringing images of *Little House on the Prairie,* but it fit Sharon Mason. She was still single at the age of thirty-seven and that was by her own choice. Although she was slim and attractive, she rarely dated or even mingled much with people her own age. She looked much younger than her true age. She was five feet four and weighed only 104 pounds, and she seemed fragile, although she was perfectly healthy. She had brown eyes and auburn hair.

Sharon was very cautious and reserved to the point of being timid. Other women took chances that she would never have dreamed of: walking alone at night, making friends by talking to strangers, and accepting blind dates. Not Sharon. She erred, always, on the side of safety. Besides, she preferred being home in her apartment to going out at night. The only way she could have been safer would have been to stay there twenty-four hours a day.

But Sharon did have a full life outside her apartment, a life that revolved around her career and her parents. She had taught the first grade at the Roosevelt Elementary School in Tumwater, Washington, for nine years. Her kids loved her, and her co-workers admired her. She was always at school for special events that involved her students.

Tumwater isn't exactly a big town, although it is a suburb of Washington's capital city, Olympia. Tumwater's claim to fame is that its natural spring water is the main ingredient of a popular beer. But Tumwater and Olympia are far more cosmopolitan than the city where Sharon grew up. She came from Aberdeen on the Grays Harbor inlet along the Washington coast. Aberdeen is a logging and deepwater fishing town and people claim it rains there more than any other spot in the state.

Born late in life to an Aberdeen couple, Sharon was to be their only child and the focal point of their lives. Every weekend, without fail, she drove home to spend the weekend with them. And, every Wednesday evening, she called them. She didn't chafe at the responsibility to her parents; she loved them and was happy to be with them.

During the week, Sharon lived near Olympia in a very nice ten-unit apartment building that was adjacent to an evergreen forest. Her balcony looked out on tall fir trees and the woods were full of bird songs. It wasn't nearly as isolated as it seemed, however, and it was only a short distance to the I-5 freeway. It was also close to the capital building so several state legislators lived in her apartment building. She really didn't know any of her neighbors well, no more than to politely nod if she met them in the parking lot.

Sharon's apartment was rather expensive for a school teacher, but she spent little money on anything outside her home. She didn't need fancy clothes to teach first grade, her car was paid for, and her home was her hobby, her avocation, her pride and joy.

She chose her furniture with care and good taste, and she coaxed house plants into luxuriant growth. Sharon's only pets were goldfish. After a hectic day with six-year-olds, her apartment was a peaceful haven.

The only jarring note in Sharon Mason's life was that she was afraid to be alone at night. Maybe it was because her parents had warned her too much about the dangers of life; they doted so on their only child. Perhaps she was just naturally timid. She hated the dark. She always kept her drapes drawn at night, her door locked, and a reassuring night light on in the hallway.

Occasionally, when the winter winds raged, there were massive power outages in the Olympia area, and Sharon was quite frightened. Then, the lowering trees seemed to close in around her apartment's balcony and she felt cut off from the world. She would either phone her mother to say she was driving the sixty miles to Aberdeen to spend the night, or she would grab the overnight bag that she kept packed, and drive to a motel. On nights like these, her locked doors, the proximity of her neighbors, or the light of candles couldn't comfort her. In the Northwest, winter days are short and the night falls before five P.M., making the darkness more pervasive.

On Friday, February 20, 1976, Sharon drove to Aberdeen as usual. It was a special weekend because her parents were celebrating their wedding anniversary. They all had a good time with friends. On Sunday afternoon, Sharon's dad polished her gold Oldsmobile for her and filled the gas tank. He always did that, a gesture to thank her for making the long drive down each weekend. Sharon headed home in mid-afternoon so that she could be in her apartment before dark.

On Monday morning, February 23, Sharon was in her classroom early, as she always was. But she was frightened. She told fellow teachers that someone had prowled the parking lot of her apartment house during the night. "My car was broken into," she related softly.

"What did you lose?" someone asked.

"Nothing," she said. "Well, nothing—except for the extra apartment key that I kept in my glove box. I told the manager about it right away, and he promised to have the maintenance man change the locks on my doors this afternoon."

None of the other cars in the lot had been touched. Only Sharon's. It made her more nervous when she remembered that her missing key had the number of her apartment on it, a clear "9" etched in the metal. And if he—she was sure, somehow, that it was a *he* who had rifled through her car—if he had wanted to know her name, all he would have had to do was check her name on her car registration on the steering column of the Oldsmobile.

It gave her a creepy feeling to think that some stranger had been sitting in her car, pawing through her things in the glove compartment and had taken her key. When she couldn't get a hold of the apartment manager to confirm that her locks had been changed, she made up her mind not to sleep in her apartment that night; she would go home only to get her overnight bag and then check into the motel where she sometimes stayed.

After classes, Sharon stayed for a brief after-school party. She stopped at an Albertson's supermarket to pick up a few items, and then cashed a check for $75 at her bank.

If she had thought to put an overnight bag in her car that morning, she probably wouldn't have even gone to her apartment. But she did, parking the Oldsmobile in the front paved part of the parking lot, facing the road, as if she planned only to stop for a few minutes.

The man who lived in the apartment directly over Sharon Mason's unit thought he recognized her footsteps on the stairs at 4:55. He heard her door open and close. But he had turned on his television to hear the five o'clock news while he was fixing dinner in his kitchen, and that blocked out any noises outside his walls.

But Sharon Mason's comings and goings were so predictable. He had *never* heard loud sounds from her apartment. Now, when he did hear something, he listened and remembered. He heard "three quick thumps," followed almost immediately by three muted cries of a woman uttering "Oooh . . . ooh . . . oh."

He stood in his kitchen, his hands poised over the sink, listening. Puzzled. The sounds weren't loud enough to be termed screams, or even alarming enough for him to be sure anything was wrong.

But his curiosity was piqued and he went to his window to peer down at the parking lot. There was a car below, and, feeling a little foolish, he jotted down the license number.

Sharon Mason's upstairs neighbor felt vaguely disturbed the rest of the evening. At one point, he even went downstairs and rang her doorbell, thinking he would ask her if everything was O.K. But no one answered the bell. He wondered if his imagination was playing tricks on him. He'd been reading *Helter Skelter* about the Manson murders, and he figured that was responsible for his being uncharacteristically suspicious.

Not another sound came from Sharon's apartment all evening, but that wasn't unusual. Sharon never had her television on too loud, she never had a party that he could recall or even entertained friends whose voices might carry.

Another man was puzzled when he tried to contact Sharon Mason that evening. He was the maintenance man who took care of the apartment complex. He'd gotten a priority assignment to change the locks on Number 9. But when he knocked on the front door late Monday, she didn't answer. Assuming that she had a late conference at her school, he had left. But he'd phoned several times during the evening and never got an answer.

After the last call, he shook his head slightly and hung up. He knew from the manager that the tenant in Number 9 was extremely upset and he had promised to have the locks changed by nightfall. But he couldn't change them unless the tenant was present. He figured she had stayed someplace else for the night, so he decided to call her the next day.

In truth, Sharon Mason's apartment was not unoccupied, but no one inside could—or would—answer the doorbell, knocks, or telephone rings.

On Tuesday morning, the first graders in Sharon's schoolroom were restless. Their teacher was late, and she was never late. One of them went to tell the teacher in the room next door.

In nine years, Sharon Mason had never failed to call in if she was ill or could not be at work. Indeed, she usually called the night before to give school authorities the chance to find a substitute teacher. Her principal and her fellow teachers were alarmed. A woman whose punctuality and dependability were legendary would not fail to appear for work unless there was something wrong.

At 9 A.M. a worried co-worker called the Tumwater Police Department to request that an officer check on Sharon to be sure she was O.K. Sergeant G. E. Miller reached her apartment house twenty-two minutes later. He knocked loudly on the front door of Number 9, and like the others who had tried to rouse someone, was met only with silence. While he waited, he glanced idly down into the parking lot and saw "a tannish-mustard Oldsmobile" parked in the stall allotted to Number 9. He noted nothing unusual about it, except that it was covered with mud.

Sharon's fellow teachers told Tumwater police officers that it was quite possible that she had driven to Aberdeen the night before. Although she hadn't mentioned that she might do that, they knew that she was very worried about her stolen key. But a call to her parents in Aberdeen elicited the information that they hadn't seen Sharon since she drove away Sunday afternoon.

Understandably her parents were frightened. They assured the officers that Sharon would have called them if she stayed anyplace but her apartment. "This isn't like her," they told the police and they asked them to go into her apartment.

With the manager leading the way with his pass key, Tumwater Police Chief Ernie Dennis and a silent trio of his officers headed toward Sharon Mason's apartment. Had it been any other woman, they would not have had the same sense of urgency; Sharon hadn't even been missing for twenty-four hours. But Sharon Mason was a creature of habit and reliability.

And the mud-covered car in her parking stall was hers, even though it was in a condition she never would have tolerated.

The police knocked again and still no one answered. As the lock tumblers clicked—still with the original lock—and the door swung open, there wasn't another sound. Sharon's apartment looked as immaculate as it always did. The investigators moved down the hall, glancing into the bathroom, toward the living room with its drawn blinds, down to the bedroom.

There, they found Sharon. The scene was as chilling as any of those she might have imagined during the dark nights that frightened her. She lay on her back on the carpet of her bedroom, mercifully oblivious to the blood-stained shambles around her.

Someone had done terrible damage to the frail school teacher. The skin on her forehead had split where some manner of blunt instrument had crushed her skull, and her fractured teeth lay scattered around her. Her throat bore the marks of a knife. She had obviously been dead for many hours, possibly since the previous night.

Sharon Mason still wore her car coat, sweater, and bra, but she was nude from the waist down. It would take a postmortem examination to say whether she had been raped, but certainly the scene before the investigators suggested that a sexual attack had been attempted.

The investigators moved slowly through the victim's apartment, finding it very neat except for the bedroom. It wasn't difficult to deduce what had happened just prior to the murder. A sack of groceries sat on the counter next to the kitchen sink. The date on the sales slip was *2-23-76* and the time was *4:23 p.m.*

Sharon must have purchased the groceries after she

left the school party. The tenant upstairs had heard three muffled cries at 4:55 P.M. Sharon still wore her coat. When the detectives learned that she had a habit of staying away from her apartment whenever she had reason to be afraid, it was apparent to them that she had intended to be there only briefly. Her neighbor gave the police the license number of the yellow car he'd seen parked in a temporary spot. It turned out to be Sharon's.

But now the car was filthy with mud and parked back in its assigned spot. No, Sharon Mason had not planned to stay in her apartment until she was sure the locks were changed. She had come upstairs, opened the door, and had probably been attacked right inside her front hallway. They believed that her killer had hidden in the front hall closet, waiting for her. The hangers there were askew and clothing was knocked to the floor. As she entered the door, the person waiting had probably grabbed her and dragged her into the bedroom.

She had been only two steps from safety; all she had meant to do was pick up her overnight bag and leave.

Although her murder was accomplished with excessive force and by several methods, it was quite possible that the slender school teacher was unconscious almost at once. The detectives hoped so.

Sharon Mason's murder was the first in Tumwater in a dozen years. Because the Tumwater Police Department had so little experience in homicide investigation, they turned to Thurston County Sheriff Don Redmond's staff for help. Wes Barclift was the mayor of Tumwater, and his brother, Paul, was one of Redmond's top detectives. Assisting were Chief of Detectives Dwight Caron and Detective Sergeant Dick Nelson.

Sharon's death sparked an all-out investigation, even

though Redmond's men sensed that her murder would go unsolved. Some homicide victims had a lifestyle that placed them in the path of homicidal violence. Sharon Mason had been a complete innocent. Any thread that linked her to her killer seemed to be so tenuous that it would be virtually impossible to detect.

"You don't make a whole lot of enemies teaching first grade, spending weekends with your aging parents, and staying at home watching television," Redmond commented.

And, of course, he was right. Sharon Mason was the least likely candidate for murder Redmond had ever encountered.

Dr. Donald Nachoneckny, Assistant Medical Examiner of King County, was asked to perform the autopsy on Sharon. An autopsy, translated, means "to see for one's self." Although victims can no longer say who hurt them, or how they died, the postmortem examination of the body can speak volumes about the truth of what happened.

Sharon had been struck forcefully on the head, and then she had been strangled manually. Human hands had left finger-shaped bruises on her throat. In a delicate victim, death by strangulation occurs quickly, sometimes within moments.

Sharon Mason had been a virgin, but while she was unconscious, her attacker had removed her slacks and her underwear and had "raped" her with a foreign object. There was no physical evidence of normal intercourse, although acid phosphatase tests on her girdle produced the bright reddish-purple reaction that indicates the presence of semen.

She had been alive, but unconscious, when the carotid

artery on the left side of her neck was severed, causing massive bleeding.

There were other, postmortem (after death) wounds on her right thigh. But these long cuts had not bled.

Nachoneckny informed the Thurston County detectives that someone—undoubtedly the killer—had moved Sharon's body some hours after death. Livor mortis, or lividity, is the purplish staining that appears on the lowest regions of a body when the heart stops pumping blood. When the body is moved before lividity is complete, a secondary pinkish coloration appears along the nether regions of the new position. This, the medical examiner said, had occurred in Sharon's case.

The investigators already knew that Sharon's killer had done a great deal of "staging" in her apartment, as if he relished the reaction of the detectives who would try to figure out who he was. They suspected he had stayed in her apartment for a long time after she died. For one thing, the witness who saw Sharon's car out front at five had watched it sporadically all Monday evening until ten—when it was gone. But then it was back the next morning, in its allocated parking spot.

The killer had carefully created the scene in the bedroom. The lower half of Sharon's bedspread was stained red, and so was the carpet beside it. The killer had deliberately driven a bloody steak knife into the carpet between his victim's legs, a phallic symbol that was an especially grim sight next to the birthday cards that spilled from her coat pocket.

More shocking and baffling, however, were the words scrawled across the mirror above the chest of drawers in Sharon's bedroom. The killer had written his message in two shades of her lipstick: DIDNT [*sic*] KEEP THE DEAL. P.S. ONE MORE . . ."

(It was a communication method used by one of the most infamous serial killers in America. In the nineteen-forties, William Heirens, 17, left a lipstick message on the bedroom wall near the body of Frances Brown, a middle-aged nurse. It read, "Catch Me Before I Kill More . . .")

What did Sharon Mason's killer mean? What kind of a "deal" could a woman like Sharon Mason have made with a man capable of such violence? It seemed totally implausible—but there it was written in scarlet on her mirror.

The rest of the elegant apartment was clean. The bathroom had not one speck of blood in it; even when the trap in the sink was removed, there was nothing to indicate the killer had washed up there; the plush bath mat was in place, as was the crystal container of fancy soaps on the sink, and the box of bath powder on the back of the toilet.

Technicians dusted every surface of the apartment for latent prints, sketched the rooms to scale, and photographed every room. Now, the real work would start. The investigative team from the Thurston County Sheriff's Office fanned out to begin questioning the first of over three hundred people who would be questioned before Sharon Mason's murder was solved.

Paul Barclift talked to the shocked and disbelieving staff at the Roosevelt Elementary School. Sharon Mason had been one of the most admired teachers there, calm and loving with her first-graders, and always ready to help out with school projects. While she had no close friends at school, no one described her as stand-offish or unfriendly; she was simply "a very private person."

Sharon had talked often about her parents. "She was superclose to them," one teacher recalled. But as far as her teacher friends knew, Sharon didn't date, and didn't even have a close woman friend.

Sharon's parents told the detectives that they felt they knew her better than anyone in the world, and they knew of no strong attachments she might have had to anyone outside the family. If there had been someone, or if she was frightened about anything, they were positive she would have told them.

Yes, she was afraid of the dark. Yes, everyone agreed that she had been unusually cautious. Was it possible that she had a kind of black presentiment of doom that some potential murder victims seem to feel? Or was Sharon's unusual vigilance due to the fear of a *real* person or situation that she had told no one about? Certainly, she had reason to be afraid during the last twelve hours of her life because she *knew* that someone had chosen her car to break into—that someone had stolen the key to her apartment.

Was it within the realm of possibility that Sharon had had a secret lover? If she had, it would have been a love unconsummated because the autopsy findings had verified that she was a virgin. Was it an affair only of the heart, or an affair that had never begun? Perhaps Sharon's lack of interest in making friends or in participating in activities beyond her parents and homemaking stemmed from a passion that was as secret as it was powerful. Had she promised to marry someone—and then reneged? Had she promised not to reveal a love for a married man—and then done so?

What was the "deal" she didn't keep? Or was it simply a red herring?

Even a woman who kept secrets from the world had to tell *someone*. If Sharon had had a lover, surely she would have entertained him at her apartment, or left at night to meet him. No one had ever seen her with a male companion in the apartment complex, in a restaurant, or at a movie. She was always alone when she registered at the motel where she stayed during power blackouts. And the motel maids said they had never found any sign at all that she had had company there.

The more they found out about the circumspect life that Sharon Mason had lived, the more the sheriff's detectives felt the lipstick-scribbled words had no connection to her at all.

But the P.S. alarmed the investigators. What did the killer mean by "P.S. ONE MORE . . . ? Did another woman have to die before they caught him?

The killer they sought was either very clever or very lucky. All the physical evidence retrieved from Sharon's apartment was sent to the Western Division of the Washington State Crime Lab in Seattle to be compared with known samples. The steak knife used in the murder could be matched exactly to others found in Sharon Mason's kitchen drawer. There were no prints in the apartment but Sharon's. The hair sample clinging to her coat was not her own—but there were no hair samples found to compare it with. The blood in the apartment was all Sharon's. The killer apparently hadn't cut himself during the violent attack.

Paul Barclift wondered how an attack of such ferocity could have taken place without Sharon's upstairs neighbor's hearing it. Barclift sent K. C. Jones to interview the upstairs neighbor who had heard the unusual sounds the night she was murdered while he himself waited in Sharon's apartment.

"I shouted and banged on the floor," Barclift said, "but K.C. didn't even hear me upstairs. With the neighbor's television on and his kitchen fan going, there was no way he could have heard Sharon as she was fighting for her life—nothing beyond those three soft cries."

There was the mystery of Sharon's Oldsmobile. The neighbor saw it at five and at ten, as clean and shining as she always kept it. The next morning, it was covered with mud and vegetation. Sergeant Dick Nelson collected samples of the dirt and weeds from the undercarriage of the car and took them to the geologists at the Washington State Highway Department's Materials Lab in the hope that they would be able to pinpoint the area where the car might have been. Unfortunately, both the weeds and the mud were common to many spots in Thurston County.

It was a long shot, a routine procedure in a frustrating homicide investigation. Another far-out possibility was that there might be something in Sharon Mason's phone records that could help them find her killer. The investigators asked Pacific Northwest Bell for a copy of long distance calls made to and from Sharon's apartment. The phone company representatives said they would forward a report as soon as the records could be compiled.

The area around the apartment house had been searched once, and it was searched again. The investigators found nothing in the building itself, and nothing in the parking lot. Several hundred yards behind the apartment property, the fir forest thickened and the shadows were deep even during the daytime. Among those trees, they found a rude dwelling—a log cabin made of saplings and interior tar paper walls. It was heated with a crude pot-bellied stove fashioned from a barrel. The floors were hard-packed dirt. It looked as if no one had lived in the shack for a long time. With the gaps in between the log walls, it would have been freezing in the wintertime.

Paul Barclift and K. C. Jones talked to people who lived in neighboring houses and learned that teenagers had built the place one summer a few years back, planning to use it as a clubhouse.

"Nobody lives there permanently," a neighbor said. "Sometimes we'll see smoke coming out of the chimney, though."

Walking back through the woods, the detectives saw the apartment house emerge in their line of vision. They came to a jerry-built ladder made of two-by-fours where someone had leaned it against a tree. Testing it first, Barclift climbed up into the tree. He realized that someone standing on this perch could look down into the windows of the apartment house below. He felt a chill and wondered if someone had watched Sharon Mason's windows and seen her as she moved around her apartment. Had her killer stood here and developed a sadistic obsession for her?

His hands sticky from the tree sap, Barclift climbed down and gestured to Jones to climb the tree. They agreed that someone had a bird's-eye view of Sharon's windows.

The two detectives looked now for the teenagers who had built the log shack, or who might have used it. They finally found two boys who admitted they had been up to the cabin.

"We met some guy up there," one of the kids said. "He's about twenty. He says his name is 'Buddy.' We gave him a lift to his friend's house—guy named Al Wilkes*."

K. C. Jones knew Al Wilkes. He was on probation for burglary, but he was a small-time crook with far more nerve than brains. He had no record of violent crimes, particularly not violent sex crimes. "He lives with his father," Jones told Barclift.

When the two detectives went to the Wilkes home, they asked about someone named Buddy. Al Wilkes nodded and said that Buddy Longnecker sometimes bunked at their place. In fact, Buddy was there now. Buddy Longnecker was nineteen, a short, skinny kid who looked as though the next wind off nearby Black Lake would blow him away. Buddy said that he wasn't working at the moment and lived mostly with friends. He readily admitted that he sometimes lived in the little log shack in the woods, but he shook his head when they mentioned Sharon Mason's name.

"Nope," he said. "I don't believe I've met her." And it wasn't likely that he had, the investigators thought. Sharon was eighteen years older, and a world apart in social status, interests and education. Buddy and Al became simply two more names on a long list of people they had talked to. It had been three weeks, and the Thurston County detectives had checked on the whereabouts of dozens of known sex offenders in the Olympia area. They hadn't been able to place any of them at Sharon Mason's apartment, in the woods behind it, or around the school where she taught.

They were holding their collective breath, but there had not been "one more" killing, and they hoped that

that message on Sharon's mirror had been an act of bravado and not a sick promise. They had been unable to find any other sexual attacks or homicides with an M.O. that was similar to the Tumwater teacher's murder. Research told them that sexual sadists enjoyed the "staged murder scene," and the man they sought had played out a flamboyantly cruel drama.

They had so many feelers out, looking for a link to Sharon's apartment that the Thurston County detectives hadn't noticed that the report from the phone company had yet to come in. It wasn't a top priority. They needed something definite, though. All the theories in the world were interesting, but not something they could take to Thurston County Deputy Prosecutors George Darkenwald and Hank McCleary who had been assigned to the Mason case by Prosecutor Pat Sutherland.

And then, almost a month after they lost their daughter, Sharon Mason's parents were sorting through mail that had been forwarded on to them in Aberdeen. They opened the envelope from the phone company and read down through the calls listed. Sharon's father looked up, puzzled. He recognized most of the numbers but there were some he did not.

This was the information that the sheriff's office had requested, but it had been mistakenly sent to Sharon's parents. When Mr. Mason brought it to the investigators, they saw why he was concerned.

There it was. Two telephone calls made from Sharon's apartment on the day she was murdered. The calls were both to San Diego.

The first call was placed at 10:40 A.M. and lasted eight minutes. Sharon Mason was teaching school miles away, unaware that anyone was in her apartment using her phone. The second call was made at 4:40 P.M. and lasted seven minutes. Less than ten minutes later, Sharon arrived home and hurried up the stairs to get her overnight bag.

It didn't take long to find out who Sharon's killer had called. The morning call had been to a middle-aged woman. When detectives called her and asked her who had called her from Tumwater, Washington, on February 23, she answered quickly, "Oh, that would have been Buddy—my son, Buddy Longnecker—Charles Longnecker, Jr."

Buddy Longnecker. Buddy Longnecker, who often lived in the log cabin in the woods behind Sharon Mason's apartment.

Buddy's mother said he had called her to say that he had a new job, and that he was on his lunch hour. He had asked to speak to his brothers and his uncle, but they weren't home. His mother said he had seemed calm, cheerful and completely normal.

When Buddy had called back shortly before five, he had talked to a male relative—a man who had once been convicted of rape, and who had since been jailed once more after an arrest for sexual assault. His mother didn't know what Buddy had said to him.

The man told the Thurston County detectives that Buddy had sounded fine, but that he had hung up hurriedly.

Buddy Longnecker's use of his planned victim's phone to make those calls was patently stupid. Didn't he *know* that long distance calls were easily traceable? Apparently not. Still, the investigators were haunted by the picture of a man who had apparently spent a leisurely day in a woman's apartment, pawing through her private things while he waited for her to come home. Sharon Mason's home had meant the world to her. She had felt safe there. It was so hideously ironic that one of the few places in the world where she felt secure was the spot where she was murdered.

It was time to bring Buddy Longnecker in. The Thurston County investigators staked out Al Wilkes' house all night on March 23, ready to arrest Buddy if he showed up there since he wasn't at the log house in the woods. It was very early in the morning when they saw the back door open and a slight figure emerge. It was Buddy. They saw that he was headed for the woods behind Sharon's apartment house and radioed ahead to Sergeant Miller and Officer Strohmeyer of the Tumwater police to watch for him and arrest him.

Buddy Longnecker was brought in for questioning, read his rights under Miranda, and told why he was under arrest. He denied ever knowing Sharon or ever being in her home.

K. C. Jones told him that they knew he had been in Sharon's apartment shortly before she was murdered. "You made calls from her phone," he said flatly. "We have the records—we can show you. You're a liar."

Buddy glared back at Jones. "I am not a liar."

K. C. Jones looked at Buddy Longnecker with disgust, while Paul Barclift sat quietly by, betraying no emotion at all.

Paul Barclift and K. C. Jones were playing a highly refined version of "good cop/bad cop," and Longnecker bought it. He announced that he didn't like Jones because Jones doubted his truthfulness. "I won't talk to you," Buddy said, "But I'll talk to *him* if you leave."

The Tumwater investigator nodded to Barclift and left the interrogation room. They didn't care *which* of them got the truth as long as he confessed. As soon as the door closed, Buddy Longnecker broke into tears. He sobbed as he told Barclift that he was ready to tell the truth.

But Buddy Longnecker scarcely seemed to recognize fact from contrived fantasy. He wiped his eyes and began a bizarre story.

"I knew her," he said earnestly. "I met Sharon a few weeks ago at the Southgate Shopping Center. She had a For Sale sign on her car—a 1972 Oldsmobile 360 Rocket Jet Automatic."

That was an accurate description of Sharon's yellow Oldsmobile, but as far as Barclift knew, she had had no plans to sell it. Longnecker continued his recollections. He insisted that he had become friends with Sharon, and that he had gone to her apartment "about fifteen times." He even drew a crude sketch of the floor plan to prove his story, pointedly omitting the bedroom where Sharon had died.

That didn't prove anything. Barclift knew that Buddy had been in the apartment. He had had plenty of time to memorize the floor plan during the day he spent there.

"I helped her correct school papers," Buddy said. "And she gave me beer and wine."

Sharon Mason didn't drink, and first-graders didn't do papers that required correcting. Paul Barclift fought to keep his incredulity from showing.

"Hey," Buddy said. "We weren't romantically involved or anything—"

"Really."

Buddy said he knew nothing about Sharon Mason's murder, only what he had heard on the radio. "I went there, all right, to make those two phone calls. But I left before she came home. I didn't even know she died until I heard the news the next day."

"She let you go into her apartment to make calls, did she?" Barclift asked. "And you just met her because her car was for sale? Nobody else told us her car was for sale."

Buddy Longnecker studied the wall behind Barclift, blinking rapidly. "Well, really I met her when I was hitchhiking. She picked me up."

Paul Barclift knew what Sharon's lifestyle had been like. She would no more have picked up a hitchhiker than she would have gone big-game hunting. The kid was lying.

"We smoked some pot together in her car," Buddy said.

Barclift wasn't as confrontational as K. C. Jones had been, but he quietly pointed out to Buddy that he could not have known Sharon Mason to be saying such things about her. "You're not even close to describing the kind of woman she was. I don't think you knew her at all."

"Yes, I did. I knew her really good," Buddy insisted.

At length, Buddy Longnecker changed his story once more, although he insisted that he had been an invited guest in Sharon's apartment. He admitted that he had been responsible for her death, but that it had all been a terrible accident. "I had these 'Numchucks' [Nunchaku Sticks], and I was playfully showing her how they worked."

Barclift knew that the sticks were deadly weapons. They were developed in the South Sea islands centuries ago. Nunchaku Sticks were made of extremely hard wood, connected by a rope or thong. Their inventors used them to thresh grain, but they doubled as lethal weapons. If one stick was held in the hand, and the other whirled, it could split a brick—or a skull—like an eggshell. Remembering the way Sharon Mason's head had been struck, her teeth shattered, made Barclift wince.

Buddy had been taught to use Numchucks by his friend, Al Wilkes. "See, Sharon found me waiting when she came home from work, and she invited me in," he said. "And she and I were smoking dope and drinking brewskis and she asked me how they worked."

Barclift asked Buddy why no one in the apartment house had seen him hanging around her front door, and he said he didn't know.

"Did you write anything in her apartment?" the detective asked quickly. Buddy Longnecker paused for a moment before he answered.

"I wrote on her mirror."

That was it. That was something that no one but Sharon Mason's killer could have known. "What did you write?" Barclift asked.

"I wrote, 'You didn't keep the deal.' See, she was pretty loose and she wanted to know what would happen if a person hit certain places [with the sticks]. The *deal* was that I would show her if she didn't get hostile. We started running around and she went in the bedroom and fell, and blood started coming out of her mouth."

"What did she hit when she fell?"

"She knocked the radio off the dresser."

There had been no radio in Sharon Mason's bedroom. "Did you take the radio?" Barclift asked.

"I broke it up, and threw it away in the garbage cans at Al's . . . I didn't mean to do it."

He was talking now about killing Sharon Mason, but

he continued in his version of their deadly encounter. He insisted that she had been playing with the Numchucks and he'd been trying to teach her how to use them when she accidentally hit herself in the mouth.

Buddy Longnecker veered off into a self-serving description of Sharon's last moments, saying that she had asked him to kill her after her teeth were accidentally broken. He recalled hitting her four or five times with the powerful sticks. Then he had gotten a steak knife from the kitchen and stabbed her in the neck.

Paul Barclift barely managed to keep his voice steady. "Did you undress her?"

"When we were running around, we started to get, you know, sexually involved. She wasn't hurt at that point. She took off her clothes." Buddy insisted that they had had consensual sexual intercourse.

"Did you ever put your hands on Sharon Mason's throat?"

"Yes. Because she wouldn't stop shaking."

He had an answer for everything, for all of Sharon's wounds, all the while maintaining that they had happened "accidental."

After he had left Sharon on the bed in her room, Buddy Longnecker said he had dumped out her purse. "And I found $75 in her coat pocket. I bent her driver's license—to hide her identity."

Buddy admitted taking the yellow Oldsmobile. "Al and I went 'jeeping' with it on the Army reservation." That would explain why it was gone for hours, and returned covered with mud and weeds.

He said he had thrown her keys in the sword ferns behind her apartment house. (When detectives searched later, they found them there.)

Buddy said he had burned his bloodied clothing in the oil drum that served as a stove in the cabin. "The Numchucks?" He had thrown the broken sticks out in the woods, but he had come back later and gathered them up.

Once Buddy Longnecker told his story, the investigators found a lot of physical evidence that tied him inextricably to Sharon's murder. What they never found, however, was a single shred of marijuana in her apartment, a beer bottle, a roach clip, or anything that would substantiate her killer's claim that the two of them smoked and drank together.

When Barclift asked him about that, Buddy said that he had "picked up all the pot and roaches and took them with me."

"Was there anything else written on her mirror?"

"Yes," Buddy said. " 'P.S. And one more.' "

"What did that mean?"

"I don't know."

"After everything was over, what did you do with the knife?"

"I was kneeling down after she was on the floor, and I poked it into the carpet—between her legs."

"Is there anything else you would like to tell me?" Paul Barclift asked.

"Yes. Before I left, I told her I loved her."

Charles "Buddy" Longnecker, Jr. was charged with Murder in the First Degree, First-Degree Rape and Second-Degree Burglary, and bound over for trial in Thurston County Superior Court. He entered a plea of guilty by reason of insanity.

There was no doubt any longer about who had destroyed Sharon Mason's safe little world in a sudden, fierce attack. Buddy Longnecker had carried out a classic sexually sadistic homicide. The question was how he got to the place where he could plan and carry out such a cruel murder at the age of nineteen.

Buddy Longnecker's parents had divorced when he was a small child, and although he called his mother on the day of Sharon Mason's murder, she did not raise him. He was separated from her when he was about six—the age of Sharon's first-graders. By the time he was in his teens, he was a drifter with no real home. He had been arrested for burglary before. The most telling arrest was for entering the bedroom of a sleeping woman. As she slept, unaware that an intruder moved quietly nearby, Buddy stole her purse and her car keys.

The progression of sexual sociopathy is relentless. Most rapists begin with seemingly innocuous crimes: window peeping and exposing. Sometimes, they move on to fetishes; they steal women's panties and bras from clothes lines and laundromats or collect their shoes. When those activities no longer satisfy, they move on to closer contact, contriving more stimulating scenarios. Buddy Longnecker had entered at least one woman's home and pawed through her things. There were probably others. He climbed a tree with his clumsily-built ladder to his perch where he could observe Sharon's apartment. He must have known her routine perfectly. He knew when she left for work, and when she came home. He knew that she left each weekend, although he probably didn't know where she went. At length, he broke into her car to get her house keys.

The horrifying aspect of it all was that Sharon probably never knew about the man in the woods watching her. She always felt safe at home except when the lights went out. And all the while, he had been out there in the forest.

Buddy Longnecker went on trial in Superior Court Judge Hewitt A. Henry's courtroom in May 1976. His trial would last ten days—shocking days for jurors who listened to testimony from the medical examiner and the investigating detectives. Dr. Nackoneckny described his autopsy findings, explaining that Sharon Mason had bled to death from the deep wound in her neck. "This was complicated by asphyxia and the blunt trauma injuries," he added.

The jurors had never heard of Nunchaku Sticks, but the force behind Sharon's injuries was dramatically demonstrated when an expert in the ancient martial art demonstrated. With one swing of the Nunchaku, he cleaved a solid concrete block in two. Everyone in the courtroom gasped involuntarily at the sound. The jurors had seen the awful pictures of Sharon's face. Now they knew what had caused her wounds.

Prosecutors Darkenwald and McCleary presented the damning physical evidence and the many confessions, however outlandish, that the suspect had made.

The Defense countered with its insanity defense. Dr. Gerald McCarty told the jury that Buddy Longnecker had "a very flaky, unreliable cognition of realities . . . some awareness and sense of reality, but no recognition of what was reality and what was not."

This was nebulous testimony, and the jurors looked puzzled. Under the M'Naughton Rule, in order to be found innocent by reason of insanity, a defendant must be shown to have been unable to tell the difference between right and wrong at the time of his crime. Longnecker had taken definite steps to cover up his crime, he had lied to the detectives who first asked him if he knew Sharon Mason, and he had told various contrived lies about his relationship with his victim. He did not seem to qualify as insane under the M'Naughton parameters.

Dr. Richard Jarvis, a forensic psychiatrist from Bellevue, Washington, testified for the State. He disagreed with Dr. McCarty and found that Buddy Longnecker showed "an awareness of the wrongfulness of his act."

It took the jury fourteen hours to return with a guilty verdict. If ever there was a murder that demanded the death penalty, Buddy's attack on Sharon Mason qualified. But he had managed to slip in under the wire. Although Washington State voters had approved the death penalty in the November elections three months before Sharon was killed, the statute decreed that it would apply only to murders *after* July 1, 1976. Sharon Mason had been killed four months too soon for her killer to receive the death penalty, and no matter how George Darkenwald argued that Longnecker's slipping through the cracks was a "travesty of justice," he could not change the law.

In a sense, Buddy had skated for a long time. *Four* years before Sharon Mason died a terrifying death, a psychological evaluation of then-fifteen-year-old Buddy Longnecker warned of trouble ahead. A psychiatrist who tested him in 1972 said flatly that there was no punishment that would prove effective on Buddy. "He should be put away," the counselor wrote. "He is dangerous. He has committed crimes simply because he wants to draw attention to himself and he has no conscience . . ."

But there were no permanent facilities where Buddy Longnecker could have been locked up. Whatever caused his disconnection from other people, he was a creature who lived for pleasure and games and thrills. He had no brakes, and no regret over what he might have done to other people to get what he wanted at any given moment.

George Darkenwald wrote to Judge Henry about Buddy's lies about Sharon, "What is not credible is the story that Buddy took a full month between the murder and his capture to concoct. It tells nothing about Sharon and too little about the events, but much about Buddy, himself. No one who knew Sharon could possibly even imagine the obscenities he uttered about her. But those who knew Buddy could understand only too well how he would like things to have happened the way he said they did. Buddy is a sociopath. His values and goals are those society cannot tolerate. He is not crazy, but he is dangerously different.

"Anyone who would even consider the possibility of releasing Buddy on society should imagine him back in the apartment, rolling Sharon's body over, placing the bloody knife between her spread legs, repeatedly carving on her dead body with the knife until he completed the hideous post mortem wound on her right thigh, and then adding to his message on the mirror in black eyebrow pencil: 'PS. 1 MORE.' No one knows what that means, but the possibilities which come to mind are chilling. It's all too possible he has told us he will kill again if given the chance."

Darkenwald had written down a statement that would survive for decades. "In a sense, writing the statement is like preparing a document for a time capsule to be opened in the year 2000—because I cannot conceive of the question of eventual parole even arising before then . . ."

The year 2000 seemed so far away in 1976. But remembering the terrible tale told in his courtroom, Judge Henry sentenced Charles "Buddy" Longnecker, Jr. to life imprisonment for first degree murder *and* life imprisonment for first degree rape, both with an additional five years for the use of a deadly weapon during the crimes. He specified that the sentences were to run *consecutively*. The lowest minimum term which could possibly be set in Buddy's case would therefore be thirty years.

As this is written, Buddy Longnecker is in the Washington State Penitentiary at Walla Walla. He is now forty-one years old. His release date has been calculated as September 28, 2031.

Sharon Mason would have been sixty years old this year, but she did not live to see her thirty-eighth birthday.

Born to Kill?

In the sixties *and seventies, prisons seemed to have revolving doors. Too many sadistic sociopaths were finding their way back into a society that had naively believed that life in prison really* meant *life in prison. In most cases, it meant anywhere from ten to seventeen years in prison. While the vast majority of convicts are neither violent nor without conscience, the sadistic sociopath is compelled to hurt other people; cruelty is an integral part of his emotional blueprint. He usually makes an ideal prisoner—because he will do what he has to do to get free. But even in prison, he doesn't change inside. And all the counseling, job training, and support doesn't make one iota of difference to him (or, to be fair,* her*). When the sadistic sociopath is released, he will murder again.*

What makes sociopaths this way? Most forensic psychiatrists and psychologists agree that there is no one answer. Early abuse certainly contributes to a child's development into a criminal later on. Quite possibly a physiological defect in the brain adds to the problem. Some researchers believe that criminals have a break in the linkage between the frontal lobe (that gives humans the ability to think and feel) and the limbic system that we share with animals. The latter says, basically, "Take what you want when you want." Some experts thought for awhile that murderers had an extra male chromosome, and that the added "Y chromosome" made them more violent than normal men. That theory, however, proved untrue when tested. In fact, Richard Speck, the Chicago mass murderer of nine student nurses, was the only infamous subject found to have an extra Y chromosome.

It is more likely that some babies are born with a genetic predisposition to violence—just as some are born with an innate talent for music or math or for athletics. If a child has an inherent tendency to be violent and he is born into an abusive situation, the perfect soil is there for growing an antisocial personality. I don't believe in the "bad seed" theory that holds that some babies are absolutely slated for a disastrous future from the moment of birth. There are too many variables, and a warm and loving home can work wonders.

The story that follows is more indicative, however, of what can happen when a child comes into the world with two strikes against him and things only get worse from there.

Michael Andrew Olds never had anything that he could call his own, not even his name. His fourteen-year-old mother was attacked in a dark alleyway in Seattle in the late summer of 1942, and he was conceived during the rape. The rapist was neither identified nor apprehended. Michael's natural father may well have been a man of inherent violence who passed it on to the son he never even knew existed. But there was also the reality that the child's first decade was as horrific as anything Charles Dickens wrote about in *Oliver Twist*. Michael was a boy nobody wanted, and he lived in sixteen foster homes before he was seventeen.

His young mother, just a child herself, didn't tell anyone what had happened to her in the alley—not until she realized that she was pregnant. When she finally confessed that she had been raped, her family was horrified. It was 1942 and good girls didn't get pregnant, or if they did, their families hid them away from the neighbors. Michael's mother was taken in at the Florence Crittendon home in Seattle. It was a good shelter, and she received excellent care while she waited to give birth, but she was lonesome and scared, one of the youngest girls who lived there behind shuttered windows and closed doors.

She bore her red-haired baby boy in April 1943, after many hours of labor. She looked at the beautiful baby and longed to keep him with her, but she was still only fourteen years old and she had no one who would support her if she kept him. She gave him away; there was nothing else she could do under the circumstances.

At some point, the baby was given the name Michael Andrew Olds. On some level, he seemed to sense that his birth had been a mistake, and that he wasn't wanted. A succession of foster parents tried—and failed—to bond with him. He didn't like to be cuddled and he cried constantly—either from temper or colic. He resisted all efforts at toilet-training; perhaps that was the only function where he had any control over his environment. He would have "accidents" until he was eight. He smashed his toys in anger and frustration and fought with other children in the homes where he was placed. Prospective adoptive parents and foster families alike threw up their hands in surrender. Michael *looked* adorable, with his mop of red curls and his freckles, but he was a prickly pear who seemed to dare anyone to love him.

He wore out the first couple who took him in when he was just a baby. The second couple who brought him home had to give up; Michael had carried the family cat to the toilet, dumped him in, and had tried to flush the frantic creature down.

Cruelty to animals is a red flag signal that shows up early in the background of many violent criminals. There was so much going on with Michael Olds that social workers barely had time to chart the latest fiasco.

Attempts at counseling failed to change Michael's behavior, and with each move, he must have felt more of an outcast. Sometimes there were other children in the homes and occasionally he was the only child. It didn't matter; he never adjusted. He was a blur of red-headed fury.

Social workers kept shuttling him around until 1959, when he was finally declared "incorrigible" after a terrifying incident in the tiny hamlet of Dayton, Washington. Given the circumstances, "incorrigible" was a mild determination. Michael, who was seventeen by then, enticed a four-year-old girl into an alley by offering her candy. There he choked and beat the toddler almost to death. She was saved only because a delivery man turned his truck into the alley and saw what was happening.

He was horrified to see Olds straddling a child on the ground with his hands on her throat, as he bellowed, "Die, damn you, die!"

When the man pulled Michael off the little girl, he was still enraged. "She called me a name," he muttered.

Michael Olds seemed to hate the whole world. During the same time period, police had caught him as he was plugging the exhaust pipes of cars with weeds and dirt and newspapers. He said he didn't like the owners, and figured they would die after they were overcome with carbon monoxide from the exhaust gas.

And so, at seventeen, Olds was placed in the Luther Burbank School, where emotionally disturbed teenagers were treated. One psychiatrist reported: "It is clear that Mike needs a placement with strong external controls. This episode, an assault on a four-year-old girl, came too close to homicide and the chances of another such occurrence are too great to consider any other disposition."

Somewhat surprisingly, Mike Olds did well at Luther Burbank; although he was there because he'd been *committed,* he at least knew where he would be for awhile.

And he did do better with external controls. He stayed a year at Burbank. On May 20, 1960, despite his history, Olds was paroled and sent to a foster home on Seattle's Queen Anne Hill.

It didn't work. He came and went as he pleased. He stayed out late, and he was consumed with gambling. He soon dropped out of school to take a job as a stock boy in a medical supply house, although he was a desultory employee at best.

Up on Queen Anne Hill, his seventeenth family was at its wit's end wondering what they would do about Michael. He frightened them because they had no idea what he was thinking. When he was home, he gulped his food and then stared at them with eyes that were as cold as a wolf's. They found comfort in knowing that soon he would be eighteen and he would be free to live on his own.

On the evening of March 28, 1961, Blossom Braham took a little time for herself. She was thirty-eight, the mother of two school-aged boys, and she didn't get that many chances for solitude. Blossom was quite beautiful; a lot of people remarked how much she resembled the movie star Donna Reed. She had once had a career in show business herself—as a dancer. But now she was a full-time mother. She stopped by the Queen Anne branch of the Seattle Public Library that Tuesday evening, returned some books and picked out some others. She needed a few items for breakfast and she walked the few blocks to Jay Samuel's Grocery Store. It was a little after eight in the evening when she got there.

Blossom Braham was a familiar customer and she shopped often at the little neighborhood grocery. Mr.

Samuels looked up from the account books he was balancing as she walked in, and called "Hello, Blossom." She smiled and moved to the bread rack and studied the breakfast rolls. The prices were higher here than at the supermarket, but it was within easy walking distance of her house and she liked Mr. Samuels.

The bell over the door tinkled again as a young man hurried into the small market. He carried a gun in his right hand.

It was a moment frozen in time. Samuels stared uncomprehendingly at the boy with the gun. He didn't say a word, but something made Blossom turn around. The gunman told them both to get behind the counter.

Then he ordered Samuels to empty the cash register and place the contents in a paper sack. There wasn't that much money—less than $40; a neighborhood grocery wasn't the kind of target a professional would have chosen.

Neither Samuels nor Mrs. Braham had resisted in any way. They barely breathed as the young gunman grabbed the sack and backed toward the door.

"Stay where you are," the man with the gun ordered—quite unnecessarily. Both Samuels and Blossom Braham remained motionless behind the counter.

The gunman reached behind him for the doorknob, and then, almost as an afterthought, he raised the gun and fired twice.

Blossom Braham fell like a stone, a bullet between her eyes. She scarcely had time to see death coming. She looked surprised, as if this could not be happening. Samuels made an involuntary move to help her and the gunman shouted, "I said stay where you are!"

It wouldn't have mattered anyway. Blossom Braham

was dying. Jay Samuels fully expected to hear the gun roar again but the gunman turned and ran out into the street.

Patrolmen E. E. Stallman and D. C. Moe received the first radio call for help at 8:43 P.M. They found Blossom Braham on the floor behind the counter; she was unconscious and breathing only sporadically. The officers knew it was the agonal breathing of a person in extremis. An ambulance crew arrived to take Blossom Braham to Harborview Hospital. Harborview's emergency room had wrenched a lot of people back from the edge of death, but there was nothing they could do for Blossom; she died without ever regaining consciousness.

Jay Samuels was in shock, but he tried to gather his thoughts for the homicide detectives who arrived right after the patrol cops. Dick Schoener and Bob Honz asked him if he could describe the gunman. "He was young—a kid, really," Samuels began. "Average height and weight but he had such piercing blue eyes. I've never seen such cold, deep blue eyes in my life."

He thought the weapon had been a .22 handgun. Schoener looked down at the floor and recognized the .22 casings there.

Detective Al Kretchmar joined the group of investigators at the scene, while a cordon of patrol cars was stationed around the area in the faint hope that the shooter was still in the neighborhood. Other officers moved in to hold back the crowds of curiosity seekers who were trying to peek into the store.

Samuels was positive that he had never seen the gunman in his store before, and he was baffled about why the man had fired his gun. "We didn't fight him," he kept repeating. "We didn't even move. He just shot."

Despite the saturation of patrol cars and foot patrolmen in the Queen Anne area immediately after the shooting, no suspect was caught. The investigators were convinced that he had to be holed up someplace. It was an unseasonably warm spring evening and there were lots of people out. A running man carrying a bag full of money would surely have been noticed by someone—yet no one remembered seeing anything. He could be hiding in a blackberry thicket in a vacant lot or he might even have gone into a nearby house. That would explain his disappearance.

The night passed without any sightings of the shooter. It had happened so quickly. Except for the blood behind the counter and the scattered bullet casings, it might all have been a very bad dream. When the homicide detectives finished their work near dawn, Jay Samuels pulled down the shade in the front door and locked the store.

Dr. Gale Wilson, the King County Medical Examiner, performed the postmortem on Blossom Braham. The fatal wound was, of course, the forehead shot; the bullet had transversed her brain, shattering as it hit the back of her skull. Wilson told the detectives observing the post that she would have lived only minutes after such a wound, and all brain function had ceased the moment she was shot. But then he detected another wound, a flesh wound in the right thigh, and the slug was still there. This bullet was retrieved intact, and it would be invaluable for ballistics tests if a suspect gun was ever located.

The *Seattle Times* and the *Post-Intelligencer* both had the story of Blossom Braham's murder on the front page. Blossom had been a lovely woman with high cheek bones, big brown eyes, and perfect features. Her picture stared back from newsstands. Her beauty drew most readers to the story. But it was the horror of her totally unforeseen death that gripped them. How many of them had run down to the neighborhood grocer for a last-minute purchase? Blossom Braham had gone to buy butterhorns for breakfast, followed the robber's orders precisely, and had died. That was what frightened people.

The Seattle Police Homicide Unit on the third floor of the Public Safety Building was deluged with tips from citizens who wanted to help, or who just wanted to get in on the notoriety of the case. None of them panned out. The killer had been swallowed up in the night and might well be thousands of miles away.

On April 1, however, grocer Jay Samuels received a phone call that made the hairs stand up along his arms. If it was an April Fool's joke, he didn't find it funny.

"I want $200," a man's voice breathed into the phone. "I killed Blossom Braham and I wouldn't be afraid to kill again—"

Even though the caller warned him not to, Samuels called the police at once. In a very short time, Detective Ed Ivey walked into the store as if he was a customer, and then he found a spot where he could act as a stake-out. If it was an April Fool's gag, there wouldn't be any more phone calls. It was a crazy thing for the real killer to have done—and the investigators didn't really expect another call, but they had to be prepared.

The phone rang shortly after Ivey was in place. Samuels picked it up nervously and the detective could sense his tension. "Tell me again what you want," Samuels said, and then he signalled surreptitiously to

Ivey to pick up the phone in the back room so he could listen.

"You heard me," the voice said impatiently. "Put two hundred dollars in a paper sack and leave it at Five Corners between five and seven P.M. tomorrow."

Stalling for time, Ivey asked for more specific directions.

"Damn you! You know where it is. It's at West McGraw and Third West!" The stake-out was working. The caller couldn't tell Ivey's voice from Samuels'.

Ivey told the caller to relax; he just wanted to be sure he got everything right, and he didn't want to chance going to the wrong spot.

"I'm not nervous," the caller said. "Not like I was when I shot the lady in the store, and I want the money."

A dummy package with cut-up newspapers between real bills was placed at the designated spot. A dozen officers hid nearby, waiting and watching. They waited until 9:00 P.M., but the killer, if indeed he had made the call, never appeared.

He did not call again.

By April 5, tension was still thick on Queen Anne Hill. Extra patrol cars did little to alleviate the citizens' concern. More than two hundred people had been interviewed, and not one had information that brought detectives any closer to the blue-eyed killer.

In downtown Seattle, cabby Ben Noyes, fifty-two, picked up a fare, a slender youth with red hair and hard blue eyes that bore right into Noyes' own. "Just drive south," he ordered, "I'll give you the address later."

This was the kind of fare that cab drivers hated. Riders without specific addresses were usually trouble. Sighing, Noyes headed out 10th Avenue South toward Beacon

Hill, but he never got an address; instead he felt a gun poking him in the back. His passenger assured him he wouldn't get hurt if he stayed calm and followed orders. They stopped in a thickly wooded area.

The gunman took all the cash Noyes had, but it was only ten one-dollar bills, hardly enough to warrant a drawn gun. "Now, turn around and head toward Queen Anne Hill," the passenger ordered.

As they drove north, he made conversation that did nothing to allay Noyes' fears. "That's where I killed a lady in a store a couple of weeks ago," he said laconically.

Just like everybody else in Seattle, Noyes had heard about the Blossom Braham killing. He was scared. If the guy was telling him the truth, he had shot an innocent woman for no reason at all. Noyes figured he was in trouble—and he was. A moment later, the gun roared in the back seat and a bullet tore into the upholstery just behind his back. He wondered if he'd been hit; maybe he was so badly injured he was in shock and couldn't feel it. And then he realized he hadn't been shot at all—only the padding in the seat behind his back had been.

"I just wanted you to know this gun is loaded," the red-headed kid said. "So no funny tricks."

They were on Third Avenue West when the gunman told Noyes to stop. "Don't call the police," he warned as he left the cab and ran down the street.

Noyes did just that, of course, calling his dispatcher.

Officer Harold Countryman was on an assignment checking parking lots for stolen cars when he heard the call. He was only two blocks away and he wheeled his patrol car around and headed for Third West. As he did so, he saw a young male matching the suspect's description jaywalking just ahead of him. When he saw the police car, the boy broke into a run and disappeared into an alley.

Countryman caught the runner in his spotlight. He turned and faced the officer with a gun in his hand. Countryman leapt from his patrol unit with *his* gun drawn and shouted to the kid to surrender. The red-haired youth hesitated for a fraction of a minute, and then he threw his gun down. Countryman handcuffed him and notified other units of his location.

Was this truly Blossom Braham's killer, or just a punk kid who had bragged about it to give himself some status?

Detectives Bob Honz and Bill Pendergast questioned the suspect. He said his name was Michael Andrew Olds, he was seventeen, and he gave them an address on First Avenue West as his home—it was only six blocks from the Samuels store.

They questioned him and he played cat and mouse with them, first hinting that he was the person who had shot Blossom Braham, and then backing off. It was four in the morning when Michael Olds finally agreed to give them details of the killing.

He was cocky as he related the story, almost like a child playing cops and robbers. It was hard for the detectives to picture this kid, whose cheeks were still covered with downy fuzz instead of whiskers, as a cold-blooded killer, but he was telling them things that only the shooter could know. Olds claimed that he thought Jay Samuels had moved his hands after he'd warned him not to move. "I meant to kill him," Olds said. "But she got in the way."

Later he changed his story. "I'm sure it was no accident. I shot her twice, didn't I?"

Olds seemed almost to revel in the notoriety he'd provoked, and over the next few days he made himself accessible to newsmen who flocked to the jail to see him. A reporter asked him if he was sorry about killing Mrs. Braham, and he gave an incredibly callous answer.

"At first I thought about the woman's family and I was pretty shook up," he said. "But I decided her husband would probably marry again anyway so I stopped thinking about it. I would have killed that cop, too, but he had that spotlight in my eyes and I couldn't see and I figured he had a gun."

Ballistics tests showed that Olds' gun was the weapon used to kill Blossom Braham. He had stolen it in a robbery in the north end a few days before the murder. Olds reveled in his infamy, and enjoyed seeing his picture in the paper, even though he was going to spend his eighteenth birthday in jail. He had never had any identity and now he did.

Michael Olds was charged with first degree murder and robbery and went on trial on December 11, 1961. He pleaded innocent by reason of mental irresponsibility. Olds' sordid and unhappy past became familiar to Seattle readers. The pictures of him in the newspaper showed him as a soft-faced Mickey Rooney–lookalike; he didn't look anything at all like a killer. The defense cited the number of foster homes he had endured and said he had been "neglected, ill-treated and ill-fed during most of his life."

The trial was a tear-jerker that fostered Olds' vision of himself as a criminal folk-hero. His real mother, now thirty-two and married, surfaced and told reporters she had come at last to stand beside her son. She sobbed as she said she regretted that she had never been in a position to help him. But there was surely no way she could help him now.

King County Deputy Prosecuting Attorney Tony Savage did not dispute the facts concerning Olds' childhood, but he questioned whether the past entitled Olds to kill capriciously and coldly. He produced a witness who said Olds had left a card game a half hour before the murder, and returned an hour later. They had all sat there, cards in hand, listening to the radio bulletins about the killing. Mike hadn't betrayed any nervousness at all.

On December 15, 1961, the nine-man, three-woman jury returned with a verdict at 11:00 P.M. They had found Olds guilty of murder in the first degree but recommended mercy. Savage didn't fight for the death penalty. "I am personally opposed to the death penalty in all cases," he said years later. "I had a deal with my boss that any time I tried a first-degree murder case I didn't have to ask for the death penalty."

Because the death penalty wasn't requested, Judge George Revelle sentenced Michael Olds to two life terms, to run concurrently. Washington State law at the time pretty much dictated that a life term was thirteen years and eight months, so the earliest date Olds could be paroled would be when he was just over thirty. The public didn't realize that; they thought he would be in prison for life.

Judge Revelle recommended that Michael Olds be given psychiatric treatment. Everyone involved expected that he would be transferred to the maximum security unit at the Eastern State Hospital where psychiatric treatment for prisoners was handled.

There is no evidence that Olds ever received psychiatric care.

Over the years, the winds of change affected many of the principals in the case. Tony Savage left the prosecutor's office and started a private practice that was to see him become one of the most noted criminal defense attorneys in Seattle. Detectives Bob Honz and Bill Pendergast rose through the ranks of the Seattle Police Department and, tragically, both died young. Harold Countryman resigned from the force. Dick Schoener became assistant chief of police.

Somewhere in the morass of files concerning Michael Andrew Olds, a psychiatrist's urgent warning was lost, or forgotten, or disregarded: "The superficial conforming facade that masks sadistic sexual impulses adds to the danger that Michael poses to the community," the doctor wrote. "Michael requires close surveillance and external controls."

Olds "really adjusted well" to prison life, according to an assistant superintendent of the Washington State Penitentiary in Walla Walla. He became an active member of the Lifers With Hope Club. He was "just a regular type resident [prisoner]," his friends and guards noted.

The memory of Blossom Braham, dead with a bullet in her brain at the age of thirty-eight, faded in the minds of everyone except for the sons and husband and family who lost her so suddenly.

By 1974, Michael Olds was no longer a hot-tempered eighteen-year-old kid. He was a thirty-one-year-old man, a "model prisoner," with nothing negative on his prison record. With so much good time, Olds was paroled on November 4, 1974. Ironically, his early release didn't even rate a line in the Seattle papers.

Michael Olds settled down in Walla Walla, the eastern Washington city where he'd finally found a home in the penitentiary there; the shadow of the walls of the prison didn't seem to bother him. He obtained a job at the City Zoo Pet Center, and he began to court a divorcée with six children. He married her, and for a while it looked as if the jury's faith in him fourteen years before had not been misplaced; they had saved him from hanging, and now he was still a young man—and free.

The owner of the City Zoo found him a dependable employee who did his job well. He didn't make a lot of money, but he tried to supplement his salary by playing cards.

Olds' marriage soured in the fall of 1976. He complained that his wife nagged him all the time and that she and the children wanted to move back to Wisconsin. He had tried to go along with that, and they all relocated to the Midwest. But after a few months, Olds was back in Walla Walla—alone. He didn't want to talk about what had happened, but he went back to work at the pet store. They were glad to have him. He found himself a room with a kitchenette and half-bath for fifty dollars a month.

The female manager of his rooming house was later to describe him as "an awfully sweet guy" who had few visitors but who would often visit with her. Sometimes, they watched television together.

At 1:30 A.M., on Sunday, April 3, 1977, Michael Olds was playing cards in a Walla Walla tavern. The other patrons noticed that he was flashing a thick stack of bills when he had always been close to broke before. It was almost sixteen years to the day since Olds had left a card game in Seattle to kill Blossom Braham.

Sometime later that night, Stephen Schmerer, a twenty-three-year-old Walla Walla cab driver, called his office to let them know he had a fare who wanted to be driven to Pendleton, Oregon, some forty-two miles south of Walla Walla.

Schmerer's cab should have been back in service within two hours, but he didn't notify the dispatcher that he was back in Walla Walla. Efforts to reach him via radio elicited only silence. The dispatcher worried, but then he figured that Schmerer had decided to call it a night after his Pendleton run.

When Michael Olds' employer opened the pet shop for business the next morning, she discovered that $356—which had been in the cash register—was gone. She didn't want to think that Michael had taken the money, but he was the only one besides herself who had the key to the cash register.

On Tuesday, April 5, Stephen Schmerer's cab was found burrowed deep in a wheat field north of Pendleton. Schmerer was found inside, long dead of bullet wounds.

Law enforcement authorities looked at the series of coincidences: Michael Olds hadn't shown up for work, the pet store had been robbed, and Olds hadn't been seen at his rooming house. All of these things had happened within the same time frame as Stephen Schmerer's departure for Pendleton with his fare. It was too much to overlook when they considered what Olds had gone to prison for in the first place.

A "stop for questioning" teletype on Michael Olds was transmitted to the thirteen Western states, and Seattle police were alerted that Olds might be heading to the coast. He had several relatives in the Seattle area and was rumored to have a grudge against some of them. The name "Olds" sent shivers through the officers who remembered him from 1961. They looked at the current photo of the suspect. The boyish facial planes were now gone; at thirty-four, Olds was a beefy man who was five feet nine inches tall and weighed 180 pounds.

Although stake-outs were set up at the homes where he might be expected to turn up, there were no sightings of Olds reported in Seattle.

On Wednesday, April 6, friends of a frail, arthritic, seventy-five-year-old widow named Mary Lindsay became concerned. Mary lived by herself in Ione, Oregon—near Pendleton—and her friends tried to check on her every day, but today she hadn't answered her phone. They drove out to her country place and found her always neat kitchen a mess and her usually well stocked ice box was empty. Mary Lindsay was a light eater; she couldn't have devoured all that food. And there was no way that the elderly woman would have left her home for more than a few hours without informing someone. They reported Mary Lindsay missing.

A call from Mrs. Tom Young* who lived near Pendleton did nothing to assuage the worst fears of local lawmen. Mrs. Young said that she and her husband, seventy-two, had been driving on a back road near Pendleton the evening before when they came upon a reddish-haired man standing in the middle of the road.

He had signalled to them to stop, and then waved a gun at them and commandeered their car.

The Youngs had been forced to drive to their home, and the gunman had held them hostage all night. "He told us he'd killed before and he wasn't afraid to do it again," Mrs. Young told Umatilla County deputies.

On Wednesday morning, the man said he was going to take their car. They were relieved just to have him out of their house, but he dashed those hopes when he said that he was taking Mr. Young with him. Mrs. Young told the deputies that she packed them a lunch of sandwiches, partly because she was worried about her husband's being hungry and partly because she thought if she was friendly to the kidnapper, he might not hurt her husband.

Asked to describe the intruder, she repeated that he had rusty hair, blue eyes and was built squarely. "He wore a white-and-pink shirt, brown trousers, and he carried an Army duffel bag. I got the impression he wanted to head toward Idaho."

The man Mrs. Young described sounded exactly like Michael Olds.

Although FBI agents, state police, and representatives of every law enforcement department in Washington, Oregon, and Idaho were looking for Olds, Mrs. Lindsay and Tom Young, another twenty-four hours passed with no word. They assumed that he had kidnapped Mary Lindsay after he had abducted Young. The officers searching for Olds and his captives knew too well that he had killed before. It was unlikely he would have any compunction whatsoever about getting rid of elderly hostages if they got in his way.

On Thursday, their fears came true when searchers

found the body of Mary Lindsay in high desert country near Burns, Oregon. Oregon State Police investigators from Ontario found that the pitiful victim had been shot and dumped near U.S. 20, the interstate that runs between Burns and Boise, Idaho.

Although the police searched the area thoroughly, they found no sign of Tom Young.

"Maybe he figures he needs Young," one trooper speculated. "He could be hiding in the back seat and using the old man as a cover. I hope we get to them before he doesn't need him anymore."

That afternoon, another woman was reported missing along the route into Idaho. Ida Burley*, a heart patient, had vanished from her isolated ranch near Hazelton, Idaho. Mrs. Burley's car was still on the ranch, but she was gone.

It was Friday night and sheriff's deputies were interviewing Mrs. Burley's worried relatives at her ranch, when they were surprised to see a car pull into the yard. The exhausted occupants were Tom Young and Ida Burley.

Perhaps in shock from their long ordeal, or led by some sense of honor, the pair said they had promised Michael Olds that they wouldn't call the police if he let them go unharmed. And they had kept that promise.

But that promise had cost the police precious time. Tom Young said that he and Mrs. Burley had accompanied "Mike" all the way to Brigham City, Utah. They let him off there to catch a bus, and they had driven all the way back to Hazelton without stopping. They had passed any number of pay phones as they traveled well over a hundred miles, but they hadn't stopped to call the police.

Tom Young explained, "We wanted to be stopped by

the police but we promised the man we wouldn't *contact* them. Mrs. Burley was driving and I told her to go like hell. 'Go through red lights,' I told her."

It was a curious code of honor but one the duo had stuck to. Young said they had agreed to report their abductor *if* a policeman stopped them. Ironically, despite the fact that Ida Burley had broken the speed limit all the way back—three hours on the road—not one trooper had noticed them. "Where's a cop when you need one?" Young joked feebly, but the officers around him couldn't force a smile.

Tom Young was able to fill in some of the missing details about Olds' path of destruction across Oregon, Idaho, and into Utah. He had been with Olds on Wednesday afternoon when he stopped at Mary Lindsay's farmhouse near Pendleton, but he'd been helpless to stop him from kidnapping the elderly woman. He wasn't sure why Olds had taken her. She rode with them in a crazy, meandering path back west across Oregon.

"He wanted me to take him to Portland by way of Mt. Hood," the old man said. "But the roads up on the mountain are treacherous in early April and I told him I didn't have snow tires."

Olds had then directed him to go south to Salem, Albany, and then east again through Sisters and Bend toward Idaho. It was certainly the long way round and had made little sense to Young. They had been close to the Idaho border when they started. He figured that "Mike" had expected a roadblock, and was trying to find an unexpected route out of Oregon.

"He told me to push it to the floorboards and get through anyway I could," Young said, "if we ever came to a roadblock."

But there were no roadblocks. They had driven end-lessly. They hadn't even stopped to eat. First they devoured the sandwiches Mrs. Young had made, and then Olds had cleaned out Mary Lindsay's refrigerator and they ate her food as they drove.

Mary Lindsay hadn't lasted even a day with her kid-napper. Frightened and sick, she had been excess bag-gage for him. They were heading east again on an insane back-and-forth trip across Oregon, and it was about midnight on Wednesday night when Olds told Young to stop the car near Burns. Olds left the car with Mrs. Lindsay, and Young said he'd tried to see where they were going. But they had walked away into pitch darkness.

A few minutes later, "Mike came back alone," Young said sadly. His captor had brushed aside questions about what had happened to the old woman. He hadn't heard gunfire so Young tried to hope that she had been left unharmed and would be picked up and taken to safety. "I had my doubts, though."

Ida Burley was next. Olds had abducted her at gun-point when she answered a knock on her door on Thurs-day afternoon. By that time Tom Young was exhausted from driving all night, and Olds told Ida she would have to drive for awhile to spell Tom.

Tom Young said the nightmare had continued as they crossed over into Idaho, and they had had a moment of terror when they saw a state police car coming up behind them. But then it had passed them at high speed.

"And then just a couple of minutes later, another state trooper was right alongside us. I thought, 'My God, man, don't you stop us!' "

He knew his kidnapper well enough by then to realize they might all die if a shootout occurred. "Mike would have started shooting if they came up to the car," he said. "God must have answered me because the police car continued on its way."

When half an hour passed and no one stopped them, Young had realized the trooper hadn't spotted them. He was partly relieved, partly worried. He kept wondering when it would be his turn to be walked into the countryside. Once he stopped being useful, he didn't expect to survive.

By late Thursday night, they were approaching Brigham City, Utah. Mike said he wanted to go to a bus station. They took him there, and watched him walk away from Young's car, half-afraid he would spin around and shoot at them. But he kept walking.

Ida Burley gunned the motor and they were free; they had outlasted him, although Tom Young hadn't slept for three days and nights. But the gunman's brainwashing power over them continued for three more hours as they raced back toward Idaho, bound by their promise not to call police, emotionally immobilized by their terror and shock.

On Friday night, an unmarked Oregon State Police car delivered Tom Young to Pendleton to be reunited with his grateful wife. Unshaven and weary, he was still able to joke, "What are all the flowers for? I'm not dead yet. I smell like a hog and I need a shave," he added, smiling ruefully.

His wife had never expected to see him alive again, but she scolded him, "Don't ever do that to me again." Then she hugged the man she had been married to for forty-three years.

"I get hell as soon as I get home," Young laughed as he hugged her back.

The investigators were relieved that Tom Young and Ida Burley were safe, but understandably frustrated that Olds had such a substantial lead on them. In the three hours that had elapsed before his whereabouts in Brigham City were reported, he could have gone anywhere. Buses leaving Brigham City were stopped and searched, but Michael Olds wasn't on any of them. He might very well have only pretended he was going to take a bus out of Utah. He could be hitchhiking, driving a stolen car or riding the rails of a train.

Robert Davenport, Assistant Special Agent in Charge of the FBI's Salt Lake City office, said that they had no leads as the weekend passed. "We just hope a lead will come up. There's a good chance he may have left the area. We know he's on the run. And he probably won't stay in one place for very long."

Davenport said his best guess was that Olds had headed east, since he was wanted for two murders in the west. It was possible he was going to his estranged wife who was thought to be in Wisconsin. Two of Olds' victims were women, and he probably was still angry at his wife for deserting him. Stakeouts were placed near her residence in case Olds showed up.

A period of uneasy calm descended. If Olds followed his usual pattern, there would be more abductions, more terrified hostages forced to accompany him as he raced across the country. Police feared they would eventually find more bodies dumped along Olds' trail.

Saturday. Sunday. Monday. The days passed without

word of Michael Olds. Where was he? Was he traveling with someone unable to call for help? He preyed on the old, the sick—people alone on farms or ranches who might not be missed for several days. There were a lot of isolated farmhouses and open spaces between Utah and Wisconsin—or wherever Olds was heading.

And then, on the night of April 11—Monday—Michael Olds surfaced. Incredibly, he had made it all the way across the country without being recognized. McKees Rocks, Pennsylvania is a suburb that edges the west side of Pittsburgh, a community a long, long, way from the vast desert stretches of Oregon, Idaho and Utah.

In McKees Rocks, a young woman left work, headed toward her parked car, and looked up to see a wild-eyed man leveling a gun at her.

"Get in the car!" he ordered.

Her mind raced. She knew that if she got in her car with an armed man, her chance of survival would probably be nil. She might die if she resisted him, but at least she figured she would have a chance. If he shot her where she stood, he wouldn't rape her. Being alone with him would be worse. She told him she wasn't going to get in the car, and started backing up, leading him away from her car. It threw him off balance; he obviously didn't want to draw attention to himself and her resistance was making him nervous. Good.

She saw another employee leaving the building and called out that there was a man with a gun on her. And then she ran. The man with the gun let her go. They called the McKees Rocks Police Department and reported the attempted abduction, describing the stocky stranger in detail.

Police dispatchers alerted officers on duty and a wide-scale search for the gunman was begun immediately. A McKees Rocks police lieutenant saw a man matching the description in the parking lot of the Eat-and-Park restaurant. As he watched from his squad car, the red-headed man walked into the restaurant. It was hard to keep him in sight in the crowded fast-food establishment.

By the time the police lieutenant entered the crowded restaurant, he realized the one place someone could hide was the rest room.

The lieutenant's heart sank as he pushed through the men's room door. The gunman was holding a seven-year-old boy hostage. There was no reasoning with him. The boy's father rushed forward and offered to take his son's place, but the gunman wasn't having any of it; he took the father hostage, too.

Captain Konkiel of the McKees Rocks police force placed a call to the restaurant phone and he, too, offered to take the youngster's place. But the nameless desperado knew a good thing when he had it. He wanted the boy and he wanted a car to make his getaway. Tense minutes ticked by as the McKees Rocks officers tried in vain to reason with him while he also debated with Konkiel on the phone. All the time he bargained with them, he held his revolver against the boy's head.

"I've got nothing to look forward to but the electric chair," the man panted. "You back off or you'll have a dead boy and his father, too. I've killed before and it doesn't mean anything more to me to kill them."

They believed that this stranger meant what he said. Again, he demanded a getaway car. No amount of psychology and coaxing was going to shake him.

Finally, it was agreed that the boy's mother would be allowed to get the family's station wagon and drive it around to the back of the Eat-and-Park. There, the gunman and his two hostages would join her. The police knew they had to get him out of the men's room and, more importantly, they had to defuse the situation to a point where he would ease the gun away from the boy's head.

Bravely, the mother pulled the station wagon up to the back door, and the man with the gun backed out of the restaurant, keeping her husband and son with him. He signaled to the woman that he would drive. He placed the boy in the luggage area just inside the rear window so that no one would be able to shoot at him from behind without endangering the boy.

Slowly, the wagon pulled away and headed toward Pittsburgh along Route 65, with unmarked cars waiting to fall in behind in a cautious caravan.

Jimmy Laurie, Chief of the McKees Rocks Police Department, pulled a few cars behind the station wagon. He was driving an unmarked detective's car. The gunman was unaware that Laurie was broadcasting his progress over all the police channels that linked the Pittsburgh Police Department with McKees Rocks.

Pittsburgh Patrolmen Howard Landers and Lewis Rauhecker were working a two-man car out of the Number 8 Precinct on the P.M. shift that night. They prepared to set up a roadblock at the McKees Rocks Bridge with an assist from Patrolmen Fred Green and Walt Long. But, suddenly the station wagon, which had been moving behind them, sped up and passed them. As it did, the man with the gun leaned out and pegged a shot at Landers. The police car braked to a screeching halt, and the bullet missed Landers by inches.

The station wagon stopped, too. Green and Long were

out of their car and headed toward the wagon from the front as Rauhecker and Landers approached from the sides. The man with the gun had a bead on Green and Long and he raised his arm to fire at them. At that moment, the mother of the boy hostage realized that at least one of the patrolmen would be killed if she didn't act. She reached from the back seat, and knocked the gunman's arm off target. He swung his gun hand and pointed the .32 directly at Lewis Rauhecker's heart.

At the same instant, Rauhecker placed his gun at the gunman's temple, and said quietly, "Drop it."

The officer was taking a desperate gamble. He had the suspect. But the gunman had him, too.

They stood like that for what seemed like an hour. If one shot, the other might die—but reflex muscle spasms action would make a dead finger squeeze off one last shot. One second. Two seconds.

Three seconds.

Four seconds.

Five seconds . . .

Rauhecker could see the man's eyes swiveling. "In his peripheral vision, he could see that he was surrounded," he said later. "Green was coming up over the hood of the car, with Long beside him and Landers was aiming in through the open driver's window. There were other police cars pulling up on every side."

The gunman blinked first and put his gun down on the seat. He was silent as he was cuffed and placed under arrest. They knew his name, but they didn't *really* know who he was. He had told Konkiel on the phone earlier that his name was Michael Olds and that he'd killed before. The Pennsylvania officers did not realize until later just what a big fish they had caught. When they contacted Washington authorities, they realized how close they had come to being blown away.

"He has killed before," the Washington detective told them. "And it doesn't bother him at all."

If Howard Landers hadn't stood on his brakes as Olds fired at him when the station wagon drew abreast of the patrol car, he might well have been Olds' fourth victim. He had felt the wind of the bullet as it whizzed by his face.

A mother determined to protect her little boy had saved Fred Green and Walt Long when she knocked Olds' gun hand off-target. Had Olds decided to take a policeman with him as he died, Rauhecker would never have lived to tell about the memorable capture.

Michael Andrew Olds's arrest pointed out the chance that a policeman takes when he begins each shift. Every one of the McKees Rocks and Pittsburgh officers involved was willing to exchange his life for those of the hostages. Many of them came close.

Although Olds was docile at the time of his arrest, he became belligerent as he appeared at preliminary hearings in Allegheny County. He was charged with attempted kidnaping, simple assault and battery, violation of the uniform firearms act, and terrorist threats. He was held in lieu of a million dollars bail.

He commented sullenly to Landers and Rauhecker that he had almost wanted to be caught. He felt he couldn't survive outside of an institution; the real world was too much for him. If Michael Olds truly wanted the security of prison, he had made sure that was what he would get. In addition to the charges in Pennsylvania, federal charges were filed in Ogden, Utah, for the kidnapping and interstate transportation of Tom Young and

Ida Burley. And then there were the murder charges in Umatilla County, Oregon, for the shooting death of Stephen Schmerer, and Malhuer County, Oregon, for the execution-style murder of seventy-five-year-old Mary Lindsay.

On Friday, May 6, 1977, Michael Olds was returned to Pendleton, Oregon, under heavy guard. He appeared before Circuit Court Judge Jack Olsen in preliminary hearings. His attorney asked that he be committed to a mental hospital for psychiatric evaluation. Judge Olsen denied the request on the grounds that there would be a profound security risk in removing Olds from the Umatilla County Jail.

Clearly, Michael Andrew Olds should never have been released from prison after his first conviction for murder.

His own defense attorney in the trial for Blossom Braham's murder agreed. "I feel terrible," he said. "I hoped that man would have been rehabilitated. Personally, I didn't believe he would ever be this way after he was released. He was a nice-appearing young fellow. The jury probably thought he had made a mistake and if he served a life term in prison, he'd be rehabilitated. But obviously it didn't happen."

But Olds had fooled any number of experts on criminal behavior. All the prison psychiatrists, counselors, guards, work supervisors, and chaplains had praised him highly in their progress reports. Apparently only the prisoner himself knew that he needed the walls and the controlled atmosphere to keep a lid on the hatred that bubbled and boiled within him.

Michael Andrew Olds was the poster boy who illustrated the end result of child abuse. Whether the seed of violence lay dormant within him is a question that can never be answered, but *he* was the first victim, a small boy whose personality was permanently damaged by too little love, too much deprivation and punishment.

The child, who was conceived during a crime of violence, ended, for all practical purposes, his own life with a series of violent crimes.

Michael Olds was convicted of two counts of murder in Oregon and sentenced to life in prison. He is serving his time at the Oregon State Penitentiary in Salem. Today, he is fifty-six years old.

As Close as a Brother

Probably nobody is more consumed by dreams than a teenage girl. At eighteen, everything seems possible: college, a new love, marriage, a baby, an exciting career in a big city. But along with the dreams, there is danger. A lot of teenagers are naive—at least to some degree. They tend to believe that the men they encounter are telling the truth. If a man is good-looking and fun, friendly and helpful, they assume that he is safe. And most of the time strangers are no real threat, even though handsome and friendly men have been known to break hearts.

Anyone who has ever tried to warn a headstrong young woman of the perils of taking strangers at face value knows it is akin to shouting into the wind. It is even more difficult to warn them about someone they already know and trust. They won't listen; they are so easily offended by anyone who tries to give them advice. Most girls eventually grow up like the rest of us in the school of hard knocks and disappointments, realizing ruefully that sometimes you have to be hurt to learn. But some, albeit a tiny percentage, put their trust in men who do more than hurt emotionally.

This case is a heart-breaker, not only for the girls who

learned too late about a deceptively friendly man, but for the people who loved them. Even though their tragedies happened three decades ago, and the victims would now be old enough to be grandmothers, I cannot forget them and the lives they never got to live.

At one time or another, every one of us has known a psychopath. Think of someone who lies when there is no need to lie, who has had just too many bizarre adventures for one person. As they grow older, these people will steal your money, step on your face to get your job, break your heart—but they won't kill you. They are garden variety psychopaths. Terms come in and out of vogue in psychiatric parlance, but the personalities involved don't change. Today, a psychopath is called a sociopath, or is said to have an antisocial personality. A sociopath remains forever in the early childhood phase of emotional development, never developing the controls or the empathy for others that mark an adult personality. He wants what he wants when he wants it. No one else matters.

He is often glib, charming, attractive, and convincing. He is not hindered by conscience. He lies with the guileless smile of a child, the clear eyes of an innocent. If you are lucky, an encounter with a psychopath leaves you only disillusioned and doubting your own judgment.

Two Washington State girls were not lucky. Their encounters with a psychopath ended their lives. Undoubtedly, many more girls would have died if not for the painstaking detective work of Seattle Police and King County, Washington, Police investigators.

On Friday, November 28, 1969, the bridge tender of the First Avenue South Bridge in Seattle reported for work somewhat grudgingly, his thoughts still on the leisurely Thanksgiving holiday just past. There was little traffic; most people had Friday off too, and even the nearby Boeing Company was closed for the holiday. Idly, he scanned the polluted waters of the Duwamish River that roiled sluggishly beneath the bridge.

Decades earlier, the Duwamish was as clear as glass, pristine as it was in the days when the Indians for which it is named lived on its banks. But it was being destroyed by industrial wastes. As the bridge tender watched the dirty water, his attention was drawn to a large object that bobbed in the waves. He had seen some peculiar things in the river, but now he felt a prickling of apprehension. The object was either a department store mannequin or a human body. As he squinted to see more clearly, he realized that it *was* a body. And it looked as though it had been in the Duwamish for some time.

And that was odd. There were so many people who worked near the bridge, who drove over it. The body could not have been there long; someone surely would have spotted it.

The bridge tender ran for the bridge shack and phoned the Seattle Police Harbor Unit. The police boat reached the river beneath the bridge at 8:20 A.M. As the officers aboard drew closer to the drifting form, they saw that it was indeed a body— the nude body of a female.

Immersion in water speeds decomposition of a body and the task before the officers was not a pleasant one. Carefully, they hoisted the form onto the police boat. They could see that she had probably been in the river for many weeks, but her age or what she had looked like in life were impossible to determine.

An assistant medical examiner waited on shore with an ambulance and the body was transferred at once to the King County Medical Examiner's office to await the autopsy that might give some clue as to the woman's fate. The dead woman appeared to have suffered some facial wounds, but that could have happened long after she was dead, damage done by floating trees or something sharp along the river banks. A rule of thumb for any superior detective is that unexplained deaths are treated first as a homicide, second as a suicide, third as accidental, and only when all other possibilities have been excluded, as the result of natural causes.

Seattle Police Homicide detectives Dick Reed and Roy Moran had drawn weekend duty and they observed as Dr. Gale Wilson performed the autopsy on the anonymous woman. Wilson had held his post as medical examiner for more than thirty years, and was one of the foremost forensic pathologists in the country. If the body held any clues, he would find them.

The woman was five feet, five inches tall, and weighed 130 pounds, but her weight could have varied up to ten percent from life weight because of bloating from gases and waterlogging. Only her hair looked alive, it was a rich auburn-brown, long and thick. Her eyes were brown. Dr. Wilson estimated her age at somewhere between twenty-eight and thirty-five, but he warned Reed and Moran that that was only a guess; it was extremely difficult to establish age on a body so decomposed.

One of the best clues to body identification are dental records, but the dead woman's teeth would be of little help. Four teeth were missing and she had no fillings in her remaining teeth. Her fingernails were well cared for; they were long and filed neatly, and were still coated with platinum-colored polish. She had small hands and feet. She wore a Timex watch, which had stopped at 3:10. But whether it was A.M. or P.M., they had no way of knowing.

There was a silver friendship band on her ring finger, left hand, and, in her hair, a white metal barrette.

She had eaten kidney beans and ham within hours of her death.

None of this information seemed likely to identify the Jane Doe victim. Like her age, the cause of her death could not be determined as precisely as it would if she had been found sooner. She had suffered cerebral contusions before she died. Someone had struck her on the forehead and around the bony orbits of her eyes causing injury to the brain itself.

There seemed to be evidence of some hemorrhaging in the strap muscles of her neck indicating she may have been strangled, too, but tissue damage made it impossible for Dr. Wilson to be sure. But one thing *was* certain; she had been alive when she entered the river, although she was undoubtedly unconscious. River silt was evident in her larynx and trachea.

Who was she?

The best chance of identifying her might be through her fingerprints. Because her fingertips were so decomposed, it was relatively easy to slip the loose skin off and send the outer layer with ridges and whorls still apparent to the FBI for possible matching.

Not really hoping to find much, Detective Dick Reed and his sergeant, Ivan Beeson, went back to the banks of the Duwamish near where the body had floated. They scoured the river banks searching for some item of clothing, I.D.—anything that might be linked to the drowned woman. They found nothing.

Dick Reed pored over all the Seattle Missing Persons reports, looking for a woman answering the description of the body found in the Duwamish. Descriptions of the "Jane Doe" appeared in *The Seattle Times* and *Post-Intelligencer,* asking for citizens to come forward with information. As always, there was a flurry of calls. Some of them even looked promising.

Two area women had told friends that they were going to Vancouver, British Columbia, some weeks before, and they seemed to have disappeared completely. The women had criminal drug abuse records in both Washington and British Columbia so their fingerprint classifications were on file.

The FBI Lab in Washington, D.C. was trying to raise the prints from the woman in the river, but it would be days before FBI technicians could complete the difficult process. It might even prove impossible.

Several people had viewed the corpse and a few had made a tentative identification. It was well nigh impossible though to be sure with only a visual observation.

A man familiar to police because he hung around Seattle's skid row told detectives about meeting a "lonely woman" at a waterfront charity shelter. "Sometimes she called herself Margie," he said. "Sometimes it was Betty—and sometimes she said her name was Sue. I expect none of those were her real name. She had a little drinking problem. Not real bad, you understand. But I haven't seen her around for a month."

The man first identified a morgue photo of the unidentified body as his friend. But then he remembered that "Margie-Betty-Sue" had had a rather distinctive tattoo in a "sort of private part of her person." The murder victim had no tattoos at all.

People seeking lost daughters, wives and friends filed through the county morgue, but there was always something that didn't quite match. The body was too tall, or the eyes were the wrong color. She was not the "lost sister" from Bothell. She wasn't the runaway daughter from a posh neighborhood on Mercer Island. Nor was she either of the two women who'd traveled to Vancouver. On December 5, the FBI was able to make prints from the dead woman's fingertips, but they did not match those on the rap sheets of the two missing women.

More devastating to the search, the FBI had no record in their voluminous file of the "Jane Doe's" prints. Apparently, she had never been printed so one of the better methods of identifying nameless bodies was lost to the investigation.

Nevertheless, the Seattle investigators made up bulletins for every law enforcement agency in the U.S. and Canada with the woman's description and her fingerprint classification. If there was someone out there who missed her the detectives would hear about it in time. Though nothing came in that shed any light on the case, they would not give up.

The lack of response was frustrating. Until the Jane Doe body could be linked somehow with the world she lived in, the people she knew, the predictable patterns of her daily existence, finding her killer would be impossible.

In January of 1970, the pitiful corpse was buried as a "Jane Doe" in Grave Lower 6, Lot 122, Section J at Riverton Crest Cemetery. Somewhere, there was probably someone who loved her and who waited for some word from her. The detectives who had tried so hard to identify the lost woman did not forget her. "Someday, we'll find out who she is," Dick Reed commented, "And when we do, we'll find her killer too."

Nine months after she was buried, on September 7, 1971, a report came in that tentatively linked the dead woman with a missing teenager from a small town east of the Cascade Mountains of Washington. Some weeks after the "Jane Doe" was buried, a Missing Persons report had come in from Mr. and Mrs. Murphy* of Cle Elum, Washington. Their daughter, Georgia*, eighteen, had disappeared while on a visit with relatives in Seattle during October and November of 1969.

Georgia was five feet, two inches tall and weighed 110 pounds. She had brown hair and blue eyes. Tragically, but inevitably, neither Seattle nor King County police connected the missing Cle Elum girl with the unnamed woman pulled from the Duwamish. The physical characteristics given for Georgia Murphy and those charted during the "Jane Doe's" autopsy were widely disparate. The dead woman was five feet five; the Murphy girl was said to be five feet two. Their weights were different and Dr. Wilson had estimated the victim's age as from twenty-eight to thirty-five, while the Cle Elum girl was only eighteen. There was really no reason to link the two.

At the time that Georgia Murphy was reported missing, Seattle Police Missing Persons detectives had done some routine checks: utilities companies, phone listings, unemployment records, to see if she had established residence in Seattle and had stayed in the city by choice. But they hadn't gone further. Georgia was eighteen and considered legally to be an adult so it was impossible for the police department in a large city to spend their time and resources trying to find someone who had the legal right to leave home.

Now, however, in 1971, King County Detective Ben Colwell and Detective Sergeant Ray Jenne had new information on Georgia Murphy. Georgia had gone missing not from the city, but from the county. Her parents had said in their missing report that she'd intended to stay with an uncle and his family who lived in a mobile home park in the south end, a park not far from the Duwamish River. But the uncle didn't know where she was.

Colwell perused the records of all the unidentified female bodies found since October of 1969. None of them came close to Georgia Murphy's description—but the woman in the river had been found very close to the trailer park. He called for a conference with Don Cameron and Ted Fonis of the Seattle Homicide Unit.

The four detectives studied the picture provided by Mrs. Murphy, and shook their heads. The missing girl smiled gently in what appeared to be a graduation photo. She was pretty in an elfin way, and she had short dark hair and light blue eyes. The handwritten description on the back of the picture described a petite girl.

"I don't think it's Georgia. The location of the body is

the only thing that fits," Fonis commented. "But we're willing to push it and see if we can find some positive identification. It's remotely possible that the height and weight could be way off. Teenagers grow and parents aren't always aware of just how tall they are. The eyes? That's rougher. Without contacts, people's eye color doesn't change. But let's see what we can turn up."

Detectives Fonis and Cameron drove to Cle Elum, a tiny hamlet on the other side of the Cascade Mountains some seventy-five miles from Seattle. Once a thriving mining town, it had become picturesque—but quiet. It was the kind of town kids often left behind as they set out for adventure in the world.

The information they received from the worried parents was not promising. Georgia had always been a girl who trusted people—sometimes at her own peril. She had longed for love and new experiences, and laughed at her family's concern for her. At eighteen, she believed that there was no situation she couldn't handle.

There were no dental records available for Georgia Murphy; she had always had perfect teeth. As far as her mother knew, Georgia wore pink nail polish—not platinum. Her eyes were definitely blue. There was no question about that. Georgia Murphy had had a very slight foot deformity on her left instep which she favored when she walked. And to the best of her parents' knowledge, Georgia had never had her fingerprints taken.

But yes, Georgia *had* worn a Timex watch with a silver band. (The Timex found on the unidentified body had a gold band.) And, yes, she had worn a silver ring of some sort on the third finger of her left hand.

* * *

Georgia Murphy's parents fought to retain their composure as they recalled the last few days they had spent with their daughter. She had been accepted by the Army as a recruit in October of 1969, and she had been excited about going into the service. Because she knew lots of people in Seattle, Georgia left a little early to go to the city to report for duty. "She left on about October 28 to say good-bye to her friends there," Mrs. Murphy said. "She was going to stay with her uncle."

Her mother said she received word from the Army that Georgia should report for duty on November 5. She had relayed this message to Georgia's uncle, and just assumed he had told Georgia.

Oddly, Georgia's uncle had shown up in Cle Elum on November 11. He said that he and his family had left Seattle for good and were moving on. He returned all of Georgia's clothes—except one outfit her mother remembered: her blue jeans, a blue blouse, blue nylon jacket, and her tennis shoes.

"He told us that she didn't need the rest of her clothes because she would be getting Army issue stuff."

Mrs. Murphy told the Seattle detectives that she'd found her brother's behavior peculiar and a bit scattered. First, he was going to stay in Cle Elum. He even found a job as a clerk at the local police department through a government funded program, but he stayed only one night and then moved on.

He didn't seem to have a plan. He came back to Cle Elum again on November 21, and asked Mrs. Murphy if she had heard from Georgia. When told no, he replied, "She probably went to Canada." On another visit, he'd advised her parents to "forget her."

The rest of Georgia's family was not about to do that,

but they tried to convince themselves that she *had* reported to the Army and was in basic training somewhere. But she hadn't written or called and that just wasn't like her.

Suspicious of the uncle's behavior, Detectives Fonis and Cameron talked to a number of people who knew him. He was younger than Georgia's parents, and he was described as a pleasant enough man until he imbibed too much, and then he could be a "mean drunk."

What the two detectives needed most was something to link Georgia Murphy to the nameless dead woman. So they checked military records to see if Georgia had had her prints taken when she applied to join the service. But her fingerprints hadn't been taken. That would have happened when she reported for duty, but she had never shown up. There was no entry in the Army records that showed Georgia Murphy as being on active duty.

Most of all, the disparity in eye color between the body in the river and Georgia puzzled the investigators. How could bright blue eyes change to muddy brown? They wondered if it was possible that the pollutants in the Duwamish River had somehow changed the appearance of the dead woman's eyes—so much so that they appeared brown? The detectives contacted plants along the river to find what chemicals were dumped into the Duwamish. The answers were startling if only from an ecological standpoint, and they could have great bearing on their investigation. Employees grudgingly admitted to getting rid of waste in the river: "Caustics, oil, oil sludge, sodium hydroxide, and hydrogen sulfide."

The investigators called forensic pathologists all over the West Coast. Their queries were without precedent. Some thought that human eye color would never change; others thought it was quite possible.

The blood in the dead woman's body had putrefied at the time of autopsy but even so a sample had been frozen. Although DNA testing was a long time away, there were fairly sophisticated techniques available to test blood in the sixties and seventies, and criminalists were able to type it. The blood samples proved to be the same type as Georgia Murphy's, although the experts could not narrow it down to enzymes and RH factors.

The Timex watch was no help at all. The number etched on the back was a model number—not a serial number.

Detectives Fonis and Cameron tried another fingerprint check through the FBI. If Georgia Murphy had simply run away, perhaps she had had her prints taken somewhere over the past eighteen months.

No luck.

"We have to find something with Georgia Murphy's prints on it," Cameron said. "Let's go back to Cle Elum."

Again the duo crossed the mountains. They gathered papers and a cosmetic bag that had belonged to the missing girl. They also took hair curlers which still had strands of Georgia's hair twisted in the rollers.

Criminalists using the Ninhydrin process with iodine fumes and heat can bring up fingerprints left on paper decades earlier. Some distinctive prints *were* raised from Georgia's personal papers and her books. On January 7, 1972, the FBI confirmed that the prints taken from the woman in the Duwamish and those on Georgia Murphy's belongings were the same. There was no question now that Georgia Murphy was dead.

The polluted river and inaccurate measurements of height and weight recorded in the missing reports circulated after Georgia's disappearance had contributed to the tragic delay in identifying the lost girl from Cle Elum. Years had passed since a much beloved daughter had been buried as Jane Doe in a pauper's grave.

Now, detectives were forced to confirm what Georgia Murphy's parents had feared all along. On February 17, the Murphys came to the Seattle Homicide office and were briefed on the detectives' work on the case. Georgia was no longer missing. But the truth behind her violent death was still unknown.

Georgia's uncle became a prime suspect. The last place she had been seen alive was near his mobile home. According to witnesses, Georgia had had a date with a young sailor, his sister, and her boyfriend on November 4—the night she disappeared. Her date had told mutual friends that he let Georgia out of his car in front of the trailer park in the early morning hours on the 5th. The uncle had told everyone that she never came home at all.

Information came back to Seattle police headquarters in late March of 1972 that the uncle was in Dallas, Texas. Ted Fonis and Don Cameron requested an address check by Dallas Police. When the man was located in the Texas city, they sent a case summary to the Dallas department and asked that a polygraph examination be administered to Georgia's uncle. Frankly, they believed he had murdered his niece; his skittishness and the way he traveled from place to place certainly made him look like a guilty man.

With a list of questions prepared by the Seattle investigators, Dallas Police Chief Frank Dyson instructed his lie detector expert to test Georgia's uncle. On April 13, 1972, he was hooked up to all the leads on the polygraph: blood pressure, heart rate, galvanic skin response, respirations. They expected him to "blow ink all over the walls."

But he didn't. He passed the test. He passed so cleanly, in fact, that he was eliminated from suspicion. This was frustrating but not unusual in police probes. Some of the "best" suspects turn out to be clean, and some of the most innocent-looking are guilty.

It meant starting over. Now, the Washington investigators focused their attention on the young sailor Georgia had dated on the night of November 4, 1969. Apparently they had gone out several times. His name was Bernie Pierce, and he was just a kid, too, not more than twenty or twenty-one. The detectives learned that Pierce had left the Navy, and was reported to be living with a sister in Flathead County, Montana.

Don Cameron called Flathead County Sheriff Curtis Snyder in his Whitefish office. Snyder assigned Detective Britt Davis to talk with Pierce's Montana relatives. Davis had no luck finding Bernie himself, but he quickly located the man who had accompanied Georgia Murphy, Bernie Pierce, and Pierce's sister on the double date in Seattle on the night of November 4.

"We went to the Double Decker Restaurant," the man recalled. "Georgia and Bernie were fighting as usual. About marriage. Georgia wanted to get married—and Bernie wanted to stay single."

"Were they drinking?" Britt Davis asked.

The young man shrugged. "Georgia wasn't. Bernie might have been. He usually drank heavily when he was on leave. Sometimes he was mean."

The quarreling pair had left the Double Decker sometime after midnight, and Bernie Pierce had told the witness later that he'd taken her home. His friend said that

Pierce had seemed genuinely surprised to hear that Georgia was missing.

The next question was, *Where was Bernie Pierce now?*

His friend told Detective Davis he wasn't sure, but thought he might be in the Seattle area. Bernie's sister was no longer in Montana, and was rumored to be back in Seattle. The informant also suggested that detectives check out a man he knew only as "Sid" who worked in an auto-wrecking yard in Seattle. "I heard he raped a thirty-eight-year-old woman," Pierce's friend said, "and I know Georgia went out with him two or three times while she was in Seattle."

It appeared that eighteen-year-old Georgia Murphy had dated or spent time with any number of dangerous men; her fate seemed almost preordained by the company she kept. As her family had said, Georgia trusted too many people. But she'd been only a teenager, enjoying the excitement in Seattle after growing up in a small town. Obviously, she hadn't been as wise to the world as they had hoped.

By June 1972, Georgia had been dead for more than two and a half years, her body returned to the place where she was loved—but her killer was neither known nor arrested. If Bernie Pierce was in the Seattle area, Detectives Ted Fonis and Don Cameron could find no trace of him. They had checked all the reputed haunts of the elusive ex-sailor, all the pertinent city and county records. They had even checked with the welfare department records. But Bernie Pierce wasn't listed anywhere. Chances were that he had long since left Seattle.

The man described as "Sid, the auto-wrecker" had evidently been a red herring; no one else had heard of him.

It looked as though the person who had bludgeoned Georgia Murphy and had thrown her away in the cloudy waters of the Duwamish was going to get away with it. Good homicide detectives hate a "loser" case more than anything so they work harder on them in their scant free time than they ever do on slam-dunk cases.

However, Don Cameron, Ted Fonis and Dick Reed agreed that they had gone as far as they could go without having some new information on Georgia Murphy's last days.

Kent, Washington, is a small town in the southeast section of King County, a town once situated in the most fertile valley of the county. But by the seventies the valley floor was being paved over for an ever expanding Boeing plant and new shopping malls and businesses. Kent is a half hour's drive at most from the Duwamish River where Georgia Murphy floated.

In Kent, on the evening of August 11, 1972, a young woman named Marjorie Knope was looking forward to the next day with great expectations. It would be her twenty-fourth birthday. Marjorie was temporarily unemployed and lived with her parents in a small frame house. She was finally getting over an event that would devastate most young women. The man she was engaged to had been suffocated and crushed beneath an avalanche at Snoqualmie Pass eighteen months before. After she lost him, nobody else quite measured up. Her old high school boy friend had wanted to renew their romance, but she couldn't do it. A lot of men had asked the slender blond woman out, and sometimes she went—but with little interest or enthusiasm. Finally, only a few days before her birthday, she met a man named Jim. She couldn't explain why, but she *knew* he was going to be special.

Marjorie stayed home deliberately on the Friday night of August 11, hoping that Jim would call. If he did, she planned to invite him to her birthday party.

She watched television with her parents, keeping one ear tuned to the phone. When "Love—American Style," ended at ten, the elder Knopes said they were tired and headed for their bedroom. Marjorie said she wanted to watch television a while longer, so her folks shut their bedroom door to muffle the sound of the TV.

Her father slept soundly; he had to be up at six A.M. Her mother fell asleep too, but woke sometime later at the sound of a neighbor's dog who was barking furiously. She saw a bright slice of light under the bedroom door and wondered why Marjorie was still up. Probably she was just excited about her birthday, or maybe she was disappointed because the call she expected had never come.

Mrs. Knope dozed off again, but it would be a restless night for her. Once more she awoke, too drowsy to know exactly what time it was. She heard voices in the living room, and assumed the television was still on. But then she heard someone walking across the kitchen floor with a heavy footfall. The shoes sounded as if they had rubber heels, and she thought that was odd; Marjorie was either barefoot or wearing thongs earlier in the evening.

Mrs. Knope heard the back door slam, and the roar of an engine revving up nearby. These were the sounds of a summer night, except they were louder than usual. There was a crunch of gravel and the sound of the car backing up and then accelerating toward the Kent-Kangley Road. She thought little of it, and half-smiled. That "Jim" that Marjorie was hoping to hear from must have come over instead of phoning. She was glad; her daughter had grieved long enough over her fiancé.

When Marjorie's dad arose the next morning, he was startled to find the TV blaring and every light in the house on. More disturbing than that, the back door was ajar. But then they lived so far out in the country in such an isolated spot that they didn't have to bother about locking doors. Mr. Knope figured that Marjorie had gone to bed and carelessly forgotten to secure the door.

But when her father checked her bedroom, Marjorie wasn't curled up asleep in her bed. Nor had the bed been slept in.

Puzzled, and with the first flickers of worry intruding, he walked outside in the bright Saturday morning sunlight. Marjorie's rubber thongs lay in the driveway beside some fresh tire tracks.

This wasn't like Marjorie. This wasn't like Marjorie at all. Mr. Knope didn't go to work after all, and when there was no sign of or word from Marjorie by 9:30, the Knopes began to call her friends. Perhaps she had decided at the last minute to spend the night with a girlfriend. She had done that once before, but when she found out how worried her parents had been, she had promised never to do it again. She was a considerate daughter who would never worry them unnecessarily.

No one they called had seen Marjorie since late Friday afternoon. The next hour passed with terrible slowness. Marjorie had to be someplace close by, but they couldn't find her. Filled with dread, her parents reported her missing to the Kent Police. Although she had been wearing baby-doll pajamas when they'd seen her last, a check of her closet led them to believe she was now wearing blue jeans and a "Captain America" shirt. "Some crazy thing with blue and white stripes," her father told the radio operator, "and a big white star on the front. And she's probably barefoot. Her shoes are in the driveway here." He said his daughter was five feet, five inches tall, but weighed only a bit over a hundred pounds. She needed her glasses to see any distance at all.

While the Kent police checked with the King County police about any accident and injury reports, her parents continued to search the house. Their fears increased when they found her blue jeans and the "Captain America" shirt stuffed in the back of her closet. That meant she was still in her baby-doll pajamas. They were positive that Marjorie would never have left the house wearing only her sheer, shortie pajamas—at least not by choice.

The morning wore on with no news of Marjorie. As the noon sun shone high in the sky on her birthday, a fourteen-year-old boy was taking a short-cut across the football field of Meridian Junior High School, a school located several miles from the Knope home. He was almost across when he noticed something lying on the west side of the field, something he couldn't identify right away but which seemed out of place. Feeling the little hairs stand up on the back of his neck, the teenager walked cautiously to within twenty feet of the object and tried to make his brain absorb what his eyes were seeing. Suddenly he realized he was looking at the nude body of a woman. She lay, crumpled in a strangely awkward position, at the far edge of the playing field.

The boy drew no closer, but whirled and ran for home. Thinking he had to be imagining things, his mother told him somewhat impatiently to get in the car, and they drove to the junior high school. When she looked where her son was pointing, she believed him. But she was too afraid to go closer. They knocked on the door of a near-by house and the man living there agreed to accompany them to the field.

He walked to the woman who half-lay, half-knelt there. He touched his hand to the sole of her foot, and found it cold to the touch. Next, he tried to find some faint pulse in her wrist and throat, but there was none.

"She's dead, I think," he told the teenager and his mother. "We won't touch anything—I'm going to call the sheriff."

The first deputies to arrive saw that the young woman who lay in the grotesque position was indeed dead. She lay half on her side, and they could see that her knees were severely gashed, although there was very little blood. These were probably postmortem wounds.

While the deputies cordoned off the entire field with yellow crime scene tape, King County Detective Sergeant George Helland and Detectives Keith May, John Miller and their supervisors surveyed the bizarre scene before them. It was almost surreal in its brutality. It was obvious that someone had driven a car back and forth across the dead girl's body, breaking bones and perhaps literally crushing the life out of her. Tire burns, tracks, and axle grease marked her pale flesh. The girl's knees were cut to the bone where some part of the vehicle's undercarriage had sliced across them.

There were some clothes lying near the dead girl's left foot. As they read over the missing report that was only a few hours' old, they had little doubt that the victim was the missing Marjorie Knope. There was a shortie nightgown, there—just as her parents had described, and there was also a quilted ski jacket.

How Marjorie had come to be on the football field dead—and miles from her home—would be harder to determine.

The detectives photographed the entire scene, taking hundreds of shots from every conceivable angle. Fresh tire tracks were evident in the dirt edging the field and in the grass itself. There were deep indentations in the manicured turf where a car's wheels had spun. The killer had clearly made at least two passes over the body.

The investigators moved carefully in a circle around the body, staring hard at the grass and dirt there. And then, they found what every homicide detective hopes for but rarely finds. There were two small items half-hidden in the grass. They spied a single Kwik-Set key attached to a ring fashioned to look like a tiny princess phone, and a brass button. The button was distinctive, almost military in appearance, with a design of two dragons etched on its surface. Had they belonged to Marjorie Knope? Or was it possible that the killer had dropped them?

Carefully, they slipped the key ring, the button, and the dead woman's clothes in separate bags, sealed them and labeled them with the date, time and their initials.

It is the King County department's habit to triangulate a body site with measurements keyed to fixed points—so that they can reestablish the location absolutely at a later time if they need to. Even photographs are not as precise as triangulation.

Hours later, when the scene had been thoroughly checked out, the victim's body was released to deputies from the Medical Examiner's Office. As they gently turned her body over, the investigators saw she still clutched some kind of scarlet material in her right hand. With rigor mortis fully established, it was difficult to pry the cloth from her hand. She had died holding onto a pair of red panties. Perhaps Marjorie Knope had been trying to find her clothes when she was hit.

"It looks almost as if she were kneeling or crawling when she was run over," George Helland mused. "Maybe she didn't even see what was going to happen. I hope not."

They had been working for hours in the hot August sun, but they were far from finished. There were two areas they had to explore at once. Residents who lived near the field had to be contacted to see if they had heard anything during the night. A sadder task was the questioning of Marjorie Knope's family to see if they could give any reason for her bizarre and brutal murder.

Deputies spread out along the streets that abutted the junior high school property. Most of the residents had heard nothing unusual, but they did provide some information that could very well prove valuable. A man, who had been up with his sick child, recalled hearing a car with a noisy engine and a worn-out muffler on the field about two the previous morning. "I heard car doors slamming," he said.

"Anything else?" Deputy Glenn Christian asked.

"The car's engine sounded like a small motor," he said. "It definitely wasn't a muscle car or anything like that."

A woman nearby told the investigators that she had been extremely conscious of time the night before. "I was waiting up for my teenagers because they had missed their curfew," she said.

The woman said she had seen a small, dark-colored car drive into the school yard at 1:20 A.M. Since her husband worked for the school district, she had watched the vehicle carefully, wondering if it was someone planning to break into the building. After it disappeared from her line of sight, she had still been able to see reflected headlights from somewhere behind the school.

"Then," she told Detective Keith May, "I heard a car start up again—precisely at 2:10 A.M. Seconds later, it reappeared at the north end of the school in the parking lot. It accelerated out of the lot and went south at a rapid pace. At this time, I could see it was like a car my son used to own—a 1961 Ford Falcon. Clean. Dark-colored. Big round tail lights, and, I think, a hole in the muffler. The car disappeared, but it was heading toward Kent on S. E. 240th."

The witness was a detective's dream, good on time and detail.

Marjorie Knope's stunned parents were at a loss to explain why she would have left their house the night before. They were having great difficulty absorbing the fact that she had been safe in her own home, only a dozen feet away from them, and now she was dead. Murdered.

Mrs. Knope went over her memory of hearing a visitor during the night, the slamming of the back door, and the sound of a car leaving. Although she had been half asleep when she heard the sounds, she was sure she would have wakened at once had Marge called for help.

The detectives checked the Knopes' yard. In front of the house, they noted that the freshly plowed dirt next to the driveway was disturbed as if a struggle had taken place there. There was also a mark that looked as if someone had dropped to one knee in the dirt. At a cursory look, the tire tracks in the driveway were similar to those at the play field—new tread on the front wheels and worn snow tires with a zig-zag pattern on the back.

Why, the detectives asked, would anyone have wanted to hurt Marjorie? Had she been afraid of anyone in her life? Was she in a relationship marked by quarrels?

"No," her parents said. "No, not at all." They said she had been mourning her lost fiancé for a year and a half, and had not dated anyone seriously since his death.

It was therefore difficult to form a motive, but the investigators reached for the most unlikely dynamics. Perhaps one of Marjorie's suitors had come to her parent's house in the wee hours of the morning and forced her to leave with him.

"He would have *had* to force her," her father said adamantly. "She would never have gone along willingly. She was little, but she was strong. And she had been working out."

It appeared possible that Marjorie Knope *had* allowed someone to enter her parents' home briefly, after throwing on a ski jacket over her nightie. She might even have walked him (or them) to his car. At that point, the unknown visitor had apparently grabbed her with such force that she was literally lifted out of her shoes. This theory was bolstered when the detectives found her wire-framed glasses in the dirt of the driveway. She wore her glasses all the time, even to have her picture taken.

What struck her parents as strange was that anyone who didn't know them pretty well could have even found their place. "Unless you have directions, it's almost impossible to find our house," her father said.

* * *

The King County detectives knew *what* had happened to Marjorie Knope on her twenty-fourth birthday, but they still had no idea who might have killed her—or *why.*

Detective Keith May was embarking on his first homicide probe and he was joined by a veteran investigator, Detective Ted Forrester. The two detectives and Sergeant Helland checked Marjorie's background meticulously, and talked to several of her girlfriends.

Her friends verified that she had no steady boyfriend. They said she dated quite a lot, but only casually. She and her friends frequented two taverns where dancing and beer-by-the-pitcher were featured. One was the Ad Lib and the other was called The Blarney Stone. They were the kind of taverns where young women could go in a group and know they were among friends. Nobody would bother them. They fed the juke box and listened to "American Pie" and Helen Reddy's "I Am Woman."

Her friends told the detectives that Marjorie had met a man at the Ad Lib on Thursday night. "Marge was in a very good mood," a good friend told the detectives. "This person was named Jim. He had long hair—medium-brown, a beard, and a mustache. He was about five foot ten, and weighed around 160 pounds. They left together, along with another couple we know.

"Marge really liked him and she told me later that he'd promised to call Friday—the night she disappeared—about a Saturday date. The last time I talked to her that day, he hadn't called."

Marjorie's girlfriend told Ted Forrester that she had had some trouble shaking a boyfriend she wasn't interested in. "His name is Scott Benti*. She told me he took her up to the mountains one day and put the make on her. She wasn't interested at all and he got mad. She said he wouldn't speak to her all the way home. And I heard that he told another one of our friends that he 'was going to have Marge—one way or another.' "

"Do you know what he meant by that?" Keith May asked.

"I don't know for sure, but it kind of scared Marjorie when she heard that."

George Helland talked to another girl who had been Marjorie Knope's best friend since they were both in the seventh grade. She nodded when he mentioned Scott Benti. "Yes, she was kind of afraid of Scott. She told me he said 'I'll get you in bed one way or another,' and that the look on his face when he said it scared her. That was the reason she was turned off about him."

Marjorie's best friend verified that she expected to have a date with Jim for her birthday party on Saturday night. "He was supposed to call her Friday, and then pick her up on Saturday afternoon and bring her to my house. She was very pleased and was looking forward to her date with Jim. As far as I know, Marge was home Friday night—waiting for his call."

This woman knew Jim's last name—it was Marrek. But that was all she knew about him.

It was a long weekend for the investigators who were trying to solve the murder of Marjorie Knope. On Monday morning, August 14, they attended her autopsy. The slender blonde woman had succumbed to the grievous damage caused by a car's being driven back and forth across her body. She had multiple rib fractures, and one sharp bone had punctured her right lung, causing a fatal hemopneumothorax. She had literally drowned in her own blood. Her nose, jaw, and thigh bones had been fractured, her knees cut to the bone, and the internal organ damage was extensive—so extensive that it was impossible to tell if she had been subjected to a sexual attack before her death. Her reproductive organs had been crushed too. However, no semen was found.

A woman who weighed 105 pounds would have been no threat even to a small man. This was overkill, and the detectives witnessing her autopsy realized that they were looking either for a man who hated Marjorie personally—or who was a danger to *all* women. They could sense the rage behind his attack, and they left the Medical Examiner's office determined to catch him before he hurt another woman.

It was easy enough to find Scott Benti. He was at home in Kent, and he appeared to the detectives from King County to be in genuine mourning for Marjorie. Moreover, he had an alibi for the late night of August 11—12. He had spent from 7:30 P.M. until well after two A.M. with a half-dozen friends at the carnival rides at Seattle Center. His friends agreed that he had been with them. His car? It was a tiny foreign model that didn't resemble a Ford Falcon in any respect.

Ted Forrester located Jim Marrek at his home in Kent on Tuesday, August 14. Yes, he had met Marjorie at the Ad Lib, left with her to get something to eat, and even taken down her phone number. "I promised to call her on Friday after work," he said, "but I never intended to. I have a steady girlfriend in the north end of Seattle. I knew she was coming to Kent for the weekend."

Forrester nodded without expression, but he thought how sad it was that the dead girl had spent the last night of her life waiting for a call from this man who had already dismissed her.

Nevertheless, Forrester and May checked out the man's alibi for late Friday night. It was good. He had been with several friends. He may not have very gallant—but he was not a murderer.

Already, two likely looking suspects—one a handsome stranger, and the other acquaintance who had threatened to rape the victim—had vanished in a handful of solid alibis. The King County investigators could not find any secrets in Marjorie Knope's life, nothing at all that would make her a likely target for a killer. She had been a sweet and friendly young woman who hoped for a second chance at happiness. Was it possible that a complete stranger had seen her sitting in her parents' living room in her frilly pajamas? Surely, he would have made noise as he forced his way in to get to her. No, that didn't fly at all; the Knope house was too far off the beaten track.

Ted Forrester and Keith May had learned only that Marjorie had been a friendly, quiet girl who was liked by everyone. She had been temporarily out of a job but was cheerfully looking for a new one. Her social life had consisted of going to the funky taverns in the Kent area—taverns that catered to people in their twenties who liked hard rock and cheap beer. Marjorie herself didn't even like beer. She seldom drank more than Coke.

The long summer of 1972 ground on, and the news stories about the small blonde woman killed in Kent went quickly to the back pages and then disappeared completely. There was bigger news as far as the world was concerned: the Olympics in Munich were the scene of a terrible massacre, and there were seven indictments in the Watergate break-in. King County detectives kept up their intensive probe, determined to find the savage killer who had somehow talked his way into the Knopes' home and taken their daughter away.

They stopped scores of cars—dark-toned Fords—and scrutinized their tires, comparing them to the moulages they had made of the tracks in the junior high field and in the victim's driveway. They combed wrecking yards for a Ford with similar tires and a bad muffler and/or an oil leak. Hundreds of people were interviewed, friends of Marge's and friends of friends of friends.

The detectives fielded the kook calls that invariably come in after a sensational murder. An anonymous caller phoned the Knopes weeks after their daughter died and breathed, "Listen carefully: Elton Joe Stark* killed your daughter."

The King County investigators found Elton Stark and quickly saw why he was not the most popular guy in his circle of acquaintances. He was a hothead who annoyed people. But he had barely known Marjorie, and he hadn't even been in town the night she was murdered.

Once more, Keith May, Ted Forrester and George Helland went back over Marjorie's past, and every event— no matter how minuscule—that had changed the dynamics of her family. They still had the key on the princess phone key chain and the button, the two items they had found next to her body. All they had to do was tie them to someone.

They learned that the Knopes were good-hearted, friendly people who had often opened their home to someone in need of help. Most stayed for a short time, but one young man stayed so long that he was almost like a son to them. In the autumn of 1965, when Marjorie was still in high school, they had taken in one of her classmates, a kid who had no place to live. The boy had lived with them for about a year.

His name was Bernard Henry Pierce.

Ted Forrester set out to find Pierce. He followed an increasingly cold trail of apartments where Pierce had lived in the past. At each address, Forrester tried the Kwik-set key. None of the doors swung open. That didn't mean a whole lot; many people get new locks when they move into an apartment. And Pierce was a long shot, anyway, someone who hadn't lived with the Knopes for six or seven years.

Ted Forrester had no idea at this point that a man named Bernie Pierce continued to be a suspect in the murder of Georgia Murphy. That was a Seattle Police case, and since he wasn't a really hot suspect in *that* case, there was no reason that the King County detective would have heard about his connection to another vicious murder of a young woman.

And then Forrester received confidential information from a young woman who had known Bernie Pierce in 1970. Suddenly, the whole complexion of the investigation changed dramatically. The woman's statement about Pierce took him out of the casual contact category. Trembling with remembered terror, the girl told Ted Forrester that she had once lived in the same apartment complex as Pierce.

"We thought he was a really great guy," she began. "My roommate and I considered him as close as a brother. He was really nice to us, helped with heavy stuff and fixed things, you know. But this one time, my roommate was gone for the weekend, and—"

"Go on," Forrester encouraged.

"Well, Bernie came to visit and I could tell he'd been

drinking. He was very talkative. He just stayed and stayed—for over two hours. I finally just suggested that he'd better go—"

She recalled that, to her shock, Bernie Pierce had asked her to have sex with him, and he did so in crude terms. When the informant told him to go or she would have to find someone who would *make* him leave, she had seen a whole different side of his personality. "He grabbed me by the throat until I couldn't get my breath. I was struggling and fighting him. I know I managed to kick him in the crotch—and then everything got black."

She told Forrester that when she came to, she was lying on the floor and Bernie Pierce was leaning over her. "He was crying and he said, 'I almost killed you. I blacked out.' " He had then confessed that he had done something like that "once before."

Terrified, the witness said that she had tried to keep her wits about her. She didn't want him to tell her what he'd done to someone else, fearful that he might get violent again. She pleaded with him to get some psychiatric care—"for his own sake." Somehow she had managed to ease him out of her apartment without any further confrontation.

"I guess I should have reported him," she told Ted Forrester. "But I was too afraid he'd get mad and come back."

"Did you ever see him again?"

"He didn't come back for six months," she said. "And then I wouldn't let him in."

Checking further into Pierce's background, Forrester learned that Bernie Pierce *had* raped a sixteen-year-old girl whose family had befriended him, and he had been arrested for that. He was currently on probation. It was beginning to look as if befriending Bernie Pierce was a decidedly unhealthy thing to do.

Forrester located Pierce's probation officer and obtained a current address for him. On September 18, 1972, five weeks after Marjorie Knope's murder, and almost three years from the time Georgia Murphy had disappeared, he located Bernie Pierce at an address on Des Moines Way South. Forrester realized that the apartment was approximately halfway between the spots where Georgia Murphy's and Marjorie Knope's bodies had been found. He left a note asking Pierce to come into headquarters—which he did the next day.

Ted Forrester had asked the Seattle detectives working the Georgia Murphy case—Ted Fonis and Don Cameron—to attend his interview with Bernie Pierce. If he was responsible for the murders of *two* trusting young women, he had to be questioned carefully.

Bernie Pierce was a softly handsome man who affected an "Elvis" look. He had wavy bangs and sideburns halfway to his chin. He was stocky and powerfully muscled in his arms and shoulders. He didn't seem particularly nervous to be questioned about Marjorie, although he gave as little information about himself as possible. He said that he'd lived with the Knope family from September of 1965 until June of 1966. Marjorie?

"I looked upon her as my sister."

"When was the last time you saw her?" Forrester asked.

"It might have been June or early July," he answered. "I went out to the house to visit her father."

At this point, Fonis and Cameron didn't ask Pierce about Georgia Murphy; he was a reluctant and seclusive subject at best, and the detectives did not want to put him on edge until they were ready. Fonis and Cameron waited.

Asked about the night Marjorie disappeared from her home, only to be found dead at the junior high school, Bernie Pierce said that he had had a fight with his new wife on that Friday—August 11. Sometime after nine, he had left and gone on a drinking binge from tavern to tavern in the southeast part of King County. A lot of the evening was fuzzy, but he recalled talking to a woman he knew at the Four Corners Tavern. He said he had no memory at all of driving home.

"What were you driving?" Forrester asked.

"It was my purple Ford—1963. I don't have it anymore. I sold it to a wrecking yard for junk."

The car was right, but none of the detectives showed their elation. Pierce was allowed to leave.

Ted Forrester found the junked Ford, and it was already partially stripped. No motor. No wheels. The muffler was gutted; it would have been very noisy. He found a blonde hair caught in the car's undercarriage, and he photographed it. He took samples of grease and oil from the undercarriage and then he took pictures of the hulk from every angle, concentrating especially on the snow tires in the back seat. They had a distinctive zig-zag pattern.

It was beginning to appear that Pierce's brotherly feelings for Marjorie Knope were as dangerous as those he had felt for the woman he'd come close to strangling two years before. Before the investigators moved in to arrest him, they needed some tangible physical evidence. The long blonde hair on the junked Ford's undercarriage was good—but even the crime lab couldn't prove absolutely that it had come from Marjorie; the most they could hope for was that it would prove to be microscopically alike in class and characteristics.

Keith May talked to the new Mrs. Pierce at their apartment. He showed her the Kwik-set key. Her face was a study of pain and dull acceptance.

"I had one like that," she said. "But I haven't seen it for several weeks. The last place I saw it was in the glove compartment of the purple Ford that Bernie sold to the wrecking yard."

She explained that the key fit the front door of a home she'd once lived in. When May showed her the brass button, she studied it quietly. Then she moved slowly to a closet and pulled out a woman's coat. She reached into the coat pocket and pulled out a button identical to the one May held.

"I lost that button when it fell off my coat onto the back seat floor of the Ford. I forgot to pick it up when I got out."

Bernie Pierce's wife recalled the bleak night of August 11 well. Bernie had come home very late, and very drunk. The next morning she'd noticed a great deal of cut grass stuck under the rear bumper of the Ford. When she asked her husband about it, she said he hadn't been very concerned. He had simply brushed the clumps of grass off.

"Anything unusual about that Saturday?" Keith May asked.

She shook her head. Bernie had spent the day with her. He had even taken her for a ferry ride. "He seemed perfectly normal—just like his old self."

Forrester and May went to the Four Corners Tavern, and

they learned the identity of the woman Bernie Pierce had talked to the night Marjorie Knope died. She remembered him well; he was hard to forget. She had danced with him, but then he had made an unwelcome pass. She'd walked off the dance floor when he became too familiar. When she told him firmly that she wasn't interested in having sex with him, his response was boorish enough that she remembered it. "He asked me if I knew any other woman in the Kent Valley who might be 'available'!"

On October 10, Bernie Pierce submitted to a lie detector test given by Dewey Gillespie, a highly skilled polygrapher. Gillespie seldom had to complete a lie-detector test; his pre-test explanations were designed to psychologically alarm the test subject. Gillespie's technique worked on Bernie Pierce, and only halfway through the test, he indicated that he was ready to make a statement about Marjorie Knope. Gillespie stepped to the door of the room, and beckoned to Keith May and Ted Forrester.

Bernie Pierce gave several statements to May and Forrester, hedging and stalling before he finally told the whole incredible story. He insisted that he had "blacked out" in the last tavern he visited, and that he had only come to his senses when he was on his way to the Knope house. He had knocked on the kitchen door, and he could see Marge sitting alone watching TV. He had simply walked into the kitchen through the unlocked door, just as he had done scores of times when he lived there. Marge had been wearing a nightie and a robe, and looked up at him with some alarm. First, he said, he told her he was drunk and apologized for that. She was nervous as she sat on the edge of the couch. She told him that her folks were just in the next room.

He had stood up then and prepared to leave, but he told the two detectives that he had suddenly gotten the idea that he should rape Marjorie. "First, though, I had to figure out some way to get Marge outside because any scuffle would bring her father out of bed with his big .44 . . ."

He said he had seized upon a ruse to get the trusting girl outside. He'd pulled out the choke on his car to flood it, and then asked Marge to come outside and help him start it. She'd slipped on the ski jacket and obligingly walked out to the driveway.

But, as Marjorie neared the driver's side door, Bernie Pierce had suddenly grabbed her by the throat and held on. The young woman had tried vainly to pull his hands away, but she became unconscious and sank on one knee to the driveway dirt. Then he had picked her up and put her in the trunk before she came to, and sped away from the home that had once been his own.

Bernie Pierce continued his sickening confession. He said that Marjorie was conscious when they got to the play field. When he opened the trunk, she had tried to crawl out. She was bewildered and asked him why he'd choked her.

"I told her, 'I want to have sex with you.' "

Marjorie had asked him where they were, disoriented by shock and being unconscious. She didn't recognize the junior high playing field in the dark of night. Apparently realizing she was trapped, Marjorie reportedly begged the man who had been like a brother to her to promise not to hurt her.

"I told her I wouldn't hurt her."

Pierce said he had removed his own clothing first, and then Marjorie's. In an ironically "gallant" gesture, he

177

said he had spread "Marge's coat on the ground so she wouldn't have to lie on the damp grass."

Asked to describe his victim's attitude, he recalled that it was one of submission. She was trying not to do anything to anger him. She had kept asking him "Why?" again and again, and she'd reminded him of his wife and his family. She had pleaded with him to "see a doctor."

Although he would not admit to it in so many words, it was apparent to the investigators that Bernie Pierce had been unable to reach a climax. It may have been because he was very drunk, or Marjorie's pleading may have distracted him.

She apparently still believed that he could be reasoned with.

Pierce recalled that Marjorie had complained that she was cold. She tried to put her coat on. "I took it away from her and told her to get in the car because it was warmer there."

He directed her into the back seat of the car, and again tried unsuccessfully to rape her. At last, he moved away from her and started to put on his clothes.

Marjorie Knope must have thought she might have a chance to get away. But, tragically, after she got out of the car she stopped to find her clothes. Had she not been so modest, she might have been able to slip away in the dark and hide from him.

"Marge had moved somewhere behind the car," Pierce continued. "It sounded like she was crying."

Sobbing, she had crawled along the ground trying to find her clothes. She was on her hands and knees when he made his decision.

"I don't recall feeling any emotion at all," he told Ted Forrester and Keith May. "I just wanted to leave, so I started the car and backed up. It must have seemed necessary at the time to back up—because I did—and I backed right over Marge. I felt it but I don't think I realized what I hit because I just put it into first gear and drove over her again frontwards and off the field . . ."

He had noticed dirt and grass under his bumper the next day and cleaned it off. Later in the week, he said the Ford's engine had thrown a rod and he'd sold the whole car to the wrecking yard for fifteen dollars. He hadn't "learned" of Marge's death until more than two weeks later when a relative told him about it. "The news shocked me. At that time, I was not aware that I had caused her death."

Not impressed with his selective memory, Forrester and May arrested Pierce and placed him in the King County Jail. On October 16, 1972, he was formally charged with first degree murder. Pierce pleaded not guilty. But, on November 20, he changed his plea and told Superior Court Judge James Dore that he was guilty of second degree murder.

The case of Bernie Pierce was far from over. Finally, Don Cameron and Ted Fonis of the Seattle Police Department could question him about Georgia Murphy. Their case was much more difficult; they had no physical evidence to link him to Georgia's murder. Even with a confession, defendants have been acquitted unless there was some strong physical evidence to back up that confession.

Bernie Pierce was cagy. He would admit only to having been with Georgia Murphy on the night she was alleged to have died. He wanted to "think about the rest of it."

When he thought about it, Pierce was not anxious to talk to Cameron and Fonis again. The Seattle Police detectives wanted Georgia Murphy's parents to have the scant comfort of knowing what had happened to their eighteen-year-old daughter. Pierce said he would take another lie detector test only if he was assured he would not be prosecuted on the Murphy case as a result of his polygraph answers.

As far as a prison term was concerned, the Murphy conviction would matter little. But, for her parents, it was essential to learn the truth. It was January 1973 when Pierce faced polygrapher Dewey Gillespie for the second time.

Gillespie found strong evidence of deception on Pierce's part when he asked the vital questions about Georgia. In the interview that followed, Bernie Pierce finally admitted his involvement in her death.

Pierce told Don Cameron and Ted Fonis that he and Georgia Murphy had gotten into a fight late on the night of November 4, 1969. He said he had pulled Georgia out of his car and she'd hit her head on some concrete. She had lost consciousness.

And then, with the flat, remorseless voice that detectives had come to expect from Pierce, he told them how he had simply rolled her into the Duwamish River. He didn't know whether she was dead or not, nor, apparently, did he care. Asked about the clothes she wore that night in early November, he said he had probably dumped them somewhere along the Pacific Highway.

Bernie Pierce was clearly a man full of rage, a rage that was exacerbated by alcohol. Beyond the two murders he had confessed to, and the sexual assaults detectives already knew about, Pierce admitting choking a

A BUS TO NOWHERE

Silas Garfield Cool in July 1994. He had come to Seattle from the other end of the country but, somehow, things never worked out well for him. *(Police photo)*

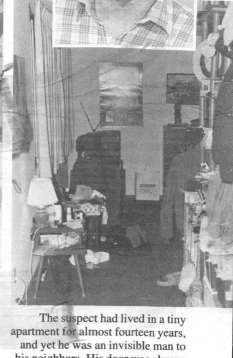

When Seattle homicide detectives went to the apartment of the mystery man on the bus, they found a profusion of bus schedules stacked on bookcases and room dividers. *(Police photo)*

The suspect had lived in a tiny apartment for almost fourteen years, and yet he was an invisible man to his neighbors. His door was always locked; his windows were covered with aluminum foil. *(Police photo)*

The tops of sixty-foot trees mark the spot where a 40,000-pound articulated transit bus carrying thirty-five people plunged through the concrete-and-metal guardrail of the Aurora Bridge in Seattle. (*Police photo*)

Seattle transit driver Mark McLaughlin was flung onto the rooftop through the windshield of the bus, which had sliced through the apartment building roof and torn the porch off a top unit. Paramedics' gear still rests at right center, where they tried to save McLaughlin's life. (*Police photo*)

The bus from the Number 359 route lies crushed against an apartment house after falling sixty feet from the bridge above. (*Police photo*)

Only six inches saved the residents of this apartment house from being crushed. Police, paramedics, and citizen heroes pried these bus doors open in an attempt to save injured passengers. *(Police photo)*

Seattle firefighters and rescue workers beneath the Aurora Bridge, looking for victims beneath the fallen bus. *(Police photo)*

The two sections of the articulated bus, virtually ripped apart, beneath the tallest bridge in Seattle after the accident. Passengers came flying from the bus as it fell. *(Police photo)*

Seattle homicide detective Gene Ramirez, wearing protective clothing to avoid transfer of evidence, searches the bus wreckage. He stands where a violent stranger stood twelve hours earlier. *(Police photo)*

The wreckage of the front half of the "bus to nowhere." Hero driver Mark McLaughlin was catapulted through this broken windshield to his death. *(Police photo)*

The shattered bus waits for detectives to process it as a homicide scene. Passengers' belongings remain where scattered by the deadly plunge. *(Police photo)*

Purses, Christmas shopping bags and, sadly, the red beret of one of those who died, still rest in the bus that fell from the bridge. *(Police photo)*

THE KILLER WHO PLANTED HIS OWN CLUES

A Thurston County Sheriff's Department criminalist dusts a goldfish bowl in Sharon Mason's living room for fingerprints. She believed the home she treasured was a safe haven but, sadly, it wasn't. *(Police photo)*

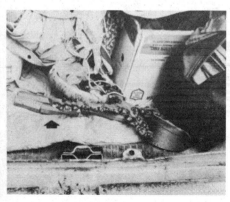

The broken Nunchaku sticks used to kill Sharon Mason were found in the trunk of the suspect's friend's car. *(Police photo)*

Sharon Mason's killer left this message written in two shades of her lipstick on a mirror in her home. The homicide investigators believed it might be a red herring. *(Police photo)*

Sharon Mason, a shy school-teacher, lived on the second level of this well-kept apartment house in Tumwater, Washington. She didn't know that someone was watching her from the woods. *(Police photo)*

The man who was obsessed with Sharon Mason hid in this rustic cabin in Washington State. He would perch in a nearby tree where he could peer into her apartment. *(Police photo)*

BORN TO KILL?

Blossom Braham, thirty-eight, shortly before she was shot to death in March 1961 by a redheaded teenager who had never seen her before.

Michael Andrew Olds, eighteen, is reunited with his natural mother in jail, after she read the publicity about the murder charges filed against him.

Michael Andrew Olds is escorted to his 1962 murder trial by King County deputies.

Michael Andrew Olds, captured in Pittsburgh, Pennsylvania, following a killing spree, after he held a family hostage and tried to shoot it out with police. Olds was extradited to Oregon and sentenced to life in prison in the Oregon State Penitentiary, where he remains today.

AS CLOSE AS A BROTHER

Marjorie Knope had no reason to fear the man who knocked at her parents' door late at night.

This man had been treated like a son by the victim's parents. He betrayed them in the worst way anyone ever could. *(Police photo)*

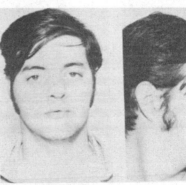

The zigzag tread of snow tires led police to the death car—and a prime suspect. *(Police photo)*

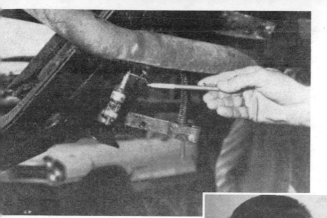

A blond hair was caught in the undercarriage of the Ford that killed Marjorie Knope. *(Police photo)*

King County detective Keith May, who investigated the murder of Marjorie Knope. *(Ann Rule)*

King County detective Ted Forrester, who discovered a long blond hair caught in the undercarriage of the suspect's car. *(Ann Rule)*

PROFILE OF A SPREE KILLER

Christopher Wilder had large blue eyes and a beard and mustache, and he could be both charming and disarming. Many of the women he approached walked away with him quite willingly.
(Police photo)

A montage of eight of Wilder's victims. He was an expert at the ruses and phony stories that tragically work so well for some spree killers.

Wilder's Path......

11 Colebrook
10 Victor • Penn Yan
7 Grand Junction •
6 • Milford Lake
8 • Las Vegas
4 • Bainbridge
5 Beaumont •
3 Haines City •
1,2 Miami

A map tracing the path of Wilder's murderous spree.

1- Feb. 26, Rosario Gonzales, **Missing**
2- March 3, Elizabeth Kenyon, **Missing**
3- March 18, Theresa Ferguson, **Dead**
4- March 20, Unidentified FSU Student, **Attacked**
5- March 23, Terry Walden, **Dead**
6- March 25, Suzanne Wendy Logan, **Dead**
7- March 29, Sheryl Bonaventura, **Missing**
8- April 1, Michelle Korfman, **Missing**
9- April 10, Dawnette Sue Wilt, **Attacked**
10- April 12, Beth Dodge, **Dead**
11- April 13, CHRISTOPHER BERNARD WILDER, **SUICIDE**

Christopher Wilder was a successful contractor in Boynton Beach, Florida. His own home had a swimming pool, and he had expensive toys: boats and a sports car. When the police asked too many questions, he simply disappeared, leaving it all behind. *(Police photo)*

THE LONELY LADY

Photo of Marcia Moore as a bride in November 1977. She was thrilled with her new life and her new husband. Sadly, her happiness wasn't fated to last long.

Barbara Easton, noted Northwest psychic consultant, came to a tragic conclusion when she read several spreads of cards about the fate of Marcia Moore. *(Ann Rule collection)*

Author Robin Moore, famous for *The French Connection* and *The Green Berets,* knew his sister would never have disappeared willingly. (Publicity shot: *Court Martial,* Robin Moore)

TO AN ATHLETE DYING YOUNG

Jane Costantino was a wonderful athlete who accomplished every challenge she set for herself. Minutes after her last victory, she met a killer on the road.

Dale Harrison, thirty-seven, turned away from one potential victim—and met Jane Costantino in a national park. *(Police photo)*

RUBY, DON'T TAKE YOUR LOVE TO TOWN

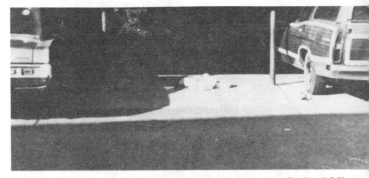

A blanket between the cars marks the spot where Amy Packard fell, shot fatally by the man who had once loved her. *(Police photo)*

Bob Fox, Des Moines police sergeant, grabbed the surviving children and saved them from further violence. *(Ann Rule)*

Brad Lee Bass, twenty-one, was a tall, good-looking young man, but he was naïve—and it cost him his life.

A police photograph of the killer, "Jackie Emerson." *(Police photo)*

Washington State corrections supervisor Chuck Wright, an expert in dealing with sexual offenders, had a difficult task when he had to recommend a prison for Jackie. *(John Nolte Photography)*

THE KILLER WHO TALKED TOO MUCH

Marcia Perkins, twenty-three, trusted someone who was infinitely dangerous. By the time she realized that, it was too late.

Detectives found two cups with instant coffee in them on Marcia's counter. *(Police photo)*

Jeannie Easley, twenty-one, the second young woman to die in two cases with many commonalities.

The apartment house where Jeannie lived. *(Police photo)*

Profile of a Spree Killer

We have become so familiar with the term "serial killer" that most of us don't remember that this appellation is relatively new to the jargon of forensic psychologists and detectives. Before 1982, all multiple killers were called "mass murderers." Indeed, when I published my book about Ted Bundy, The Stranger Beside Me, in 1980, even he was called a mass murderer on the cover copy—and no one questioned that. It wasn't until my dear friend, Pierce Brooks, retired Captain of the Los Angeles Police Homicide Unit, invited me to present the Bundy case to the VI-CAP (Violent Criminals Apprehension Program) Task Force in Huntsville, Texas, that I first heard the term "serial killer."

Serial killers kill one or two victims at a time over a long period of time. They are addicted to murder—just as some people are addicted to drugs, alcohol, or gambling—and they do not stop until they are dead or arrested. At first they kill out of curiosity and a deeply imbedded rage, and it gives them a chilling kind of "high." They may not try it again for a few years. Gradually, their killing games grow closer together until they must *kill just to feel what they term "normal." The "substance" they abuse is, of course, not drugs or alcohol; it is the power of controlling the life and death of another human being.*

A mass murderer, unlike a serial killer, who is considered "sane" by current medical and legal standards, is almost always psychotic. The mass murderer makes headlines for just one day's activities, when his paranoia sends him into a business, a restaurant, or, too many times, a post office, where he attacks every human being he encounters. The mass murderer's toll is high, but rarely as high as the overall body count run up by a serial killer. The serial killer takes infinite pains to keep his identity secret and to escape detection. The mass murderer is often bent on suicide. He either kills himself or places himself deliberately in the path of police bullets. Charles Whitman, shooting at hapless targets from the Texas Tower in Austin, was a mass murderer, and so was James Huberty at the McDonald's in San Ysidro, California, and Howard Unruh in Camden, New Jersey, in 1949. Whitman and Huberty died the day of their crimes and Unruh still lives in a mental hospital.

There is another, less known, category of multiple murder: the spree killer. The spree killer borrows certain traits from both serial killers and mass murderers and yet he is neither fish nor fowl. (I say "he" advisedly in all three groups because serial murder, mass murder, and spree murder are all male-dominated crimes.)

A spree killer erupts suddenly, metamorphosing from a seemingly normal—even charming and successful—personality to a killing machine. Once he begins, he is a juggernaut who selects and stalks his victims day after day after day until he is stopped. His binge as a self-

proclaimed executioner may last a week or even a few months, and, like the serial killer when he reaches his endgame, the spree killer begins to lose control and he takes chances that make it more likely he will be recognized and caught.

Andrew Cunanan was a spree killer, committing murder across America in July 1997, finally exposing himself to the public when he shot designer Gianni Versace in Miami. He committed suicide in a nearby houseboat, where he was hiding out. And so was Christopher Wilder, whose crimes inspired blazing headlines in 1984—although few people remember him today. Wilder was among the cruelest—and wiliest—killers I have ever researched.

Christopher Wilder was born in 1944 in Sydney, Australia. Early on, the blue-eyed, blond-haired boy demonstrated signs of sexual aberrance. He was involved in a gang rape at the age of fifteen, a terrible crime against a young girl. Wilder told her that if she had sex with him, he would protect her from the other teenagers who held her captive, promising her that he wouldn't let anyone else bother her. Desperate, she agreed—and Chris Wilder laughed as he broke his word.

Fantasies of rape enthralled young Chris Wilder. He was given therapy and even electroshock treatments in an attempt to get him to re-focus his energies. On the surface, he seemed normal, although he exhibited symptoms that bespoke an underlying obsessive-compulsive disorder. He washed his hands until they were raw, and he drank gallons of water a day—as if he were trying to cleanse himself inwardly as well as outwardly. But he kept his deviant sexual fantasies to himself.

In his twenties, Chris Wilder was investigated after two teenagers disappeared on a lonely Australian beach, but somehow he slipped through the cracks in that country's judicial system. He emigrated to America with no criminal record, and eventually became a naturalized

American citizen. He lived an upper middle-class life on the east coast of Florida where he became a successful contractor. With a partner, Wilder built fine homes and small office buildings in Boynton Beach and Boca Raton. He himself owned a very nice house located on one of the many canals snaking into the area; it was somewhat isolated from other homes, made more so by the trees and shrubs that grew high around it.

On the surface, Chris Wilder would seem to have been a man that single women would find attractive. He owned his own home, complete with a swimming pool, plus a thriving business, and one of his avocations was race car driving. He had a customized Porsche 911 which he drove expertly on various tracks in the area. He also had a boat. At thirty-seven, Chris Wilder was a good looking man just under six feet tall, although his hairline had receded until he had only a single stray lock on top that he combed forward to a point in the center of his forehead. He made up for the thin hair on his dome with a luxuriant mustache and well-trimmed beard. His eyes were deep blue, his features even, and his smile expansive.

But there was something about Wilder that turned women off. Lots of them wanted to be his friend, but few accepted dates that might turn romantic. Perhaps it was a sixth sense, a gut feeling that he was a little dangerous. It may only have been that he seemed to be a little nerdy.

In 1981, Wilder made a real effort to find someone. He joined a dating service, paying a hefty fee up front for the professional video that promised to introduce him to available women. Gazing into the camera, Chris Wilder spoke in a soft voice that had the slightest trace of a lisp, but no Australian accent at all. "I want to date," he said. "I want to meet and enjoy the company of a number of women. I want to meet someone special."

His words sounded like every ad ever placed by a "swinging" playboy in a lovelorn column. "I have quite a few playthings at home," he bragged. "I like sports cars. [But] bar hopping is not—and never has been—one of my greater joys . . . I would like a family one day."

Perhaps. "Between the ages of fourteen and twenty-four, I was heavy into surfing," Wilder continued. "That was my sole game in life. Arriving here and finding no surf, I went from one extreme to the other. I was completely non-work oriented prior to coming here."

Apparently, he wanted to come across as a good, solid, marrying kind of guy—but also as an exciting man. He sounded too perfect. Why—at almost forty—was a man with so many sterling qualities still single? Why did he have to pay somebody to find him a date?

In truth, Wilder had met many women already; he just hadn't met any who wanted to be involved in a serious relationship with him. He took out Vicki Smith, who was also a race-car driver. They certainly had a lot in common and they went dancing once a week. "He was so polite and gallant," Vicki remembered. "He never let me open my car door."

But politeness and gallantry weren't enough for Vicki. And their dancing dates became sporadic when Wilder met a woman he found completely perfect for him. Her name was Beth Kenyon and she was twenty-one in 1982 when she met Wilder at the Miss Florida beauty pageant. Wilder introduced himself as a professional photographer. He had an expensive camera around his neck and was taking pictures of many of the contestants. Beth liked his easy manner and his smile.

Beth was tall, slender, and classically beautiful. She had been a cheerleader through high school and college, and she was a finalist in the Orange Bowl princess beauty contest. When she graduated from the University of Miami, she became a teacher of special education classes at a high school in Coral Gables. She coached the cheerleading squad and the girls were thrilled to have her.

Beth Kenyon and Christopher Wilder were never a couple, not in the way he visualized it. For one thing, he was sixteen years older than she was, and she had a number of men in her own age bracket whom she dated. Beth's family was wealthy, and she was scarcely impressed with Wilder's construction business, his house, cars and boat. She never considered him anything but a buddy. And she talked about him that way to her mother, Dolores Kenyon. Chris was someone she occasionally had dinner with, a good friend who was always available to her.

Dolores Kenyon met Chris Wilder sometime after Beth did, when he invited Beth and her family out for dinner in an expensive French restaurant. "He was very polite," she recalled. "He brought flowers for the women, and he stood when we entered the room."

Later, when Dolores would have a tragic reason to try to dig deeper beneath Wilder's courtly facade she recalled, "There was nothing menacing about him at all. Actually, Beth found him a little boring . . ."

Shortly after this "family dinner," both Beth and her parents were stunned by what happened the next time Chris Wilder saw Beth. "He asked Beth to marry him!" her mother said. "Beth was shocked. She had never given him any encouragement. She told me she explained her feelings to him, and afterward she thought that everything was fine—they were just going to be friends. She said he took her refusal very well."

Beth Kenyon got over her surprise at Chris Wilder's unexpected proposal, and decided that they had simply been miscommunicating, but that they had worked it out. Chris had taken her explanation that she just didn't view him as more than a very good friend without any sign that he was hurt or angry. Had Beth known that he was devastated, she would have been even more shocked. He didn't betray his feelings by so much as the flicker of an eye or a flush of embarrassment.

Beth continued to see Chris and to trust him as a friend. She was serenely oblivious to the fact that he was totally obsessed with her. He had buried his secret fixations for most of his life, and by the age of thirty-nine, he was expert at hiding them.

Chris Wilder had arranged to race his Porsche in the 1984 Miami Grand Prix during the last week of February. The dark sports car, Number 51, was as familiar to race fans as Chris himself was. On February 26, he was seen around the track, and so was twenty-year-old Rosario "Chary" Gonzalez, a pretty dark-eyed girl with dreams of succeeding as a model. A pharmaceutical company had hired Chary and several other attractive young women to pass out free samples of a new pill containing aspirin to the race fans. The "models" all wore red shorts and white t-shirts.

Chary Gonzalez left her home in Homestead, drove north for twenty-three miles, and arrived at the parking lot of a hotel close to the racing action. She picked up her tray of samples at the pharmaceutical company's tent at 8:30 that Sunday morning. She was a little tired because she had been on the phone with her fiancé until almost two A.M., making plans for their June wedding. But she was young and her smile was vibrant as she moved through the sea of people on Biscayne Boulevard near Flagler Street and the Bayfront Park.

It was shortly after one P.M. when Chary dropped her sample tray at the company tent, saying she was going to take a lunch break and then return. But she never *did* come back to finish the day's work. There were so many girls in white t-shirts and red shorts that no one noticed one of them was missing.

Rosario Gonzalez had told her parents she would probably be home for supper in Homestead between six and seven that Sunday in February. When she wasn't there by nine, they were worried—worried enough to call the Florida Highway Patrol to see if there had been an accident involving their daughter. There hadn't been, but Chary still wasn't home at 3 A.M. Some sixth sense told the Gonzalez family that Chary was in terrible danger. "We were so hysterical, screaming and crying," her father said, "We couldn't control our emotions long enough to say a prayer."

Miami Homicide detectives were handed Chary's case the very next day, Monday morning. Miami has a tremendously high homicide rate as well as a high number of adults who simply disappear for their own reasons. But the vanishing of Rosario Gonzalez was treated seriously from the beginning. She was happy at home, madly in love, and thrilled to be planning her wedding. She had no reason at all to run away.

Detectives' questions produced only a few witnesses who remembered seeing Chary on Sunday afternoon. One of the other models who handed out aspirin samples said that she and her mother had seen Rosario. "She was following a man, or maybe just walking behind him in the crowd," the girl said. "He was white, and looked as if he was in his late thirties."

It wasn't much to go on, but a police artist produced a sketch of the man from the other model's description and distributed it to the media. The *Miami Herald* printed a story about Rosario's disappearance, and a scattering of "sightings" trickled in. A man on the Pompano Turnpike called police to say that he'd seen a girl resembling Rosario jump out of a car near the Turnpike Plaza and run. But two men had chased after her, caught her, and it looked as if they were struggling with her and beating her as they forced her back into the car.

The motorist said he'd followed their car to the turnoff to Boca Raton and managed to get the last three numbers of the license plate. It was a little help — but not much; the Motor Vehicles Department at the Florida State Capital in Tallahassee fed the numbers into their computers and got back *12,000* cars which had that combination of numbers on their plates. It would be virtually impossible to check out the whereabouts of all the registered owners.

Beth Kenyon didn't know Rosario Gonzalez, although she may have read about her disappearance in the paper or seen the story on the evening news. Beth's school was in Coral Gables, just south of Miami. On Monday, March 5, only a week after Rosario Gonzalez's disappearance, Beth didn't come home to the apartment she shared with a roommate on Ives Dairy Road.

Her roommate assumed that Beth had gone to her parents' home in Pompano Beach, about thirty miles up the Florida coast, so she was not really worried—not until someone at the high school where Beth taught called the next morning to ask why she hadn't come to work. Beth's roommate called Bill and Dolores Kenyon, and learned that they had not seen Beth nor did they know of any plans she might have had that would have kept her away from her apartment all night. Frightened, they notified the Metro Dade County police.

Three days passed with no word from Beth Kenyon. On Thursday, March 11, Beth's Chrysler convertible, the car she had driven away from the high school in Coral Cables, was found parked at the Miami International Airport. But Beth's name wasn't listed on any flights going out of Miami during the previous three days.

The Kenyons hired Ken Whittaker, Jr., a private investigator and the son of a retired FBI agent, to search for Beth, even though the Miami-Dade County police were doing everything they could to find her. It was a daunting task for everyone; there was *nothing* in Beth Kenyon's past that might explain her sudden disappearance. As a beautiful woman, she certainly had had a number of boyfriends but, as far as her parents knew, she had never had an acrimonious breakup. She had no enemies. Like Rosario Gonzalez eight days before, Beth Kenyon had seemingly stepped into another dimension.

Beth's photograph became familiar to people who lived in southern Florida. One man who learned she was missing worked at the service station in Coral Gables where she usually bought her gas. He remembered the last time he had seen her—on Monday, March 8, shortly before his shift ended at three o'clock. She had been driving her convertible, but she was talking with a man who drove a Cadillac Eldorado.

The attendant recalled their conversation to investigators, "She was asking, 'Am I dressed all right?' and 'Who will be taking my picture?' When I went to clean her windshield, she told me, 'Don't worry about that—I'm late for the airport.' "

The man in the Cadillac had paid for her gas, and she had followed his car out of the gas station.

This was the last reported sighting of Beth Kenyon. Who was the man with Beth on Monday afternoon?

Beth Kenyon's mother went through the photo albums her daughter had kept updated so meticulously. Dolores Kenyon slipped all of the pictures of men out of their transparent envelopes. It was a difficult task because she had to look at photo after photo of her daughter smiling into the camera, and it heightened the terrible sense of loss and anxiety she had fought for days. She knew some of Beth's boyfriends, some of her platonic friends, but a few of the photographs were of men she didn't recognize.

Dolores Kenyon gathered up the pictures and took them to the gas station where Beth had last been seen. The attendant thumbed through the photos, and paused as he stared at a picture of Beth with a balding man at the Florida Derby Horse Race.

"That's him. The man in the Eldorado."

Dolores looked at the picture. It was Chris Wilder. She shook her head slightly in disbelief. Chris Wilder was the most polite man she'd ever met. She remembered the flowers, the lovely French dinner, how deferential he was to all women. She recalled how he had confessed his love to Beth, and then been so understanding when Beth gently refused his unexpected proposal. It was difficult to picture him as an abductor.

Investigator Whittaker and his dad called the number

after Chris Wilder's name in Beth's address book. He answered, and said that he *did* know Beth, but that he hadn't seen her for awhile. Told that he had been placed with Beth on the previous Monday, he said that wasn't possible. He said he'd been working in the Boynton Beach area and hadn't been anywhere near Miami or Coral Cables. He did, however, agree to call Beth's parents to "reassure" them. And he said he would be happy to talk to the investigators.

Ken Whittaker, Jr. and an associate drove to Wilder's home on the canal in Boynton Beach. No one answered their knocks and all the window blinds were tightly drawn. They left and visited the offices of his construction company, restaurants where he was known, and, finally, the Boynton Beach Police Department. There they found someone who was not disbelieving when they suggested that Christopher Wilder might be connected to Beth Kenyon's disappearance. The local police department knew that Wilder had a criminal record, which included three charges of sexual assault and abduction, and that he had left Australia under a cloud, after his last visit.

Even while he was dating Beth Kenyon, Chris had been on probation after he pleaded guilty in 1980 to charges of attempted sexual battery brought by a teenage girl in West Palm Beach. He had, however, denied any connection to the charges to his friends—insisting that he had only been questioned about the girl, and that police had admitted it was a case of "mistaken identity." Wilder had violated that probation almost immediately when he flew to Australia. There he had kidnapped and sexually assaulted two teenage girls. He had been arrested the next day, but Australian authorities released him on $376,000 bail that his parents had posted. He then left Australia, after promising his parents he would return for his trial, which was scheduled for April 1984.

With all the charges and trials pending, Chris Wilder had managed to maintain his equilibrium. He continued to race his Porsche, date a number of women, and act as the good and generous friend that everyone in Boynton Beach and Boca Raton knew. But now, the world was clearly closing in on Chris Wilder. He was apparently *anything* but the perfect gentleman and the considerate and understanding "buddy" that Beth thought he was. He had demonstrated that he was a sexual predator. It was Ken Whittaker, Jr. who saw the link that might connect Beth's disappearance with Rosario Gonzalez. When he learned that Wilder drove a race car, he recalled that Rosario had vanished during the Miami Grand Prix.

Armed with this information, Miami Homicide Detective George Morin checked Wilder's name against the roster of competitors on the weekend of February 25–26. He found that Chris Wilder had driven his black Porsche 310HP sports car on Saturday, the twenty-fifth. He had placed seventeenth out of the large field of drivers and had won $400.

More ominous was the statement of a photographer who had been at the Grand Prix that weekend. He told detectives that Chris Wilder had presented himself as a photographer as well as a contractor and race car driver, and had had an expensive camera around his neck on Sunday, February 26. The two had walked past the pharmaceutical company's tent, and Wilder had stared openly at the girls who were handing out free samples. The witness could place Chris Wilder within ten feet of Rosario Gonzalez shortly before she disappeared.

Neither Beth Kenyon's parents nor the investigators doubted now that Wilder had taken her away. Dolores and Bill Kenyon went to Boynton Beach with the investigative team on Monday, March 12. Beth had been missing for a week, and Rosario for fifteen days. It took everything her parents had not to knock on Wilder's door and demand that he let them in, but they waited at the Boynton Beach Police Department as they were asked to do.

The investigators, in plain clothes, went to Wilder's construction offices and asked to speak to him. And then they waited. Several hours later, a Cadillac Eldorado drove up and Wilder got out. They confronted him and asked to talk with him, and he nodded amiably and invited them into his office.

Smiling at them, he fixed his clear blue eyes on their faces as he said he couldn't have been with Beth in the gas station the day she vanished. "I was always working," he explained. He called in an employee who gave him a somewhat halting alibi, "Chris is always down in Boca in the morning—then back here in the afternoon," the man said. "He's *always* here in the afternoon."

Boca Raton—the posh seaside resort town, whose name flows so easily off the tongue. Few realize that it actually means "the mouth of the rat." There *was* a tremendous amount of construction going on there. Any contractor worth his salt could make good money.

The man who gave Wilder his alibi had blurted out something about "a girl's car found at the airport," and then acted as if he'd wanted to take it back. "That's what you told me, wasn't it, Chris?"

Darting a cool glance at his talkative employee, Wilder had said quickly, "Yes, her mother told me that."

He gave the detectives permission to accompany him to his home—as long as he was back at work by five. But first, they checked with Dolores Kenyon. She was adamant that she had *never* told Wilder about Beth's car being found at the airport. That was information that the police had chosen to keep quiet so that they could weed out the compulsive confessors from the real person who had abducted her.

And yet Chris Wilder had known exactly where Beth's convertible was.

At this point, Ken Whittaker, Jr., and his associates pulled out of the intense probe, allowing the Metro detectives to carry on a full-scale investigation of Christopher Wilder. The Kenyons still hoped against hope that Beth was alive somewhere; nothing mattered except that she be found as soon as possible.

Up until this point, the investigation into Beth Kenyon's disappearance had been conducted mostly by private detectives; when adults go missing, it is a rule of thumb that police departments wait from twenty-four to forty-eight hours before they get actively involved, simply because the vast majority of those missing come home. But eight days later, there was no physical evidence that Beth had been harmed. No blood. No signs of any struggle. No bullet fragments. No torn clothing. Nothing.

It is difficult to obtain a search warrant without probable cause and a list of what detectives hope to retrieve by going into a car or a house or a boat, "tossing it," and searching for evidence of a crime. The Metro police didn't have that probable cause—at least, they felt they did not. Wilder's background file showed a pattern of his skipping away from prosecution. They wanted to be sure they had him so solidly that there was no way he could slip out of the net they were weaving.

Theirs was, perhaps, a tragic reluctance to move forward. Chris Wilder had been seeing a woman counselor about his sexual obsessions, a condition of his probation on the rape charges in 1980. Although professional ethics forbade her saying anything to anyone, his therapist suspected he might be dangerous. He seemed to her to be a "walking time bomb."

She knew that he was obsessed with sex, fantasizing about holding women captive. His ideal relationship with a female would be that *he* was dominant and his "partner" submissive. As a boy he had wanted to become a white slaver. A decade or more earlier, he had read John Fowles' *The Collector*, a novel where a man kidnaps a woman and keeps her in a sealed room, trapped like some exotic butterfly, totally in his possession.

Now, Chris Wilder failed to show up for his appointment with his therapist on Thursday, March 15. He headed instead to the ocean and checked into a Daytona Beach motel. He wandered the sandy strip, stopping to talk with young women he met there. None of them would recall that he said anything obscene or suggestive. They remembered only that he had distinctive blue eyes and a soft voice.

A fifteen-year-old girl named Colleen Orsborn disappeared in Daytona Beach on that Thursday, gone as quickly and certainly as Beth and Rosario were. No one can say if Chris Wilder was responsible for her vanishing; she would never be found.

Wilder had less than a month before he was scheduled to go on trial in Australia. Florida police were focusing on him, and, on Friday, the *Miami Herald* broke the story about a race car driver who was a suspect in the disappearance of both Beth Kenyon and Rosario Gonzalez. They did everything but print his name and a photograph.

It spooked him. He had slipped out of control a few days before, and now he saw surveillance teams everywhere he looked—even though they were only in his imagination. He told acquaintances that the police were parking vehicles close to his house and business so that they could watch his every move.

The Miami detectives had taken a calculated risk that a man with as much property and as many ties to Boynton Beach and Boca Raton would not bolt and run. In every contact with him, Christopher Wilder had been as cool as ice cream; he never got angry and he never got flustered.

But now, driven by his obsession and his paranoia, he blinked. Quietly, Wilder withdrew savings from his bank account, using some of the money to purchase a 1973 Chrysler New Yorker with low mileage. He took his three big dogs to a kennel and left them.

And then he left South Florida far behind. He may have had nothing left to lose, but Chris Wilder intended to make a large and horrible statement.

Each serial killer and his evil brother, the spree killer, has a plan in mind, and a preferred victim type. While their obsessions are insane, they themselves are not. These murderers know exactly what they are looking for in a victim, and they are always prepared with a ruse, a device, a *plan* that they can activate when they spot a potential victim. Chris Wilder was fixated on beautiful young model types, the tall slender girls who were caught somewhere between the innocence of a teenager and the sophistication of a woman in her twenties.

Despite his bizarre compulsion, Wilder was a very intelligent man and he knew exactly where to go to find girls like that: amateur model shows in the malls of America . . .

Would-be models and starlets are made vulnerable by their ambition. Chris Wilder would take advantage of that. He was immaculately dressed with a neatly trimmed beard as he blended in with the crowds surrounding the temporary stages in the malls. Long-legged coeds and high school girls strolled and strutted, some smoothly and some with the awkward coltishness of adolescence. Wilder was well prepared with fake business cards that identified him as the representative of a model agency. With an impressive camera on a strap around his neck, he watched the amateur models and smiled at them encouragingly.

St. Patrick's Day found Wilder a hundred miles north of Boynton Beach at a shopping mall on Merritt Island. Teresa Ferguson was twenty-one, the stepdaughter of a police captain in Indian Harbor. Terry hoped to become a model and she was certainly lovely enough. She had huge brown eyes, a full mouth and clouds of dark hair. She sometimes affected a sultry, pouting expression when she gazed at a camera, but she was really a sweet-natured girl.

Terry Ferguson took her time shopping in the mall that Saturday afternoon. At some point, she was approached by a man with sandy hair and a neat beard. Shoppers in the mall would recall seeing her talking earnestly to a man with a camera. She didn't seem at all alarmed; she was smiling and nodding.

In a seemingly unconnected incident, a man whose car was stuck in the sand near West Cocoa Beach had to call a tow truck that day. Merritt Island is a long, narrow, offshore spit of sand, and it wasn't unusual for people to get stuck. It was sometime between three and three-thirty when the call for a tow came in. The truck driver responded, to find a man about forty, balding, with a short beard. His 1973 Chrysler was trapped along a local road known as a lover's lane. In his frustration at finding himself in the soft loam, he had revved his engine until the rear wheels of the car were deeply embedded. He said his trunk was locked and he didn't have a key, but that he didn't have anything in there that would help him dig out, anyway.

The Chrysler came out of the sand easily enough, he paid the tow truck driver, and drove to a Cocoa Beach motel, where he didn't check in with his real name—Chris Wilder; he signed the name of his business partner.

Like Rosario Gonzalez and Beth Kenyon, Terry Ferguson failed to return home, and her parents reported her as missing.

On March 20, three days later and 250 miles away in Tallahassee, a nineteen-year-old Florida State University student named Jill Lennox* was shopping at the Governor's Square Mall. Slim and blonde, Jill *looked* like a model. It had been six years since Ted Bundy entered the Chi Omega sorority house at Florida State and had left two coeds dead and two others gravely injured. Six years since he had sprinted across campus to attack another woman on the same night. The fear that had gripped Tallahassee then had long since dissipated. Jill Lennox had been only thirteen then, and if she'd ever heard of Ted Bundy, she knew he was safely locked up on Death Row in the Florida State Prison in Starke.

When a man walked up to her and held out a business card, Jill was a little startled—but not afraid. He explained that he was a professional photographer and that he could not help noticing that she had the kind of beauty that modeling agencies were looking for. Jill smiled but shook her head when he offered her a job. He had a commission for a "shoot" and he needed a young blonde who looked like a coed. "That's you," he grinned. "You're perfect. I have things set up back at my studio."

"No," she said. "I don't think I'm interested."

When he couldn't convince her to take the job, the bearded man shook his head good-naturedly. "O.K.," he said, holding his hands up in a gesture of defeat. "I took some shots of you as you were walking—" He offered to send them to her if he could use them, too.

"But my release forms are back in my car. It's parked right outside the entrance, there."

It seemed safe enough. Broad daylight in the parking lot of a busy shopping mall. Jill walked with the man toward his car, a car that wasn't quite as close as he'd described. He talked amiably as they strolled toward it, lifted the trunk lid, and rummaged around inside.

And then he half-turned and his arm shot out as rapidly as a snake striking. His closed fist hit the softness of her belly, knocking the wind out of Jill Lennox. An instant later, she felt a blow to her head that left her dizzy. Before she could gather her wits to run or fight, the man lifted her off her feet and tossed her into the trunk, slamming the lid down hard and plunging her into complete darkness. She was tossed around as the car hurtled out of the mall lot.

After several minutes, the car stopped, the trunk lid opened and Jill rolled toward the lip of the compartment.

They were out in the country somewhere, but she didn't get to look long; he tied her hands and feet, and slipped a gag in her mouth. As the car started up again, Jill tried frantically to think of some way to call for help, but she was totally helpless.

Although Jill Lennox didn't know where they were when the car finally stopped, they were across the Florida-Georgia state line, about seventy miles northeast of Tallahassee in Bainbridge, Georgia. When the trunk lid opened, it was dark outside and all she could see was the blurred shape of her abductor.

Chris Wilder was far from finished with Jill. He forced her to crawl and wiggle into a sleeping bag and he zipped it completely around her head and threw her over his shoulder like a sack of potatoes. Still gagged, she couldn't make enough noise for anyone to hear her.

He tossed her roughly onto a bed in the motel room. Desperately hoping for a chance to escape, Jill Lennox underwent a terrible ordeal of sexual sadism. She was raped and subjected to every variation of abuse that the man who held her could think of. When he was satiated sexually, she realized dully that he wasn't done with her.

Wilder cut the cord of the bedside lamp, and peeled back the insulation from the bare wires. Then he plugged the cord back in the wall, and holding it where *he* would not be shocked, he held the bare wires to her feet. The shocks were terribly painful, but not enough to kill Jill. He demanded that she dance and do aerobics in time with the shocks. It took him over two hours to get bored with his electric torture.

Now, he wanted to see if Super-Glue really worked, and he drizzled a bead of the glue on the lids of her eyes and forced them closed, using a hair dryer to make it dry faster. The glue worked only too well, and Jill could barely open her eyes, but she did have a narrow slice of vision. She realized that *he* didn't know that.

Confident that his captive was helpless and blind, Chris Wilder allowed himself to concentrate on some television show that had grabbed his interest, pausing only occasionally to zap Jill with the power cord.

Suddenly, Jill tugged the cord from the wall, and tripping over it, she used the slight vision she had to head for the door. He whirled and cracked her over the head with the hair dryer. She felt her head split and bleed, but she managed to get into the bathroom and lock the door behind her.

Now, Jill freed herself of the gag and screamed until she was hoarse, pounded on the walls and the floor. When she stopped yelling for a minute to listen, she could hear him scurrying around the motel room, the click of his suitcase, and then a door slamming. Not trusting that he was gone, she waited for another half hour before opening the bathroom door.

Jill opened the door a crack and peered out. The room looked empty. Terrified that he was waiting to surprise her, she came out further and looked around the room through the slits of her glued eyes. If she could just get her clothes on and get out, maybe she could make it to the motel office.

She stepped all the way out of the bathroom and grabbed a sheet and wrapped it around her naked body. It was only when she reached the motel manager's office that Jill believed that she might be going to live after all.

One call to police brought an instant response. Jill Lennox didn't know her kidnapper's real name, but she had memorized his face, determined to be able to identify him if she ever had the chance. Every cop in Florida was looking for Chris Wilder, and one of his mugshots was included in the "lay-down" of eight photos shown to Jill.

"That's him, absolutely," she said immediately, pointing to the picture of Christopher Bernard Wilder.

Five young women had been abducted in less than four weeks. And all but Jill were still missing. Jill had been abducted and taken across state lines against her will, a federal crime. Now the FBI entered the case. Chris Wilder was infinitely dangerous to beautiful young women and every law officer who read the case followups believed that he wasn't going to stop unless he was captured.

A federal warrant was issued for Wilder's arrest.

Jill Lennox's statement made it clear Wilder was a sadistic sociopath, a man who derived pleasure from his victims' pain. He was not abducting women solely to rape them. His cruel games only *began* with his sexual release.

Although little hope had been held out for the women who had vanished, the extent of the Ferguson's tragedy became known the next day. Terry wasn't missing any longer. A crew from an electric company had come across her body in an isolated creek in Polk County, more than a hundred miles from where she had disappeared. Terry had been savagely beaten and strangled. Authorities followed Wilder's trail to the mall where Terry vanished, to the bogged-down car in the sandy lover's lane, and then to where her body floated. Sickened, they concluded that she had probably been in the trunk of his car while it was being towed.

There was even more urgency to their search now.

Wilder had obviously zig-zagged around Florida for weeks, but, with Jill, he had crossed into Georgia. There was no telling where he might be by now. He wasn't a serial killer—not unless he was in the final stages of his "addiction." He was taking victims in too narrow a time frame. He wasn't a mass murderer; he clearly wasn't psychotic. Wilder was too well organized. Crazy as his behavior seemed, he knew what he was doing and he was quite capable of seducing his victims with a charming story and a winning smile and then his escapes were well-planned.

They concluded that Chris Wilder fell into that rarest of multiple murderers: the spree killer. He was off on a spree of murder, and there was no telling when he would stop.

Now that he was headline news all over Florida and the southeast, people who had known Wilder shook their heads in amazement. Friends at the race track told FBI Special Agents that the man they had known and raced with was "a really nice guy, a little shy . . . very kind . . ."

One of the most shocked of Chris Wilder's acquaintances was a homicide detective in the Palm Beach County Sheriff's Department. Tom Neighbors read a BOLO (Be on the Lookout For) that had come into his office and was stunned. He knew Chris well—or, rather, he thought he did. A racing fan, he enjoyed following Chris's competition. He liked the guy, and found him friendly and generous. He had invited Chris over to his home many times—the last being on March 8. They had both been excited about an upcoming race.

Try as he might, Tom Neighbors had trouble picturing

Chris Wilder as a roving rapist/killer. But then he remembered something. He himself had worked a case of sexual assault in 1983 where two barely pubescent girls had been pulled into a Chevy El Camino pickup in Boynton Beach. The driver had taken them to a lonely road and molested them—and then, surprisingly, he had driven them *back* to where he abducted them—and let them go.

The case had never been solved, even though it happened very close to the police station, and, Neighbors now realized, close to Chris Wilder's office. An artist's sketch done from the girls' description showed a man with a thick head of hair, which Chris hadn't had for a long time. But Neighbors wondered if Chris might have been wearing one of the toupees he occasionally affected.

The Palm Beach County detective arranged for the 1983 victims to look at a laydown of mugshots, and like Jill Lennox, they picked Chris Wilder at once.

His personable mask off at last, Chris Wilder was on the run. He didn't linger long in Georgia, but headed the Chrysler west.

It was March 22, 1984. Cutting south and then heading due west from Bainbridge, Georgia, Chris Wilder traversed the southern borders of Alabama, Mississippi, Louisiana, as he hastily put miles between himself and the Florida authorities. He may not have known yet that the FBI was after him too, but he must have realized it was only a matter of time and he had much to do before anyone caught up with him. The sun was warm and the wind fierce off the Gulf of Mexico as Wilder pulled off U.S. Highway 10 and turned his road-dirty white car into a motel in tiny Winnie, Texas. He was still using his partner's name and credit card.

The next day was Friday, and Wilder backtracked a short distance to Beaumont, Texas. There, the bluebells that dot the landscape were beginning to respond to Spring. Terry Diane Walden was 24, married, and the mother of a four-year-old daughter, but she found time to study nursing, too. Terry was a beautiful blonde, and she often drew admiring stares. In fact, a man had approached her the day before in the parking lot of her college and told her she should be a model. She laughed when she told her husband about it, dismissing the stranger's offer of a posing job as half peculiar and half compliment.

Terry had almost forgotten about that encounter by Friday morning in the rush of activity that was her life. She took her little girl to day-care in the three-year-old Cougar that the Waldens had recently purchased. Terry was headed off to study with a friend so they could quiz each other on all the minute medical details they suspected would be on the next test. And she had to pick up a few things at a Beaumont shopping mall. She planned to be home in plenty of time to pick up her daughter from day-care.

Chris Wilder had a reason to retrace his journey and go back to Beaumont. He couldn't get the blonde woman he had seen out of his mind. No one will ever know if Terry had agreed to meet him in the mall to discuss his offer of a high-paying modeling gig, or if he somehow knew where she would be.

Terry Walden's husband was the first to realize something was terribly wrong that Friday evening. His daughter's day-care called to say that his wife hadn't come to pick the child up. Only then did the worried young husband remember her telling him about the man who owned a modeling agency. The local police and the FBI took Terry's disappearance seriously from the very beginning, and they organized grid searches of the area around the mall.

Law enforcement authorities knew that Wilder had left Florida and Georgia in the white Chrysler, and they were concerned when a teenaged girl reported that she had seen such a car along a little-traveled dirt road that afternoon. Something ephemeral had made her watch the car as it drove by slowly. "There was a man with a beard driving," she recalled. "And there was a woman in the passenger seat. I didn't see her well because she was kind of leaning her head against the window."

The white car had turned off through some rice fields, something that was also unusual. "I saw it again later," the young witness said. "It was coming back along that rice-field road. But I couldn't see the woman that time."

Although a massive search for Terry Walden began in that area, the searchers didn't find her for three days. Her body, bound tightly with rope, bobbed face-down in a canal near the road where the girl had seen the white Chrysler. An autopsy revealed that Terry had been stabbed three times in the breasts, thrusts so powerful that the blade had gone completely through her body. She might have lived—if only she had gotten medical help soon enough; she had succumbed to exsanguination—bleeding to death. It was impossible to tell if she had been raped; any trace of seminal fluid would have dissipated in the waters of the canal.

Terry Walden had probably died on the afternoon she was abducted, but it was possible she was still alive, if unconscious, when the witness saw her leaning against the passenger window of the Chrysler.

The Waldens' 1981 Cougar was missing, but there was no way of knowing if Terry's killer was driving it. The white Chrysler hadn't been sighted again, either.

Every cop in the South knew now that Chris Wilder was a virtual killing machine, and he was hurtling across their territory, so slick in his approach to his victims that he was able to take them away from safety without so much as a scuffle or a soft cry for help. Back in South Florida, detectives and special agents were learning more about him.

Apparently Wilder had used his "model agency" and "fashion photographer" ruses for a long time. Some girls who had been approached by the man with the beard saw his photograph in the newspapers and on television and came forward. The investigators learned that he had used a number of aliases, but he had always seemed to have business cards that made him seem reputable. Sometimes, he had actually taken photos of young women without making a remark or gesture that was out of the ordinary. One woman said she had gone with him to an empty house someplace in Boca West. "He said it was a 'photo test' for a BMW ad," she said with a shiver. "But he never called me back."

Back in Florida, the Kenyons, the Orsborns, and the Gonzalez family hoped against hope that their daughters were still alive, perhaps held captive somewhere. In a sense, their endless waiting was worse than the grief the families felt who *knew* that their daughters were dead. Their dreams were haunted with visions of torture, horrific captivity and their own helplessness.

Searches of Chris Wilder's home and business produced no clues at all that might indicate any of the missing girls had ever been in either spot. Wilder had had a boat——he could have dumped their bodies far out in the ocean where no one would ever find them, and this was plausible since he seemed to have a fetish about putting his victims in water after he was finished with them.

The fact remained: while Wilder was living in his own house, he had managed to hide the missing girls completely; now that he was on the run, he dropped dead bodies off with alarming regularity. What was there about his being in Florida that had made it easier for him to hide his activities?

A map in the investigator's command center showed Chris Wilder's slashing course across America. On March 25, the marker moved north from Beaumont, Texas, to Oklahoma City. He had spent the previous night at a motel there. And then, that Sunday afternoon, he was seen at the Pen Square Mall, although no one thought much of it until Monday.

Suzanne Wendy Logan, twenty, was a new bride on that spring day in 1984. Suzanne had a great smile and thick, taffy-colored hair with blonde highlights. Her ambition was to be a model, and she had painstakingly put together a portfolio with various photographs of herself. She went to the Pen Square Mall on March 25 and met Chris Wilder there.

Wilder's luck in finding women who fit perfectly into his victim profile was uncanny. With shorter and shorter spates between his killing days, he was somehow able to spot his victim, cut her away from those who might have saved her, and destroy her at his leisure. How did he *know* that Suzanne dreamed of being a model? Did he have some magic power that drew his targets to him?

In truth, it was more likely that Chris Wilder had simply become completely conversant with the longings of vulnerable, naive girls. He knew how to look like a professional photographer, and he had used that guise to dupe Suzanne. When she turned up missing, there were witnesses who recalled seeing her there in the mall Sunday afternoon, talking with a bearded man with a camera around his neck.

They found poor Suzanne two days later and more than three hundred miles away. Continuing north, with his helpless victim in tow, Wilder had driven up I-135 to Newton, Kansas, away from the warm days and into wind-driven snowstorms. He had found a motel with thick walls where he beat and tortured Suzanne Logan, who wasn't as lucky as Jill Lennox had been. The next day, a fisherman found her bound body on the shores of Milford Lake, although it would take time to positively identify her.

Chris Wilder's rage was building; he inflicted pain that was beyond the imagination of someone who felt empathy for other people. Suzanne's beautiful hair had been cut short and her pubic hair shaved. She had been "teased" with a sharp knife, bitten, and stabbed through the left breast.

Because Wilder was still using his ex-partner's credit cards, he left a trail that was easy to follow. The investigators were frustrated because they knew where he had *been,* but they had no way of predicting where he would go next. He had abducted seven women since the end of January, and only one had escaped.

Chris Wilder turned west again after he abandoned Suzanne Logan's body. Still driving the Cougar that he'd stolen from Terry Walden, he roared across Colorado on Route 70. Apparently, he was confident enough that the police and FBI didn't know where he was that he didn't even bother taking the back roads, and he made good time on the freeways. On the night of March 28, he stopped in Rifle, Colorado, not far from the state's western border. Once again, Wilder was in Bundy territory. He had sailed right through Glenwood Springs where Ted Bundy escaped from jail on New Year's Eve, 1977. But even Ted Bundy had never killed so many women in such a short window of time.

Chris Wilder was nearly a thousand miles west of the lake where he had thrown Suzanne Logan away, and he was ready to troll for a victim again on March 29. He was audacious enough to ask for a particular type when he showed up at the Mesa Mall that Thursday. With his camera and other photographer's gear, Wilder was observed in the mall as he asked if anyone knew of a "cowgirl-type" model; he needed one, he said, for a specific photography job commission.

Sheryl Bonaventura, eighteen, was exactly what he had in mind. Although she had never heard of a man named Chris Wilder, she dressed for the part, unaware. When she arrived at the mall, she wore a white sweatshirt with a Cherokee logo, blue jeans, cowboy boots and a lot of chunky gold jewelry. Sheryl didn't plan to shop long; she was going to meet a girlfriend soon so the two could head to Aspen for skiing, and all she needed were a few toiletry items.

With her thick ash-blonde hair, her slender figure and her perfect features, Sheryl Bonaventura looked like a model. And although she looked sophisticated, she was only eighteen and a sitting duck for a man like Chris Wilder. Somewhere in that Mesa Mall, Sheryl met Wilder, believed his story offering her a modeling job with a big Denver agency, and walked away with him.

Sheryl's friend waited and waited for her, but she never arrived at their prearranged meeting spot. Somehow, Wilder had managed to convince her that it was all right to leave her friend stranded. There is evidence that Sheryl did go with Wilder willingly; the pair were seen in Silverton, a little mining town on the way to Durango. That was a hundred miles south of the mall where she was last seen. They stopped at a restaurant there where Sheryl was known—her grandfather once worked there. She talked with the owner who remembered how excited she was about becoming a model. A man with blue eyes and a neatly-clipped beard had stood right beside her, smiling, as she bubbled over with enthusiasm. The couple bought a sack of doughnuts before they moved on.

There was no possibility that Sheryl Bonaventura was being held against her will—not at that point. Her last name meant "Good Luck" and "Happy Adventures," and she believed she was on a wonderful trip.

And it may have been, but only for a very short while. For some reason, Wilder did not harm Sheryl for several days. The couple were spotted at several locations in Colorado and Arizona. They seemed to be an especially close pair; the man with the beard never left the pretty blonde's side. In retrospect, Sheryl's sometimes "odd" behavior may have been her futile attempts to signal for help—with darting eyes and exaggerated expressions when the man beside her looked away for a moment.

The couple were seventy miles south of Durango the day after they were seen at the restaurant. They seemed like any tourist couple as they visited the Four Corners

Monument where Utah, Arizona, New Mexico and Colorado's borders touched.

The night of March 30, they checked into a motel in Page, Arizona, as a married couple. The desk clerk didn't notice anything untoward, but then motel clerks have learned not to look too closely at "married" couples. Shortly after dawn, someone noticed Chris Wilder as he whisked the blonde woman out of his room and rushed her to his car.

From that point on, there were no more sightings of the woman in western garb and the man twice her age. Nor were there any calls from Sheryl. Back in Grand Junction, her family was frantically worried. On their own, they gathered friends and relatives to search for her. Their desperate search party fanned out from Grand Junction to Durango and down toward Las Vegas. They hoped that Sheryl had left on some kind of romantic adventure, and that she wasn't in terrible danger.

But the FBI's revisiting of the trail Wilder left with his credit cards didn't make things sound promising. Wilder had registered a woman thought to be Sheryl Bonaventura as his wife in Durango, and again in Page. However, the next night when he stopped in Las Vegas, he didn't list a wife. If Sheryl was still with him, he might have had her wait in the car and then sneaked her into the motel room.

Although Sheryl's family kept up their search for her, she had vanished somewhere along the trail from her hometown to Las Vegas. Hunting for the beautiful teenager was an impossible task; no one could check all the thousands of square miles with lakes, rivers, mountains, and endless barren prairie lands. Sheryl could be anywhere. As much as her family hoped that she was somewhere safe having a heedless adventure, they knew in their hearts that she was dead.

Chris Wilder's terrible killing spree continued unabated; he was clever enough to move on before local authorities even realized he had entered their jurisdictions. By the time the pathetic bodies were found, he was somewhere else, searching for his next victim.

Seventeen-year-old Michele Korfman was as guileless a target as anyone could be. She was very pretty and very young as she parked the new car her father had given her at the Meadows Shopping Mall in Las Vegas. It was April Fool's Day, an ironic date in retrospect for a beauty contest. Michele and many other young women were excited about the competition. Some, like Michele, came to the mall alone, but a lot of them had their mothers chaperoning.

The man who approached at least four of the girls who waited to compete seemed innocuous enough. Later, when they were asked to describe him, there wasn't much they could remember: "middle-aged . . . not much hair—but a short beard." "He had a soft voice, and nice blue eyes."

The man asked all of the girls basically the same thing. He was a fashion photographer and he was looking for models. He had a portfolio of photographs he had taken of beautiful women, and he showed it to the pretty teenagers. He had a very expensive camera in a leather case. He promised the potential models a good fee up front and, more important, the chance to be seen by top modeling agencies.

Even so, three of the girls shook their heads; they didn't want to leave the mall and go with him to his studio. He didn't seem angry or disappointed at their reluctance. Rather, he had returned to his seat on a bench near the stage, watching the contest with interest. One of the mothers in attendance was taking pictures as her daughter strode confidently across the stage, and without realizing it, she captured the "professional photographer's" image in several frames. He may have been unconcerned; he was probably unaware that she had taken his picture.

When the beauty contest at the Meadows Mall was over, the man lingered. Several people saw Michele Korfman talking to him, and then the two of them headed slowly toward an exit. Nobody took a picture of that; it didn't seem important.

Michele looked a lot like Cindy Crawford. Like Terry Ferguson who had been seen leaving a mall on Merritt Island, Florida, two weeks before, Michele had long thick hair and she usually posed for pictures with an unsmiling, sexy look on her face. Like Terry and the other girls who had been led away from bustling shopping malls, Michele had perfect features. She *would* have made a wonderful model.

And then Michele Korfman, the darling of her daddy's eye, a girl with everything to live for, was gone. And another family was left to search and to live with agonizing doubt. All authorities really knew—or *believed*—was that Michele had not left of her own volition. Her prized car, in perfect condition, was found a few days later in the parking lot behind Caesar's Palace.

Chris Wilder left Las Vegas and Michele was with him at least part of the way. By the fourth of April, Wilder was alone again, and still driving the stolen Cougar.

Since he had just made the FBI's Ten-Most-Wanted list and lawmen all over America were looking for him, he had had incredible luck. His mugshots were on the wall of every post office in the country. That did not mean, however, that young women intent on shopping in a mall or in attracting enough attention to get a modeling contract would see it, or remember it if they did see it. By this time, Chris Wilder must have felt invincible.

The FBI attempted to warn as many potential victims as possible by releasing the eight-minute videotape he had made for the dating bureau. His image flashed across television screens in every state, the image of an almost shy man with a slight speech impediment, a man who was lonely for female companionship and had resorted to this awkward method of matchmaking.

And apparently, he was *still* lonely. That sounds like a bad joke and an odd thing to say about a ruthless killer who had systematically destroyed eight young women and left another physically and psychologically maimed, but it is perhaps the only way to explain the way he related to his next captive. The tenth victim may have lived because she didn't argue with him or threaten him. Her very helplessness may have saved her life.

On April 4, Toni Lee Simms*, sixteen, was headed to apply for a job at a delicatessen in Torrance, one of the many cities whose boundaries blend into one another south of Los Angeles. Toni Lee wasn't looking forward to the job and it paid only minimum wage—but she and her mom were more or less alone in the world. As young as she was, she was a survivor who wanted to pull her own weight, someone who was used to a side of life that wasn't always comfortable or safe. When she encountered Chris Wilder, she was easy game.

He came up to her outside the deli, and he didn't look frightening at all—just an older man with a beard and friendly blue eyes. He told her that she was just the right type for an ad campaign that a company he worked for was doing. She saw his camera and a bunch of other photographic gear he had with him. He looked straight and honest and safe.

Toni Lee was a little bit chubby, and she wasn't used to having someone tell her she could be a model. She was flattered and intrigued when the man—"Chris"— offered her a hundred-dollar bill if she would come to the beach near Santa Monica with him and pose for some ad shots. She calculated how many hours she would have to work to make that much money—*even* if she got the job in the deli.

It was kind of fun at first. The sun was shining and there were people around, but later she realized that the wind was getting chilly and everyone but the two of them had left the beach. She told Chris that she had to be getting home. His friendly persuasion disappeared in an instant, and he seemed terribly angry at her.

Before she could think fast enough to run, a pistol appeared in Chris's hand and he grabbed her by the back of the neck with one hand and forced the gun into her mouth with the other. She heard a click as he aimed the gun down her throat.

"Your modeling days are over," he breathed.

He dragged her over to his car, pushed her into the back seat, and held her down as he tied her arms behind her and then looped the rope down to her ankles.

And then the car was racing away from the beach,

away from Torrance. Toni Lee had no way of telling what time it was, but it seemed as though they had driven more than six hours when her captor finally slowed to a stop.

Michele Korfman, gone from her safe life in Las Vegas, was dead; her unclaimed, unidentified body lay in the Los Angeles County Morgue. (On June 15, when Nevada and California authorities finally connected her sad little corpse with the beautiful seventeen-year-old who had vanished from Las Vegas, she had been missing two and a half months.)

Wilder and Toni Lee were still in the Cougar, although it now bore stolen plates from New Mexico. Except for using his partner's credit cards, this was Wilder's sole effort to hide his identity. He headed out of Los Angeles County to El Centro, California, twelve miles from the Mexican border at Calexico. He may have planned to attempt a crossing at the border, and thought better of it. The pair, he, thirty-nine, and Toni Lee, sixteen, checked into an El Centro motel.

Long before it was light, Wilder put Toni Lee back in his car and they crossed the desert into Arizona, and then turned the Cougar north to Prescott. They stayed the night at a motel there, and then something changed; maybe Wilder *knew* that he'd made the Ten-Most-Wanted list; perhaps he saw the flyer with his picture in a truck stop cafe or in a gas station. There were no sightings, no motel receipts—nothing for four days.

During those four days, Toni Lee Simms was subjected to multiple sexual assaults. She didn't fight him. She had survived with passivity for a long time, learning to watch people quietly and to evaluate what *they* wanted so that she could just get along. She listened to her captor as he talked of his fantasies, his obsessions, his hopes and fears. Somehow, her very helplessness soothed Wilder. All of the other captives had been dead within a day or two.

For some reason Chris Wilder didn't kill Toni Lee Simms. He kept her with him in his headlong race back east across America. Toni Lee was caught in the grip of the Stockholm Syndrome, an intricate psychological process that virtually turns the mind inside out. A more familiar term is brainwashing. Anyone can be brainwashed; it is only a matter of how much terror, loneliness, time and repetition it will take. There are four steps: (1) the subject suffers a profound psychological shock; (2) the subject is taken away from every person and place where she felt safe; (3) the "programmer" repeats his message over and over and over, and (4) he holds out the promise of a reward—usually the captive's life.

Toni Lee Simms had been brainwashed. She was kidnaped, terrorized, raped, and taken far from home. Amazed that she was still alive as the miles zipped by, she began to be mesmerized by Wilder's deceptively soft voice. He had not killed her yet, and she hoped that he wouldn't kill her if she just listened to him and did what he asked of her. After four days with Chris Wilder she began to think only as he gave her permission to think.

By the time they crossed the Indiana state line, Toni Lee was prepared to do whatever Wilder asked of her. He had convinced her that even when she was out of the car and away from him, he could still hurt her. In order to stay alive, she would have to follow his orders. In Gary, Indiana, on April 10, Wilder ordered Toni Lee to go into the West Lake Mall and bring back a girl. He gave her the script. She was to offer a likely-looking girl a good job, and then bring her to the car.

It turned out to be nowhere near as difficult as Toni Lee thought it might be. She walked around the mall, no longer even psychologically capable of escape, until she saw a girl about her own age filling out a job application on a bench outside a clothing store.

"I work here," Toni Lee said. "You look as if you'd be fine for the job. If you'll come outside this mall exit here and wait, I'll call the manager and tell her."

Chris Wilder was waiting for his next prey, Carrie McDonald*, sixteen. Now, as the Cougar sped away, Toni was no longer the prime captive; Carrie had taken her place and lay trussed up and gagged with duct tape in the back seat of the car. Her ordeal would last for three days as they drove across as many states. Even in her terror, Carrie wondered about the other girl—the girl who had led her to the cruel man who enjoyed torturing her. The girl he called Toni seemed to be in a trance. She wouldn't help Carrie or even look at her.

The last place Wilder's partner's credit card had been used was in Arizona, and so law enforcement agencies were concentrating their efforts there. And yet they knew that they couldn't be sure *where* he was; he had covered over six thousand miles already in a crazy, zig-zagging pattern. And then they tracked him to a motel in Wauseon, Ohio. He was moving northeast.

That, combined with the disappearance of the girl in Gary, Indiana, made them suspect that he was still abducting women. There was no way of knowing how many women might have gone missing between Arizona and Ohio.

On April 11, the credit card was used again in a motel

southeast of Rochester, N.Y. No one there recalled seeing anyone with the man who had checked in. For that
matter, the clerk couldn't really describe the man, either.

On Wednesday, April 11, a tractor mechanic was driving on a meandering two-lane road in the woods near
Penn Yan, N.Y. It was an easy place to get lost, and the
tractor serviceman finally accepted that he was headed
for a dead end. He sighed and wheeled his rig around. As
he did so, he saw what looked like an apparition lurching
toward him. It was a young woman who was nearly
naked. Her breasts were scarlet with blood as she tried to
stanch the flow with her clothing.

The mechanic blinked his eyes as if to clear the
"ghost" from his sight, but the girl was still there. He
jumped out of his truck and helped her into the passenger seat. She was real, and begging him to take her to a
doctor.

The closest medical help was at the Soldiers and
Sailors Hospital in Penn Yan, and the man floored his
accelerator, afraid that the injured girl would die before
he could get her there.

Carrie McDonald proved to have incredible recupera-
tive powers, despite the stab wounds in her chest. Sheer
luck had prevented the thrusts from piercing vital organs,
and she was anxious to talk to the FBI agents who
flocked to the Yates County District Attorney's office.

For the first time since Jill Lennox had escaped from
Chris Wilder, the investigators had a living witness who
could look at a laydown of mugshots and identify him as
her attacker.

It was Christopher Wilder all right. He had gone from
Florida to Georgia, Louisiana, Alabama, Texas, Okla-

homa, Kansas, Colorado, Utah, Nevada, California, Arizona—back to Indiana and Ohio, and now he was somewhere south of Lake Ontario between Buffalo and Syracuse, New York. Only God knew how many women he had killed and thrown away on his sojourn of sadism, but the FBI and task forces around the country agreed that they had names for nine to twelve victims that matched his M.O.

What shocked them the most, perhaps, was Carrie McDonald's statement that Wilder had a girl with him, not another victim but an accomplice! She told them how the girl she knew as Toni Lee came into the mall in Gary, Indiana, where Carrie was applying for work. "She lied to me—to get me to go out by the car where he was waiting."

She described Toni Lee as being about her own age—sixteen—and said she was pretty but a little plump. When she had followed Toni Lee outside the mall, she'd been led to a Cougar, and a man with a beard. He had pulled a gun that she identified as a .357 Magnum as he bound her hands and feet. When they stopped at night, Carrie said she, too, had been subjected to electric shock torture, along with other horrible abuses.

Carrie didn't know why he hadn't killed her, and she had been determined to find a way to escape. But she was bound and gagged during the days as they traveled, hog-tied in the back seat and hidden beneath a rack of clothing Wilder had strung up there.

But it was hopeless. At night, she was hustled into various motel rooms, and the days were long stretches of bondage. "When we went through Niagara Falls," Carrie remembered, "he and the girl got out to look at the falls, and they left me there in the parked car . . ."

Chris Wilder had been so confident; he had somehow managed to control Toni Lee Simms so completely that she was on an invisible tether. And Carrie had been controlled with a gag and tightly-wound layers of duct tape. But then something happened. They woke in their motel room on the morning of April 12, and Wilder turned on the television. Toni Lee gasped. Her mother was on the screen, sitting there on "Good Morning America," and begging for news of her missing daughter.

Maybe that was the first time Wilder realized that he was big news, and big news meant the roads would be lousy with cops. Carrie told the FBI agents that he panicked, and hurried them into the car. He drove to the narrow and isolated road where the tractor mechanic had found her.

She had known that he meant to kill her, even though she couldn't see what he was doing. She was blindfolded, bound and gagged, as she followed his directions to "walk here . . . keep walking." She sensed that they were in an open field, that they had broken out of the woods she'd seen before she was blindfolded. And then he forced her roughly to the damp ground. He clamped one hand over her mouth and pinched her nose shut with the other, but she had tossed her head back and forth in her frantic efforts to breathe and stopped him from suffocating her.

Then it felt as if he had hit her hard in the chest and twice on the back. Blinded, she didn't realize she had been stabbed until she felt something warm and wet, her own blood. She had willed herself to lie perfectly still and she took breaths so shallow that she longed for oxygen. But she wanted him to think that she was dead. She had heard him standing over her, breathing heavily, and then, finally, the sound of his footsteps going away.

At last, she rubbed the blindfold along the ground to strip it off her eyes. Her own blood made it possible for her to slide her wrists out of their bonds, and she had been able to untie her ankles. But even without the blindfold, she was disoriented. She had staggered first into the woods, and then she had found the road—and the man who saved her.

Although Carrie was in critical condition, doctors believed that she would live. Courageously, she had told the investigators everything she knew about the man named Chris and the girl named Toni Lee. Toni was wearing blue jeans, she said, and had short hair and a round face.

It was anybody's guess where Chris Wilder and his captive—whom they now knew as Toni Lee Simms—had gone. They wondered if Toni Lee *was* still a captive or if she had joined forces with Wilder. Carrie said she had not hurt her, but she hadn't helped her either. If Toni Lee continued to assist Wilder in snaring victims, detectives feared there would be more deaths.

The investigators had assumed that Chris Wilder would continue moving north and east, although they knew that assumptions made about a sexual renegade are seldom predictable. Going over the thick stack of follow-up reports they had gathered from anyone and everyone who had ever known Wilder, they found something interesting. An old girlfriend of his in Florida had told detectives that Wilder had once visited her home in New Hampshire with her. He was getting closer to the small New England state. He hadn't made it over the border to Mexico, so they figured he might be trying for Canada.

But then Carrie McDonald had said that Wilder had threatened to send her to Mexico City, not once but several times. He might just as easily backtrack and head toward the Southwest again.

Beth Dodge was thirty-three, a wife, mother, and Sunday School teacher. She did not fit Chris Wilder's profile in any way, save that she was female. She was sweetly pretty, but she was no winsome long-legged teenager with hopes of becoming a model. Beth had a lunch date to keep with a friend in the Eastview Mall near Victor, N.Y., which was a small town just off I-90 about forty-five miles northwest of Penn Yan.

Doctors were still monitoring Carrie as they had been for the three hours she had been in the Emergency Room when Beth got into her gold 1982 Pontiac Firebird. It was a flashy car for a Sunday School teacher but she loved it and kept it spotless. Beth wore a lilac-colored suit in keeping with the pleasant spring day.

Chris Wilder sat behind the wheel of the road-worn Cougar in the Eastview Mall. He watched carefully as cars approached and parked. When he saw the gold Firebird, he nodded, half to himself. That was the one he wanted.

Wilder and Toni Lee waited for more than an hour, and he never took his eyes off the Pontiac. When a slender woman in a pale lavender suit came walking back toward it, he motioned to Toni to get out of the car. She knew what to do.

Listening to the story that Toni Lee told about needing some help, Beth Dodge believed her and walked with her to the car where Wilder waited. He ordered her into his car at gunpoint, took her keys from her hand, and tossed them to Toni Lee. "Get in the Pontiac and follow me," he instructed.

The two-car caravan ended up at a gravel pit. He made Beth get out of his car and walk into the gravel pit area. There was no one else around to hear the boom of his gun as he shot the young housewife in the back. Chris Wilder left the battered Cougar at the gravel yard, and he and Toni Lee drove off in the gold Firebird.

Toni Lee had lost hope that she would ever escape; she tried simply to live through each day. Had anyone seen her, she might have looked normal enough, but a closer look would have let them see a vague, glassy look in her eyes. Torrance, California, was a whole country's worth of freeways away; she didn't believe she could ever go back there to her mother, her boyfriend or her life. That was another world.

Shortly after nine that night, Toni Lee was shocked and stunned when Chris Wilder turned the gold car into the airport access road in Boston, and followed the signs to Logan Airport. She wondered if he was going to shoot her there—in front of everyone. Instead, he pulled out a thick chunk of bills and handed it to her, telling her to buy a ticket to Los Angeles. She sat, disbelieving, for a few moments—and then she crawled out of the car. The door swung wide and slammed as he pulled rapidly away.

No one in the crowded airport looked twice at the disheveled teenager in blue jeans, although her hair was cropped so close to her head that she looked like a Marine recruit or a refugee from a concentration camp. No one saw that her expression was strangely blank. She bought the ticket home, and boarded the "red eye" flight.

Toni Lee had no idea why her captor had let her go, but her mind was in a fuzzy, odd place where she could not put one thought together with the next one to make sense out of anything.

Beth Dodge's body was found a few hours after she died, and so was the Cougar that had once belonged to Terry Walden and her husband. There was no question that Chris Wilder was still in a killing mode. The ugly bullet wound in Beth's back marked her murderer as a heartless coward. It took only a short time for investigators to send out a nationwide alert for her missing car. Surely, a car as visible as a stolen gold Firebird would soon draw attention no matter where Chris Wilder was headed.

Three thousand miles away from New York State and Boston, Toni Lee took a cab from LAX airport to Hermosa Beach. She was virtually home, but she didn't call her mother, her boyfriend, or the police. Instead, she wandered into a shop that featured sexy lingerie and began picking out underwear. She had worn the same undergarments for more than a week, but that wasn't why she was there. She was so emotionally traumatized that it was almost as if she was still under Wilder's control.

At some point during her bizarre shopping spree, Toni Lee walked up to the clerk at the counter and blurted out, "I've been kidnapped!"

Before the clerk could stop her, Toni Lee left. She went home but that didn't feel right either. She made her way to the Torrance Police Department, and smiled at the officers on duty there in a foggy way. They thought at first that the girl might be intoxicated, but then they looked beyond the almost-shaved head and recognized a face they had seen on "Missing" posters.

She had to be Toni Lee Simms, who by this time, they all believed, was dead. And here she was, walking right into headquarters alive and well—but definitely emotionally disturbed.

They questioned her carefully about where she had been. And she looked at them with eyes full of shock and fear and said simply, "I've been with a madman . . ."

Indeed, she had. Toni Lee was taken to a hospital. Her physical wounds quickly became apparent. Her breasts bore peculiar dark bruises that doctors said had come from multiple electric shocks. She had lost weight and looked exhausted. Worst of all were her psychic wounds. A psychiatrist questioned Toni Lee gently, drawing out just the top layer of the horror she had seen.

"She has been terrorized far beyond ordinary threats to her life," he said later. "Wilder communicated with her very little."

He had instinctively or by design programmed Toni Lee according to the Stockholm Syndrome parameters, telling her that she must obey every single one of his commands if she wanted to live. Toni Lee had not known *who* her kidnapper was, but she learned his identity from the police. Knowing that she had been with a man who had killed almost a dozen young women only exaggerated her fear. At the psychiatrist's request, Toni Lee was put into a quiet room where the only sound was the hum of the air-conditioner and the soft footsteps of nurses. Policemen stood guard outside her door so that no one could get to her.

As she felt safer, Toni was able to tell the Torrance

detectives a few more details of her abduction. She related her intense fear when Wilder had shoved the pistol in her mouth and said quietly, "Your modeling days are over." She had expected to die then—and every day since then. She could not really believe that he had allowed her to leave him. That he had allowed her to live.

Toni Lee Simms admitted that it was she who had lured the girl in Gary, Indiana, to Chris's car. She had had no choice. She hated what he did to the girl named Carrie—but she had been helpless to stop him. She was happy to find that Carrie was *alive,* and not dead in the woods near Penn Yan, New York, as Chris had told her.

"You were in a different car from Chris—after he stole the gold Pontiac," a detective asked. "You could have driven away from him after he kidnapped Mrs. Dodge—"

Toni Lee shook her head. "No. He was a race car driver. He told me. He told me that he could catch up with me, that I couldn't go fast enough to get away from him—and then he was going to kill me."

Toni Lee said she hadn't seen what happened to the woman in the lilac suit because she and Chris had been out of her sight at the time.

The psychiatrist who was overseeing the teenager's treatment explained brainwashing to the detectives. She had been reduced to a creature so afraid for her very life that she would have done *anything* to stay alive.

How long could it go on? How could one man evade police officers and FBI agents all across America who were determined to stop him from his killing spree? Although he didn't appear to be disguising himself and although he had only changed cars three times in his eight-week murdering spree, Chris Wilder seemed to be as elusive as the ground fog that clung to the rural highways of the Northeast in the very early morning.

On that Friday—the very day that Toni Lee Simms walked into the Torrance Police Department, the man who had released her was prowling once more. A nineteen-year-old girl in Wenham, Massachusetts, well north of Boston on state highway 1A, was sitting in her stalled car beside the road. The starter ground ineffectively until the battery gave out, and she was relieved when a friendly-looking man in a gold Pontiac slowed down and asked if she needed help. She accepted the ride he offered, as he said he'd take her on up into town to a service station.

She knew the area well and began to give him directions to the closest garage. But it didn't take long for her to realize he wasn't turning where she told him. In fact, he was heading *away* from town. She glanced at the man, and felt the skin at the back of her neck tighten. She'd seen the papers and the television news bulletins asking people in the Boston area to be on the lookout for a killer. Now, to her dread, she realized that she was sitting beside Christopher Wilder.

They came to a stop sign. As Wilder slowed down, the girl pushed the door handle and tumbled out. She hit the ground running and never looked back until she was on the front porch of a nearby house. The Pontiac had picked up speed and was disappearing down the road. Frightened that he might only be turning around, she pounded frantically on the door, and was vastly relieved when it opened. She had escaped from horrors she could never have imagined.

The police knew where he was. In a sense, Wilder had

boxed himself into the northeast corner of the U.S. He didn't have the wide prairies of Colorado and Texas to hide himself in now. Like all serial and spree killers who play their killing games too long, he was making mistakes, grabbing victims without planning his escape, leaving a trail. Like any *addict,* he was taking too many chances to get the substance that he lived for. Addicted to murder, he had lost control.

Sometime that Friday morning, Chris Wilder crossed over into New Hampshire, and he made good time as he headed north and then veered slightly west to Colebrook. There, he was only eight miles from the Canadian border. He may have figured that he would find shelter there; Canada often hesitates to return prisoners to the U.S. if they are going to face execution. He may only have been blindly running, putting miles between himself and the dead and kidnapped women he'd left behind. He probably didn't know that Carrie McDonald was still alive; she had feigned death perfectly when he walked out of the woods in Penn Yan. He had to know that Beth Dodge was dead. He knew he'd be identified by the young woman in Wenham. The world was closing in on Chris Wilder when he pulled into a gas station in Colebrook.

It was 1:30 P.M. on Friday, April 13, 1984. Chris Wilder, the master at putting on a friendly mask, got out of the gold Firebird and walked around as casually as any ordinary tourist might. He pumped his gas and then strolled into the cashier to pay. There, he asked how to get to the Canadian border.

In a moment of synchronicity, two New Hampshire state troopers were paying their tab for lunch in a little restaurant just down the street. Colebrook only had

1,200 people and the only strangers in town were people headed for the border, and there weren't that many of those. The troopers, Leo "Chuck" Jellison and Wayne Fortier, got into their unmarked station wagon and headed down the main street of Colebrook. Their trained eyes spotted the gold Pontiac Firebird sitting at the gas pumps. It had Massachusetts plates while the bulletin had listed a New York plate—but that didn't mean anything. If Wilder could shoot a woman and steal her car, he could easily have stolen license plates.

Jellison and Fortier pulled into a business parking lot just next to the gas station, their eyes never leaving the Pontiac. They saw the man walking casually from the cashier's booth. He looked right. Age. Height. He did, however, seem awfully laid back for a man who had to know that he was one of America's Ten Most Wanted felons.

Chuck Jellison, thirty-three, eased his huge frame out of the station wagon and Fortier moved their vehicle onto the gas station apron.

"Hold on a minute," Jellison said easily, "Wanted to ask you something—"

The man turned to look at him for an instant and Jellison saw the blue eyes, the familiar face. And then he sprinted for the Pontiac, with Jellison right behind him. Fortier leapt out of the police vehicle with his gun drawn. Almost in slow motion, the troopers saw that the wanted man now held a .357 magnum in his own hand.

Chuck Jellison literally leapt on Wilder through the driver's door of the Pontiac; it was akin to being hit by the offensive tackle of a pro football team. For a frozen few moments, the two men were nothing but a tangle of struggling arms and legs. And then there was a tremendous "BOOM!!!".

Fortier kept his gun pointed at the gold car, watching in shock as his partner almost fell back toward him in an awkward stumbling gait. "I'm hurt—" Jellison said, and Fortier could see blood. Fortier covered him as he limped back to their station wagon to call for help.

There was no movement from Wilder's car, but Fortier was taking no chances. He waited, his gun leveled, afraid for his partner, but knowing he couldn't drop his gun and go check on him. Time inched by, and suddenly there was another shot. The man everyone had hunted for weeks sat dead in the driver's seat, his heart literally blown apart by the .357 magnum bullet.

Chuck Jellison had been critically injured by a bullet that had been slowed down—but not stopped—as it passed through Wilder's body front to back and *then* penetrated the trooper's chest as he grasped the fugitive from behind in a bear hug. The slug missed Jellison's liver by an inch. Had it hit him in the liver, he probably would have bled to death before help arrived.

And help was arriving rapidly. The Colebrook Police first, and then state troopers from both Vermont and New Hampshire.

Jellison was rushed to the hospital for surgery, but the only doctor who would examine the body of Chris Wilder was a forensic pathologist. The second blast from his .357 was a puzzle. The first had undoubtedly been a fatal wound, and quite probably, he had done it deliberately—fired into his own chest to commit suicide. The second shot had probably been the result of a muscle spasm in the dying fugitive's hand. But this was the wound that blew his heart to pieces.

It was, perhaps, a fitting end to a man whose cruelty suggested that he had no heart. And the day—Friday, the 13th—was an apt date for the denouement of the most savage spree killer America has ever known.

The news of Chris Wilder's death was a terrible blow for the Gonzalezes and the Kenyons. He had carried within him the knowledge of where their daughters were—and if they were alive or dead. The Kenyons wept when they got the news of the shoot-out in New Hampshire. "We were hoping and praying that they wouldn't kill him," Bill Kenyon said. "I know he killed himself. But we don't know how we'll ever find Beth now."

And they never did. Although Sheryl Bonaventura's body was found in Utah on May 3, where the remains of Beth Kenyon, Rosario Gonzalez and Coleen Orsborn are and what their fates were has never been known to this day, fifteen years later. Of all the terrible things Christopher Wilder did, this may be the cruelest—to leave families wondering and worrying for the rest of their lives.

The Lost Lady

Thousands upon thousands *of adults disappear in America every year. Some go because they choose to; the stresses and disappointments of life can make the concept of "running away" seem very appealing. Some actually do suffer from amnesia, that much beloved plot device of the television soap opera writer, but it is an exceedingly rare psychological phenomenon in real life. Lots of people vanish because they are victims of foul play. And some human beings actually seem to evaporate into the mist that forms between midnight and dawn, gone forever without explanation.*

I have never researched a police case as unearthly as the story of Marcia Moore. Marcia was an altogether beautiful woman, a psychic of international reputation, an heiress to a large fortune, and a well-published author. And at the age of fifty-one, she had found the kind of perfect love that all women long for in their secret hearts.

Years before I ever wrote about Marcia Moore, she was familiar to me. I first saw her image in the seventies when so many of us were caught up in the yoga craze, hard on the heels of the study of reincarnation and astrology. The lithe, gorgeous woman who demonstrated yoga positions in Jess Stearn's books was Marcia. She seemed to all of us in that bemused decade to be the very essence of perfection. My friends and I would have been shocked to know that her life had been as beset by heart-break as it had been blessed by wealth and genetic gifts.

Seeing her then as she posed in leotards and tights, a study in grace and beauty, no one could ever have imagined the tragedy that lay ahead of her.

In 1928, Marcia Moore was born into a family of high achievers. She was the cherished daughter of Robert Lowell Moore, a thirty-two-year-old Bostonian with a scrupulously blue-blooded background. Undeterred by the financial climate of the Great Depression, Marcia's father founded the Sheraton Hotel chain in the 1930s and his business knowledge made the luxurious hotels flourish. The Sheraton Corporation stayed in the family until it was sold to ITT in 1968 for an estimated $20 million.

Marcia's parents were involved in the New England Theosophical Society, which she always called laughingly, "kind of blue-blooded spiritualists." Later, they built a "meditation mount" in Ojai, California, where they often joined friends who were interested in the same spiritual pursuits.

One of Marcia's brothers became a successful attorney in Greenwich, Connecticut. The other was Robin Moore, whose books *The Green Berets* and *The French Connection* stayed at the top of the best-seller lists for months and then were made into blockbuster movies.

Marcia herself was a talented writer, but her field of expertise was far more ethereal than her brother's. She saw beauty in nature, secrets of life beyond the veil of reality, and she trusted more than the average human, using her special sense to guide her. She was considered a true psychic by those who believed that the mind was capable of perceiving far more than the concrete things that can be rationally explained.

Marcia Moore's life story and her expertise in the mystic arts of yoga became familiar to a million readers when Jess Stearn wrote a book about her in 1965: *Youth, Yoga, and Reincarnation.* Stearn, who also published *Edgar Cayce, The Sleeping Prophet* and *The Girl with the Blue Eyes,* spent three months with Marcia Moore and her third husband at their Boston home, and he, too, became a devotee of the yoga philosophy.

Marcia appeared in the picture section of the book, wearing leotards and demonstrating the complicated yoga positions or "asanas," her body so perfect that there wasn't a hint of cellulite or the slightest bulge of fat. She was almost forty, but she was completely flexible, her muscles elastic and trained. Indeed, she appeared to be a girl in her teens. That was important to her; she had a fear of growing old.

Oddly, although Marcia was a brilliant woman with an exceptionally strong mind, she had never been successful at choosing men. By the time she was fifty, she had four husbands. The first three were men who had disappointed and hurt her. Though she charted her life through her knowledge of astrology, letting the stars guide her, they often failed to guide her well when it came to romance.

There were dark sides to the men she chose. "Marcia was drawn to brutal men," a friend said sadly. "She was so lovely and so good—she deserved better."

Marcia Moore referred to her first three marriages as

"unfortunate," and didn't say much more. "She felt her first husband treated her like a writing machine," her friend recalled. "She was basically kept behind the type-writer—being a little 'word merchant,' as she called it."

When Stearn wrote about her in the mid-sixties, Marcia Moore was in the midst of her third marriage—to a man who was twelve years younger than she. He was also an astrologer, but their marriage was to be no adver-tisement for selection by the stars. Marcia probably knew that when she spoke with Jess Stearn. He quotes her in the book as saying that her destiny and her hus-band's might not always lie together. She told him that she only knew that it was meant for them to be together at that point in their lives.

After the excesses of the sixties, America was ready for a lifestyle that was pure and healthy. Marcia Moore was right at the forefront of all the new fads. She espoused vegetarianism as well as yoga. Except for her relation-ships with men, it all worked for her wonderfully well. She had everything, seemingly, that anyone might need to be happy—beauty, intellect and vibrant health. Indeed, Marcia had such control over her body and mind that she could actually control her heartbeat, her breathing and her blood pressure. She taught these techniques to her then-husband. By following her directions, he was able to beat a lie-detector test in a clinical situation by controlling those responses that would indicate he was not telling the truth. With his mind alone, he stopped perspiring, slowed his heartbeat, and lowered his blood pressure.

Marcia Moore's whole life was directed toward learn-ing as much as she could about the other side of reality. She believed there were hidden doors she might step through, ways to step beyond her physical body into a world most people never glimpsed. Even as a young woman attending Radcliffe College, Marcia had been fascinated with the world of the occult. She took correspondence courses in meditation and traveled to India to study yoga. Blessed—or cursed—with psychic ability, she searched for keys to open doors to the "other" world.

Despite the bitter disappointment she felt when her marriages failed, Marcia Moore continued to believe she had the ability to make the right choices about her future through astrology charts and her psychic gift.

Initially, and despite urging from associates who had taken pharmacological shortcuts to enlightenment, Marcia found nothing that convinced her that drugs were the answer. Later, she reluctantly tried marijuana, mescaline, LSD, and even ingested seeds from the heavenly blue morning glory, but she was not impressed. None of them expanded her mind enough.

She wrote that ". . . these endeavors left me with the tantalizing sensation of having caught a few sneak previews of a show that never came to town."

Always seeking, Marcia Moore wrote or co-authored seven books dealing with the psychic world, including the popular *Diet, Sex, Yoga and Reincarnation,* and *Key to Immortality.* She coined the term "hypersentience" for a technique she had discovered that seemed to open her mind and let her get in touch with other lives she had lived before her current existence on earth.

Reincarnation as a philosophy is as old as mankind. It predicates that all of us have lived many times before. Proponents believe that souls choose each life as a vehicle that will help them refine and perfect their souls to a point where utter bliss, purity, and Nirvana are reached.

Believing in reincarnation allows believers to deal with the tragedies and disappointments in life, because they can be seen as being preordained by karmic design. Sadness and disaster give the believer the opportunity to cope in order to achieve spiritual growth.

There was a tremendous interest in reincarnation in the seventies. Even the Beatles were spending time with gurus and mystics. With deep hypnosis, many people said they had been able to go back far beyond birth to recall past lives. Interestingly, the most vocal of the previous life travelers had all been someone famous—or *infamous*—in their earlier lives.

Marcia Moore took reincarnation more seriously than most. She believed that while hypnotized, she had gone back into Egypt, back to the days before Christ. She described former lives and deaths. It was a fascinating theory that could not be proven or disproven.

Marcia Moore, in her present life, resembled Cleopatra. Her silky black hair was cut in a sleek cap; her features were perfectly symmetrical. She had many suitors. Although her first three marriages fell apart, Marcia bore and raised three children to adulthood. She rarely spoke of them to her friends on the West Coast. Sometimes even *her* life seemed mundane and disappointing, but she searched continually for answers to questions that most of us never think about seriously.

Marcia didn't have to worry about money; there was the trust fund set up by her family plus the money that she received from her lectures and books. She was involved with groups who were searching for meaning, just as she herself was.

Marcia had a talent for friendship; she was sincerely concerned about her women friends and kept in touch with notes and cards, always urging them on to better things. She often drew pen and ink sketches of flowers on her cards and included quotations from Thoreau and Emerson.

One of Marcia's dearest friends was Elise Devereaux* who was president of the Seattle Astrological Society. The two women had met through a mutual friend, a psychologist in San Francisco, who had known Marcia since the sixties when he was in college. Elise was responsible for bringing Marcia to Seattle in 1975 to speak to the Astrological Society. "She was a most gracious and professional guest speaker," Elise would recall. "She helped the society significantly."

In 1976, Marcia wrote to Elise:

Dear Elise,

Delighted to have your letter of May 23, and especially to hear that you are regressing people. As for the truth or falsity of the material in terms of scientific validation, it is still too early to judge. All we know is that some of them do check out. . . . Interesting about your life as a monk who ran an orphanage in the valley. But actually these *were* the ones who did such fine work in raising abandoned children. It is easy to imagine you in such a situation.

Marcia wrote that she hoped to come back to the Northwest, but would have to wait until she had a paid book tour. "But I'd love to plan on the regional conference in the summer of '77. That sounds a long way away, but it isn't really. By then, I should have some genuinely new conclusions and not just a bunch of case histories as I have now. I have a fairly long story with the astrological correlates in the September Bulletin. In fact, I plan to give more space to Karmic Astrology from now on . . ."

Marcia Moore and Elise Devereaux had become fast friends, even though they didn't see each other in person that much. Elise was living in the foothills of the Cascade Mountains and Marcia was either traveling or headquartered in Ojai. They kept in touch by letter and the occasional phone call. "Marcia was very reserved," Elise said. "If it had not been for my friend [who introduced them] I would never have guessed there had ever been anything seamy in her life. She was just attracted to the wrong men. Marcia was like a princess, small, beautiful and wealthy; there was a sadness about her. I think she was always looking for a 'Bright World.' She was very eloquent and educated, and somehow she could make the damndest things seem reasonable."

Sometime after she posed for the pictures in Stearn's books, Marcia had a face lift. She was nearing fifty, and she had the kind of fragile thin skin that showed wrinkles early. The operation was a complete success, and she looked under forty again, although she never actually admitted to having had plastic surgery. One thing that Elise noticed was that Marcia never showed her legs; she wore either long flowing skirts or slacks. Elise remembers that Marcia was in a fire as a child, and suspected that her legs were badly scarred as a result. She never spoke about it, though.

After three marriages, Marcia Moore was essentially alone. She still hoped to find the man in the world she was destined to be with. Elise Devereaux was alone too, divorced and raising her small daughter. She was giving astrological readings, and an older woman who was cutting down on her clientele sent Elise several referrals. One of them was a handsome, dark-haired man named Steve Monti*. Monti was an anesthesiologist who was on staff in a Seattle hospital. Although he was awfully good-looking and masculine, Elise was somehow not attracted to him.

"I did his chart," Elise said. "And gave him a reading in my home. Dr. Monti recorded the reading. But then I received a call from him saying that the recording was blank—and he asked if I would do the reading again."

She told him that, of course, she would. At the time Dr. Monti was going through a divorce, and talked to Elise about it. He showed her pictures of a very pretty blonde woman and explained that this was his *second* divorce from the same wife. There were children from their marriage, and Monti said that his family lived in North Bend, Washington.

It wasn't unusual for Elise's clients to confide their most intimate concerns. Steve Monti told Elise that he hated his name—that he had always hated it because it was his stepfather's name. He said the man had sexually abused him when he was small, and he was going to get rid of the name as part of a healing process for the scars left behind. Henceforth, he would be known as Walter "Happy" Boccaci*.

Monti-Boccaci had had a life full of catastrophes, it seemed. He told Elise that he had survived a terrible car accident a few years before. He had been driving his Volkswagen which was crushed by a larger vehicle. "I think the only reason I survived," he confided, "was because the doctors knew I was a physician, too, and they went to extraordinary effort to save me."

Dr. Boccaci said that his aorta had burst, which was usually a "death sentence." Indeed it was; unless a patient is actually on the operating table when the main artery of the body tears or bursts, death by exsanguination almost always follows. But Happy Boccaci had survived, although he was in sorry shape. He showed Elise pictures of himself on crutches. His legs seemed to be limp and paralyzed.

However, by the time he'd come to her for an astrological reading, he looked to be in perfect health. The only sign that he'd been in an accident, he said, was that he could no longer drum or roll his fingers on a hard surface. He had lost control of those nerves.

If Elise had begun to wonder if Dr. Boccaci was full of tall stories, she soon had proof that he *was* on the staff of a highly respected hospital. "I have a genetic bone disease," she said. "One morning, I woke up with stress fracture of my knee. Happy had me come to his hospital and I was given the royal treatment. I didn't have to pay for anything. I really felt that Happy took a real, altruistic interest in my health."

Elise was in her thirties and attractive; Dr. Happy Boccaci was about forty and newly single. Soon he began to visit her on a social basis, although she tried to keep their relationship platonic. It wasn't that he wasn't attractive because he *was*. But there was something that put her off.

"He began buying my two-year-old daughter gifts," she said. "This was making me uncomfortable and I tried to make some distance. I remember my daughter crawling on his lap once and asking, 'Are you nice or are you mean?' He told her he was a nice Italian man."

The question of Dr. Boccaci's interest in Elise Devereaux soon became moot. Marcia Moore came back to Seattle to speak for a second time in the summer of 1977. Happy Boccaci was in the audience and was totally taken with the fragile heiress. He learned that Elise was a friend of Marcia's and began a campaign to get an introduction to Marcia.

Something made Elise hold back. She knew that Marcia was involved with a young man, whom Marcia sensed to be a reincarnation of Lord Byron. She had always been fascinated by Lord Byron, and felt they had had a connection in another life. Although the man she was seeing was much younger than she was, she was drawn to him. He had a lot of medical problems, and Marcia was taking care of him. He was her "Lord Byron."

Even so, Elise knew that Marcia was often lonely, and so was Happy. There was no real reason they shouldn't meet, although Marcia was about a dozen years older than Happy. "He kept badgering me to introduce them," Elise recalled. "I was reluctant. He actually called me on the phone and had a temper tantrum. I must have felt intimidated because I invited him to a private reception. The rest is history. Marcia and Happy were drawn to each other immediately."

Anyone could see that they made a striking couple—the big bear of a man with thick dark hair, beard and mustache, and heavy features, and the petite woman with the features of a porcelain doll. Dr. Happy Boccaci swept Marcia Moore into his arms and she felt, finally, as if she had come home.

Walter "Happy" Bocacci at forty was the deputy chief of the anesthesiology department at Seattle's Public Health Hospital. He had held that highly responsible position for ten years. Until his second divorce from his wife, his interests had been in the scientific world where everything was explainable. It would seem that he would be an unlikely mate for the ethereal Marcia Moore, but he had already plunged into the world of astrological projection by the time he met Marcia.

They both felt a karmic link. Who could argue that the meeting of Bocacci and Marcia Moore did not seem preordained? It *did* seem as if they were meant to be together.

Happy always told the story of their meeting in a way that did not include Elise Devereaux. He explained that he had been browsing in the Quest Bookstore in Seattle, a shop specializing in works on the psychic world, in late May 1977, when he picked up a volume titled *Astrology, the Divine Science.* "I was mesmerized by the picture of a woman on the dust jacket."

It was Marcia Moore.

As he confided to Marcia later, "It flashed through my mind. Wow! Would she make a perfect wife! I actually felt some electrical impulse coming off the page and penetrating me—such as we visualize with magnetism."

And so when Marcia came to Seattle to lecture, Dr. Happy Boccaci was there, sitting in the front row, taping her remarks so that he wouldn't lose the sound of her voice or her insights into this new world that enthralled him. He knew that he would see her again, that he was already half in love with her.

After Elise's private reception, Happy invited Marcia to walk with him. They strolled through the fragrant summer night and talked until the sun came up.

Marcia had to leave Seattle for lectures in Vancouver, British Columbia, but Happy Boccaci pressed his suit with letters he had a friend hand-carry to Marcia in the Canadian city. He invited her to visit him in Seattle, saying, "Marcia, I know my destiny is either with you or through you."

She agreed with him. She had missed him terribly, and they spent a week together and, as Marcia wrote later, took "two incredible mind trips together." Marcia Moore had been traveling for five years, never spending more than three months in one place before moving on.

Certainly, a lot of men had come on to her, had desired her, but this was the first man in a long, long time who had seemed right for her. With him, she'd felt that she had "come home" at last.

Marcia and Happy were married on November 25, 1977. Two days later, she wrote to Elise Devereaux, "Little did you know what forces you set in motion when you invited me to stop off in Seattle this last July! Anyway, here I am married to Walter, and very much enjoying life in our clean, fresh, and shining new home near Lynnwood. We would both love to see you! Do come by whenever you can. Also, we are having an open house on Friday night, December 23. So much news to catch you up on . . . You won't believe what we are doing!"

One would never expect to find a woman like Marcia Moore living in a duplex apartment in Alderwood Manor, Washington. She had always seemed to belong in Los Angeles or Shanghai, or, even India, studying the masters of the occult.

But Marcia's own particular karma had intervened. The man she had fallen in love with lived in Washington and, when she joined her life with his, she, too, would settle in the principally rural area of Snohomish County.

Fir forests, lumber mills and farms instead of incense, tapestries, and mystery.

One of the subjects Marcia and Happy discussed at length was the capability of drugs to alter the mind. Marcia was still trying to find a way through the looking glass of life. She mentioned a relatively little known drug, ketamine, to Happy and he surprised her with his familiarity with it. She shouldn't have been so surprised; as an anesthesiologist, he had used it on children and in animal experiments.

Normally, ketamine was used in such strong doses that it would produce unconsciousness, but Marcia felt ketamine had properties that could unveil age-old secrets of the psyche if it were taken in much smaller quantities.

Happy wondered if she might be right. She was exquisite, brilliant, and she seemed to have, almost within her grasp, the answers he sought.

Marcia Moore became more and more convinced that ketamine was the answer to what she was seeking, and Dr. Boccaci soon was almost as enthusiastic about the mind-expanding properties of the drug as she was. Boccaci was convinced that ketamine would one day be recognized as one of the brightest tools in psychotherapy. He called it "ketamine psychotherapy." He left behind the job at the hospital that was paying him $47,000 a year, to prove his theories.

Walter and Marcia received government approval to research ketamine. They called their research "the samadhi therapy." They set up a foundation and lived off the $1,400 a month that Marcia received from the family trust fund. They began to call ketamine hydrochloride "the goddess Ketamine."

Marcia charted their experiments, and wrote of her reactions to her first 50-milligram injection of ketamine.

". . . I became aware of a tingling warmth and a sense of relaxed well-being . . . In this and subsequent ketamine voyages, my impression was one of making the circuit of a vast, multi-dimensional wheel. *Walter!* I repeated the name and the syllables shone forth like a glowing crown of light . . . 'Walter, flower, power.' I kept on chanting the words, watching the equivalent images blossom forth."

Both Happy and Marcia were injected with the drug daily for about six months, but Boccaci soon found that he wasn't getting the insights that Marcia was. He said later that he felt he didn't have her mind, her psychic capacity or the spiritual growth that she had possessed before he met her. So he stopped.

But Marcia Moore continued. For fourteen months, Marcia took the drug daily—the only human on earth known to have ingested it with such regularity.

One of Marcia's friends, an author himself who had written a number of books about the human mind, begged her to stop. He told her that he had experimented with it, too. He warned her that he had become addicted to it. "Marcia," he pleaded, "my wife found me face-down in the swimming pool. I barely survived. I'm telling you, you are a damned fool to mess with ketamine . . ."

Marcia wouldn't listen. She was even able to convince a few of her close friends to try ketamine, but none of them liked the sense of falling away from themselves that resulted.

Marcia and Happy invited Elise to spend the night with them in their duplex. "It was a small town house," Elise remembered, "but it was attractively decorated with all the treasures that Marcia had purchased on her travels to the East."

Although she had never been much of a homemaker before, Marcia cooked a lovely meal of stir-fried vegetables and tofu. "The two of them were just like little kids telling me about their plans with ketamine," Elise remembered. "They felt that they were a perfect duo—he an anesthesiologist, and she with her background in psychology. It was as if the sixties had passed them by and they thought that ketamine could do what Leary thought acid would do with psychotherapy."

Elise didn't want to hurt their feelings, but she felt they were deluded. "I thought it was all nonsense."

Undeterred, in 1978 Happy and Marcia published *Journey into the Bright World,* a book about ketamine. Everything seemed to be working beautifully for them. Marcia's capacity for creative work had always been high, but now she had multiple projects going. She was writing a book using astrological projections about the Kennedy family for her brother's publishing company. It would be timely, considering the upcoming presidential elections. Marcia confided to her brother that Ted Kennedy must not run for president, that his karmic involvement was such that he didn't deserve to win, couldn't win, and would be destroyed trying.

She was also working on another book that unveiled the beauty secrets of Cleopatra, whom Marcia felt she had known in a past life.

Marcia Moore was thrilled with what she had discovered; she felt she had something to tell the world, and wondered, "Can it be that the so-called common man is as deserving of a mystical experience as he is of the opportunity to take a plane trip?"

And so, by January 1979, Marcia Moore appeared to finally have reached the happiness that she had sought for half a century. She was fifty-one, still beautiful, wealthy, married to her one love for fourteen months, and engaged in work that consumed her.

What happened on January 14 is as inexplicable and eerie as anything Marcia Moore ever visualized as a psychic or experienced under the effects of ketamine.

On that Sunday evening, Happy Boccaci asked his wife if she cared to see a movie with him. She shook her head and smiled, he recalled, saying that she was going to get up early the next morning to begin work on a new book. He left her cozily ensconced in their apartment and went to the show alone.

When he returned at one A.M., he was a little alarmed to find that Marcia was not in their duplex. Her purse, her wallet, and all of her cash were there. Her passport was still in their home too. He expected her to pop in at any moment; perhaps she had gone to visit a neighbor in one of the other units. Boccaci searched the place inside and out, and then, even though it was a bitterly cold night, he walked over to the nearby Floral Hills Cemetery to look for her there. Unlike less hardy and more fearful women, Marcia often enjoyed solitary walks in the huge, well-kept cemetery. But she was not there. She wasn't anywhere that Happy Boccaci looked.

Early in the morning, Boccaci called the Snohomish County Sheriff's Office, and reported that his wife was missing. Sheriff Bob Dodge, a retired long-time Seattle police officer, dispatched investigators to check the Boccaci duplex. There was no sign that anything criminal had taken place. The doors and windows showed no evidence that they had been forced, and there was absolutely nothing that would indicate a struggle. The ground outside was frozen hard, and would not have held any impressions from shoes or tire treads.

Dr. Boccaci wasn't sure what clothing his wife was wearing, but detectives found her kimono lying on the floor of her closet, something friends would say wasn't at all like her. She was almost compulsively neat.

Marcia Moore became a "missing person." Lieutenant Darrol Bemis took over the probe personally, assisted by Detective Doris Twitchell. For detectives trained in scientific investigation, the search for Marcia Moore would be a whole new experience.

It was not out of the scope of rational reasoning to suspect that Marcia Moore might have been kidnapped. Her family was both well-known and extremely wealthy, but no requests for ransom money came in. And kidnapping the woman without trying to collect for her safe return didn't make sense.

Suicide? How? And where?

A woman whose life's work involved writing about life and those areas beyond life would certainly have left a note. Moreover, Marcia Moore believed devoutly in reincarnation. And for believers, suicide is the worst possible death. Suicide destroys the natural karmic pattern. At best, the individual would have to come back again and start all over, making the same mistakes, suffering the same disappointments and agonies of the life they have just left. At worst, some proponents of reincarnation believe that a suicide is doomed in every life hereafter. Moore's friends said that Marcia had espoused the latter theory. For her, suicide would be sentencing herself to endless lifetimes of misery, with no hope of spiritual growth.

Could she have been abducted by a killer? Possibly. It was unlikely that she would have allowed a stranger into her home, but she could have gone for a walk in the cemetery and been attacked there. But, if that were the case, where was her body? Most murder victims turn up sooner or later. Most—not all. Snohomish County was full of rivers, lakes, much of it on the shores of Puget Sound. There were abandoned mine shafts, and mountain passes covered in deep snow.

Could Marcia have decided to leave of her own accord? Neither her husband nor her brothers felt she would do that. She was happily married, involved in her work. And she was very considerate of her elderly parents. "She would communicate with us if she were able," attorney John Moore insisted. "She wouldn't do that to the folks."

Robin Moore concurred. "My sister and I were quite close. She would not have disappeared without letting me know. She was writing a book for my publishing company. If there's one thing she had, it was a very strong sense of deadlines. She would have called."

Most of her friends were baffled by Marcia's disappearance, but Elise felt an ominous cloud that had nothing to do with her skill at astrology. "I watched Marcia deteriorate very rapidly after she started experimenting with ketamine," she said. "She had complained of pain in her hip. That was why she took walks around Floral Hills. The paths were a flat surface on which to walk. She didn't want to talk about her hip, but she did say that someone was 'bewitching' her . . ."

But Elise didn't think Marcia would have gone walking in the cemetery at night.

Robin Moore's wife had spoken long-distance with

Marcia on Saturday, January 13. She had found her sister-in-law very enthusiastic about her new projects, if a little repetitive and "slightly confused" about her theories.

Robin Moore, himself familiar with police investigations and mysteries from research on his books, had two theories about his sister's fate. "I really think it's at least a fifty-fifty chance she was kidnapped, but not by an ordinary kidnapper. It would be a grotesque kidnapping by one of the people who knew [of] this very unorthodox spiritualism she was involved in.

"Then maybe her husband is right. Maybe the ketamine caught up with her. Maybe something snapped and she took off walking."

Agonized, Dr. Boccaci said he had come to that theory as a possibility. Although he had never seen any profoundly detrimental effects from the drug, he realized that Marcia was a special case—the only human in the world known to have ingested so much for so long.

Could she have suddenly been gripped by amnesia without his seeing its approach? The *PDR (Physicians Desk Reference)* warned that a side effect of ketamine is "confusional states" during a patient's recovery from surgery. Temporary amnesia was a possibility.

But Marcia's dosage had been far less than that used for surgical anesthesia. If she had been building cumulative residuals of ketamine, a physician of her husband's experience would surely have noted it.

Boccaci described the immediate effects of the drug in small doses by injection. "After the first two or three minutes, you begin to feel the initial effects, like hearing the chirping of crickets. Then, after five minutes, you begin to leave your body behind. There is no cognition of the fact that you have a body, but you are aware that you are still alive. You have a center point of consciousness. You go out of the planet of Earth and into the astro planes."

This is the opposite reaction to the street drug known as "angel dust." With angel dust, the ingester feels dead and those who have overdosed are convinced that they are, indeed, dead.

Some of Marcia's friends told the Snohomish County investigators that, with deep meditation, there were documented cases where the "soul" had gone so far out into the astro planes that the body left behind had died. But, even if it had succumbed without its "soul," it was still there. Marcia Moore's body was nowhere—nowhere where anyone could find it.

Lieutenant Darrol Bemis had to take a crash course in the psychic world, spending half his nights reading Marcia Moore's books and others like it, "so I can understand the terminology psychics use," he told reporters.

He was deluged with tips from mystics who believed they knew what had happened to Marcia Moore. In a case with no clues, the investigative team tried to remain open-minded and consider every possible source of information carefully, no matter how far-fetched it might be.

The phone bills run up in the probe were astronomical. Lieutenant Bemis and his team called every telephone number they could locate in the missing woman's duplex, without finding anyone who had heard from Marcia. Marcia Moore's family on the East Coast never heard from her. No one in Ojai, California—where she had scores of friends—heard from her.

There was one strange incident that might have had

bearing on her disappearance. On either January 15 or 16, the twelve-year-old daughter of one of Marcia's closest friends answered the phone and a woman with a Boston accent like Marcia's asked, "Is your Mummy there?"

The child said she was not and there was no number where she could be reached, and the caller said she would call back later. She never did.

"If she were in trouble, that would be the time she would call me," the friend offered. "She has called me to her side several times in the past when she needed me."

The search for Marcia Moore grew eerier and eerier. Some psychics maintained that the ghosts of the dead were able to use phone lines to get messages through, even years after they passed over. Was it possible that Marcia Moore would try to contact someone from the other side? Bemis and his fellow investigators found themselves considering the most bizarre possibilities when regular detective work netted them nothing at all.

Marcia and Happy Boccaci were to have attended the International Cooperation Council's Rainbow Rose Festival in Pasadena, California, on the weekend of January 27 and 28 as featured speakers. This was America's largest gathering of psychics and it was a function that Marcia would never have missed if there was any way she could be there.

One of the festival organizers had a theory on Marcia's disappearance. "I guess this sounds kind of far out, but a lot of psychics here think she dematerialized. In the Indian philosophy, you can raise your consciousness, keep developing yourself like Jesus Christ and some of the gurus, and reach a point where you just zap out."

Bizarre? Of course. But then the whole of Marcia

Moore's life had bordered on the bizarre, and there were no rational explanations about where Marcia had gone.

Marcia had also written a speech that she planned to present at the World Symposium on Humanity in Los Angeles in April. Happy Boccaci went in her place. He wrote to Elise, "I just got back from L.A. where I delivered Marcia's brilliant speech, entitled, 'Where is the reincarnation movement heading today?' And I got a lot more people praying. I don't have much to say except I am terribly depressed and ever so lonely. I do cry a lot. Again, thank you for your note and do keep praying . . . Light and love, (not so) Happy."

The husband of a missing woman is always suspect. So was Dr. Walter "Happy" Boccaci. Marcia's family considered him the prime suspect in her disappearance, although he stood to gain nothing financially in case of her death. He would actually be poorer because her trust fund wouldn't go to him—but to her three children.

Boccaci seemed remarkably sanguine about the suspicions of the Moore family. "I realize that if my daughter were suddenly to marry somebody on the East Coast that I had never met—and six months later she disappeared, I would say, 'Damn it. It's the husband who did it. He's the culprit!' That's just a natural thing to believe."

Her family used Marcia's trust fund to hire private detectives. They came to the Northwest, and had no better results than the Snohomish County investigators. Although they looked hard at Dr. Happy Boccaci, and reportedly tried to trick him into believing he would get an inheritance if Marcia's body was found, he told them what he had told everyone: "I wish I knew where her body was, her soul, whatever. But I don't."

* * *

Because Marcia Moore was herself a psychic, I consulted two psychics whom I knew to be amazingly accurate in their assessments and predictions. What would happen when the cards were thrown down a year after her disappearance and questions were asked about Marcia? Would there be two diverse opinions—or would they agree?

Barbara Easton, a well-known Northwest psychic who reads ordinary playing cards, did several spreads on Marcia Moore. She knew only a little about the case. She was asking the question, "What were the circumstances around Marcia Moore's disappearance?"

The answers came swiftly. "Just before she vanished," Barbara said, "she received a long-distance phone call from a woman concerning a contract in which a lot of money was involved. There is a man involved, too—a man concerned about a real estate contract on which a great deal of money hinged."

According to the cards, Marcia Moore's marriage had been in trouble, and she was in the process of making a decision to get rid of emotional ties that had never worked. She had been very disappointed and frustrated. Moreover, she had recently heard from a man out of her past and received an invitation which had made her happy.

"The cards tell us that she wanted a divorce—even if no one was aware of it," Easton said, shaking her head.

Easton spread the cards four times, and each time the ace of spades (the death card) appeared side by side with the nine of hearts (the wish card).

"I think she's dead," Easton sighed. "Someone wished her dead, but the cards indicate that she was also blessed with very good women friends who were lucky for her, women she had turned to in the past for help."

Easton also picked up repeatedly on "hospital" and "court (or trial)" as she did further spreads of cards. Could Marcia Moore be in a hospital some place where no one knew who she was? Could there eventually be a trial for her murder?

The blonde psychic explained that, although death showed repeatedly in Marcia's cards, these could also be interpreted as the death of the personality as it has been known. "She could have been so enlightened by the drug that her known personality died—leaving her body. There's possibly a five percent chance that she's hospitalized or sitting on a mountain top some place—meditating," Easton said. "It's called going to the void."

The elements of Marcia Moore's disappearance, then, that Easton elicited from the cards again and again were:

1. Marital problems, disappointments, frustration.
2. A renewed relationship with an old love.
3. A real estate transaction involving a lot of money.
4. Concern over another woman.
5. Phenomenal success ahead for Marcia in her work.
6. A hospital.
7. Death. Violent death.
8. A court trial.

"I think the decision was made for Marcia Moore to die," Easton summed up flatly.

Another popular psychic based in the Northwest, Shirley Teabo, read Tarot cards. Like Easton, she had a high success rate.

Shirley Teabo was not told about Barbara Easton's

reading on Marcia Moore, nor did she know more than the bare facts about the woman's disappearance.

Could a second psychic home in on whatever astral projections Marcia Moore's entity was sending? Would Teabo's interpretations be entirely different from Easton's?

Teabo was able to pinpoint the date of Moore's disappearance (without knowing when it was) as between December 20 and January 20, 1979. "At that time, there was a passage away from difficulties—a journey over water," she said. "A journey over water far enough to leave the state of Washington. I see her on a ferry boat and I see the rays of a lighthouse crossing over her. She has—or had—a woman friend who was very good for her, someone from the past."

Teabo picked up a "retreat, a meditative state, a convalescent state after much anxiety."

"For some reason, I pick up the San Juan Islands. She has ties there, but I pick up a sunny day and she is happy. It may be something that has happened in her past."

The next card was not so cheerful; it was a coffin, a sarcophagus—a sign that someone is buried. "Sheets and things are wrapped around her," Teabo said. "Her 'fear' card revolves around a real estate transaction—something involving a great deal of money."

The psychic spread cards asking about what had happened in Marcia Moore's home on the last day she was seen. These cards showed the end of a cycle, a finishing-up. "She was preparing for a change, and she was well able to protect herself."

Oddly, Teabo, too, saw trouble with another woman—a woman of a violent nature who could have caused

Moore real problems. "One woman is her friend—the other was a danger to her."

According to Teabo's reading, Marcia Moore had been about to advance tremendously in the world of her art. The books she was working on would have been highly successful. "But I see an illness . . . a hospitalization. She may be in an institution."

According to Shirley Teabo, Marcia Moore had been subjected to great stress. "Quarrels over money, over land, and someone was trying to make away with something that belonged to her."

Marcia's brother Robin had theorized that, if she had been kidnapped, it would have been because of the "unorthodox spiritualism" she was involved in. Teabo turned up cards that indicated that this might very well be true. Twice in succession, the anti-religion and cult cards turned up side by side. "She was at a crossroads and the path she chose was faulty, dangerous."

Marcia's marriage had not been serene, according to the Tarot cards; the couple had each felt bondage and restriction, frustration in the marriage.

As Barbara Easton had, Shirley Teabo saw violence on the last day of Marcia Moore's known existence. She picked it up again and again. "Oddly, I don't think she's dead . . . but I don't see her alive, either. It's as if her mind isn't hers any longer. If she is dead, she's earthbound."

A summary of Teabo's reading has many points of similarity with Easton's.

1. Trouble in the home.
2. A real estate transaction involving a lot of money.
3. Great success ahead in Moore's career.

4. Concerns about another woman who was dangerous to her.
5. Hospitalization.
6. Violence.
7. A "death" state.

If Marcia Moore was alive, the cards of both psychics
suggested that she was incapacitated to the degree that
she couldn't let anyone know where she was. If she was
dead, her body had been secreted so carefully that it
might never be found.

While Lieutenant Darrol Bemis and Detective Doris
Twitchell worked the case from the scientific viewpoint
of trained police officers, Dr. Walter Boccaci tried to
reach his wife through less orthodox methods. After fast-
ing all day and doing yoga, he injected himself with ketamine at midnight.

"The sole purpose of this is to reach my wife. We
were telepathic. We were soul mates. Ketamine is the
only way I can get out of my body. And I have been
reaching her. I see her so clearly. She's sitting in a lotus
position, lovely and beautiful. But she doesn't talk to
me. I know why. She's amnesic. That's the only possibility, don't you see. The only way that makes sense."

Dr. Boccaci published one last issue of "The Hypersentience Bulletin," the newsletter he and Marcia had
mailed to their followers. He wrote a "Final Note" to
Marcia: "When you walk along the beach and listen to
the sound of the waves, listen also to the roar of my
voice, reverberating, 'Marcia, I love you. I'll always love
you . . .'"

Despite his protestations that his life was over now

that his wife was gone, Boccaci remained a suspect in her disappearance—or death . . . or transformation, whatever had happened. He told Erik Lacitis, a *Seattle Times* columnist, about his troubles. "The tragedy of this whole thing is what's happened to me. I am just hanging on by the skin of my teeth. I am destitute. I'm surviving by selling furniture and other personal possessions.

"I just spent a whole year of my life devoting all my energy to trying to find my wife . . . I tried everything. There's nothing more I can do to find my wife. Now, I'm trying to pick up the pieces of my life. I am forty-two, and I have another forty-two years ahead of me. And I can't get a job. I have been blackballed."

Although Boccaci said he had never lost a patient because of anesthesia or even had one with an adverse reaction, he felt he had been unable to find work in his profession because of all the publicity about Marcia's disappearance, and, perhaps, their ketamine research.

Boccaci left Washington State and took a residency at a Detroit hospital where his story was not so familiar. At length, he *did* find a job as an anesthesiologist at a tiny hospital on the Washington coast. Happy Boccaci wrote to Marcia's friends that he was finally doing well, jogging five miles a day, and feeling much better.

Marcia Moore's family members were divided in their opinions of what had become of her. Her daughter recalled how often Marcia had spoken of her dread of growing old. "It bothered her a lot. What do *I* think really happened?" she asked. "I would have to say that she committed suicide in some way."

But committing suicide without leaving a body behind is not easy to do. If Marcia Moore had leapt from a ferry boat on its way to the San Juan Islands, her body might have sunk—but, more likely, it would have eventually washed up on some spit of land.

It would be two years after Marcia Moore vanished before those who loved her and those who sought her would have at least a partial answer to a seemingly incomprehensible mystery.

A property owner was clearing blackberry vines from a lot he owned near the city of Bothell on the first day of spring 1981. He reached down and almost touched a partial skull that lay hidden there. There was another bone, too. The site was less than fifteen miles from the town house where Marcia and Happy had lived. The skull had well-maintained teeth, and that would help in identifying the remains.

When the Snohomish County investigators asked a forensic dentistry expert to compare Marcia Moore's dental records with the teeth in the skull, they knew, at long last, where she was.

A meticulous search of the area produced nothing more, however. No clothes. No jewelry. No hiking boots.

Could Marcia Moore have walked so far on the freezing night she vanished? Possibly. But she would have had to skirt a busy freeway and pass any number of areas where people lived, shopped, and worked, and no one had ever reported seeing her. Could she have been murdered, and taken to this lonely lot? Possibly. Although the detectives didn't release the information, there was profound damage to the frontal portion of her skull.

One of Marcia's close women friends made a pilgrimage to the spot where her last earthly remains had lain. She wrote to a mutual friend who also mourned for their dear friend, and it was both a comforting and a disturbing letter.

"I went over and saw the exact spot where the skull was located," she wrote. "And it was a beautiful place, on top of a bed of soft, dry leaves, encircled by some very large trees. And growing all around the circle were trilliums beginning to come up. Of course not in bloom yet. My first thought was, 'Marcia would have loved this place!' It was almost like a gigantic fairy ring, those big trees in a circle. A little boy showed me the place; he is the son of the man who found the skull. The little boy said there was a hole right in the front of the skull, and I said, 'That sounds like a bullet hole,' and he agreed."

But he was only a little boy, and the investigators were never convinced that Marcia Moore had been shot in the head; her skull was so fragile and it had lain out in the elements for more than two years.

To this day, no one really knows what happened on that Sunday night in January 1979—no one but her killer, if, indeed, she *was* murdered. Marcia had always longed for a glimpse into another, brighter, world. Once there, she sent no messages back to the friends who waited for some sign.

Had she lived, Marcia would have been seventy years old now. Her last husband is sixty-one, but no one has heard from Happy Boccaci for a long time.

To an Athlete Dying Young

Many athletes pursue *an inner radiance that comes only when they exceed what they believe their bodies can do. The young woman in the following case was a tremendous athlete, and she had realized many goals she had set for herself, often against great odds.*

She had seen many dreams come true. But dreams can be addictive, especially when they come true. She wanted to crowd as many into her life as she could before time and fate ended them. The last dream seemed, in many ways, the easiest to bring to life.

Sadly, even though she accomplished the task she had set for herself, there was someone determined to smash her triumph even as she exulted in success.

It is a bleak commentary on society that city parks have become dangerous places for women. They may be safe enough in the daylight, or if one is accompanied by a large dog. But the isolated trails of city parks have gradually become off-limits for women when shadows grow long. Too often these parks are oases within the inner city, bordered by streets filled with predators. The next case deals with the dangers women face when they venture too far off the beaten path—even in cities.

The huge sprawling national parks of America once seemed safer than metropolitan parks—at least when it came to human predators. Although there have been horrendous headlines about women who were dragged off and mauled to death by grizzly bears, man remains the deadliest creature of all.

Jane **Costantino** was a beautiful, vibrant woman with masses of long blonde hair, and a perfectly toned body. She considered the world her home, particularly the outdoors. She had always met life head on, and never used the fact that she was a female to avoid hard work and daunting tasks, but sometimes it seemed that Jane almost dared the fates to challenge her. She was an adventuress not unlike Amelia Earhart, another independent woman who came of age in her thirties, and who broke barriers that most women were afraid to challenge. Jane would brook no fear in herself; she liked to say she wasn't afraid of anything. Of course, that was an exaggeration. Like everyone, she had her fears, but when something frightened her, she set out to conquer it.

Jane was an easterner by birth. She grew up on Long Island, attended Fordham University in New York City, and worked for a few years as a social worker there. But she felt confined in the city so she went west. She sought hotter deserts, higher mountains, broader prairies. But before relocating to the west, she went first across the Atlantic to Europe.

During her tour of Europe, Jane Costantino met a Colorado man who seemed to share many of her interests.

When he told her he owned a string of pack horses in his home state, she was hooked. She married him and moved with him to Denver. Their marriage survived only two years, but Jane loved Colorado and she stayed on in the Denver area. Still, she used the mile-high city only as a home base. She would always be a traveller at heart who couldn't resist the call of the road.

Jane wasn't wealthy, and she had to plan carefully to be able to afford the trips she took. She had to work seven days a week for most of the year as a waitress to save money for each new summer's adventures. She lived, if not frugally, *sparely*, during the eight or nine months she was in Denver. It was a trade-off that she accepted gladly. The possessions that most people sought meant little to her and she happily drove a beat-up old Volkswagen bug. She lived in a tiny apartment in an old brick apartment house in Denver. Everything extra went to buy the best in hiking and camping equipment. In an era when many women were floundering to find their identity, Jane Costantino knew exactly what she wanted and she worked hard to make it come true.

She was a good waitress, "the best we've ever had here," according to one Denver bartender. She was blessed with a great personality and a smile that went with her strong good looks. It wasn't an act; she genuinely liked the people she waited on, and they rewarded her with generous tips that she kept in glass jars at home until she saved enough to add to her savings account.

There aren't many people who can quote a poem or song that absolutely sums up their philosophies of life, but Jane could. She lived by the lines of her favorite poem— Robert Service's "Rolling Stone."

The mountains are a part of me. I'm fellow to the trees. My golden years I'm squandering. Sun-libertine am I. A wandering, a wandering. Until the day I die. Then here's a hail to each flaring dawn. Here's a cheer for the night that's gone . . . And may I go a-roaming on. Until the day I die. . . .

Despite her sunny disposition, there was a shadow that sometimes crept into the edges of Jane Costantino's world. She had long had a premonition that she wouldn't live to grow old. She wasn't sure where it had come from, although it seemed an integral part of her, a kind of gut feeling that she didn't fight. If she wasn't meant to be an old woman sharing memories of her glory days as she rocked on a porch somewhere, that was the way the universe's plan was designed.

Jane had lived with an awareness of her own mortality for as long as she could remember. Maybe it was because by the time she was thirty, she had already had ample experience at jousting with death; she had come so close too many times. She took chances and she knew it. She probably assumed she would die at the hands of a capricious Mother Nature since she was a risk-taker. In the nineties, studies suggested that those addicted to danger are programmed genetically to be that way—that there exists a spot in the DNA of the mountain climber, the ski jumper and the race car driver that propels them into life on the edge. But, in the seventies, Jane Costantino's family and friends worried and cautioned her and finally shook their heads; she was who she was, and she seemed to be living a glorious life.

Jane was twenty-seven years old in 1974, when she was struck by lightning as she climbed the Grand Tetons.

She was at the 14,000 foot level when it happened. She was hit by a powerfully searing jolt that would have knocked her off the mountain if she hadn't clung tenaciously to her perch. Seriously burned and with her shoulder badly injured, she climbed and rappelled down the mountain and walked several miles to a ranger station. When the ranger on duty saw that the lightning bolt had burned her shoulder to the bone, he almost fainted. A lesser woman—or man—would have been dead, or at the very least, would have had to be airlifted off the mountain.

Jane was hospitalized for a month. When she was finally released from the hospital, she carried the blazing keloid of a huge burn on her shoulder. She called the scar her "badge of life" because it served to remind her to live life to its fullest; she told friends that she knew that any day might be her last.

There was only one thing that really frightened Jane Costantino, and that was water and her fear of drowning. So she forced herself to become adept at water sports—scuba diving and kayaking down white-water rivers—to overcome her phobia. Even when she nearly drowned while fording a river in the Katmai region of Alaska, she continued to risk her life in deep and raging waters, stubbornly refusing to give in to her terror.

Jane Costantino taunted Nature. While she was mountain climbing in Yosemite, she slipped and literally fell off a cliff. Fellow climbers watched in horror as a cascade of rocks plummeted down on her, almost burying her—and yet she survived with only a broken ankle and a concussion.

In 1979, Jane climbed Mount Rainier, Mount Baker, and Mount St. Helens all in one nine-day period, and then bicycled to Mexico for good measure. She missed the disaster that befell Mount St. Helens months later, and sometimes spoke a little ruefully about the fact that she hadn't been there for all the fireworks. Jane was the kind of adventuress who would have happily camped in the shadow of Mount St. Helens even as the peak threatened to blow. If she hadn't been so busy on her winter job, she would have been there when the mountain finally blew its domed top on May 18, 1980, spewing tons of lava and mud down its slopes, taking a number of victims. And, if Jane Costantino had died that way, no one would have been surprised.

Because she was in great shape, it seemed to her that she would be in her twenties forever, but one day Jane woke up and realized that she was thirty-two, and in eight years she would be forty. It was a sobering thought. She was still young at thirty-two, but she knew that she wasn't "young-young" any longer. Already, old injuries ached when the weather was changing, and she sometimes thought that her lung capacity wasn't what it was when she was nineteen.

Typical of her personality, Jane raised the bar, setting harder tasks for herself, willing her body to remain as trim and tautly muscled as a ballerina's. As if she hadn't already proved herself enough in 1979, she set off to bicycle alone from Nova Scotia to New York. Along a dark stretch of road, she collided with a truck and was carted off, bleeding and bruised, to a hospital. After a stay of several days, she insisted on finishing the trip.

If Jane Costantino had been a cat, she would have had five lives yet to go. But she was, after all, only a human, only a woman alone in a world fraught with dangers far more menacing than lightning or an unlit country road.

Jane Costantino's carefully charted 1980 trip was the most rigorous adventure she had ever attempted. She and her brother bicycled from Denver to New York City. They had a wonderful time, their time together turned out to be everything she had hoped, and the summer season was far from over. She had pedaled her way to one coast, and intended to make it to the West Coast, too.

She flew back to Colorado and began another bicycle trip west, but this time she was all by herself. She liked her own company and she always met interesting and friendly people so she never really felt alone. There was no question at all that she could manage the second trip physically.

Jane's plan called for her to go to the shores of the Pacific Ocean first. She would dip her bicycle wheels in the ocean at Cape Alava off the Ozette Indian Reservation. This was on the farther-most northwestern tip of the Olympic Peninsula in Washington State. After that, with her trip symbolically over, she would bicycle leisurely back to Seattle to meet with friends on Thursday, July 24.

As she knew she would, Jane made it to the Pacific Ocean all right. Tanned and healthy, she attended an archaeology lecture at the Ozette digs. She was a woman that people always remembered and several would recall seeing the lovely, blonde woman headed toward the beach. Although it didn't seem that ominous at the time, they also remembered seeing a man walking on the trail behind her, also headed toward the ocean. He was big, burly, and had black hair.

It was early afternoon then. The sun was shining. In

the forty-second year of its existence, the Olympic National Park had been a safe haven. It was a place for communing with nature, for renewing one's soul after a long winter, and that was all Jane Costantino had on her mind. She was a short walk away from her goal; she was about to swish her bike's tires through the salt water in the shallows of the Pacific Ocean. And then she would head toward Seattle. Seattle was well over a hundred miles and a couple of ferry boat rides away, but it wasn't much of a challenge after she'd just traversed the entire country.

Jane Costantino didn't know that another woman in the park had been approached by a hulking man in a black cowboy hat and a purple shirt, nor that the woman had been alarmed by the way the stranger acted.

Jane didn't know that this man was just behind her on the trail, stealthily keeping out of range of her sight and hearing as the rugged trail fell away behind her. Even if she had known, she might not have been frightened. She was full of stories about eccentrics she'd met on her travels. She would be the first to say that most of them were harmless enough. Maybe just a little crazy or lost or lonely.

The afternoon sun grew warmer, but it wasn't oppressive because the wind from the ocean was cool and fragrant with the special salty sea smell that cannot be duplicated. Wild roses and berries vines gradually gave way to sea grass. Beyond, there was nothing but wave after wave as the Pacific Ocean rolled on into infinity.

It was 3 P.M. on that Wednesday in 1979: July 23. A group of hikers trudged toward the ocean; when they rounded a turn in the trail they came upon a woman who appeared to have fainted. She lay beside the beach trail two-tenths of a mile from the ocean. Moving closer and calling, their voices became hushed and then silent as they saw that her blouse was soaked in wet blood. Try as they might to find a pulse or to catch even a faint rising and falling of her breasts, they were unsuccessful.

Here, on a perfect day in a perfect paradise of a park, a woman was dead—and not by accident, but by violence. Her body was fully clothed, and there was no sign at all that she had been sexually assaulted.

Notified by a phone call from one of the hikers, three separate law enforcement agencies responded: Clallam County Sheriff's deputies, tribal police from the Ozette Indian Reservation, and rangers from the U.S. Park Service. The Ozettes, the Park Service, and the Clallam County Sheriff's office had worked together for nearly half a century to keep the park safe. Although the Clallam County Sheriff's office was sixty miles away in Port Angeles, the sheriff's detectives were on the scene within minutes. They had waited on a windy narrow finger of land named Ediz Hook, until a Coast Guard helicopter winched them up and shuttled them to the beach trail where the dead woman lay.

Park Rangers Gordon Boyd and Steve Underwood and Deputy Michael Lenihan saw that the victim had not died accidentally or of natural causes. She had multiple stab wounds in the chest, so many that she had probably died almost instantly. Either she had been part of an intensely violent argument with someone she knew, or she had been stalked by a maniac along the lonely trail.

Gingerly, they fished her wallet out of her backpack. It

was pathetically easy to identify the tanned woman. There were numerous pieces of I.D. in the pack—listing addresses in Denver and Long Island. She was Jane Costantino, thirty-two. The description on her driver's license and the photograph fit. She had come here from far away, but for what reason? Had she come alone or with a lover or husband?

The investigators organized a grid search of the vast national park, and they fanned out through the area, talking to other hikers and campers. Even though the murder had been discovered within a very short time of its occurrence, a national park is not an ideal crime scene to work. The killer might well have slipped away unseen, and already be headed back toward a city where he could lose himself. It had to have been a man—surely, no woman would have been able to overpower a victim who had been as ruggedly healthy and perfectly muscled as the woman who lay before them.

When the officers at the scene finished searching the sandy banks and the brushy areas off the trail, they released Jane Costantino's body to the coroner.

Roads into the vast park were sealed off by deputies and rangers. Every car leaving the park was stopped and searched. Women hiking alone quickly joined up with other groups. It was still a long time until dark on a July day in the far Northwest, but every shadow cast in the forested area seemed threatening now.

The officers and rangers feared they were looking for a killer who might well strike again. Every male camper was suspect, even if he had a wife, a bunch of kids and dogs, and a picnic basket with him.

The probers were exceptionally fortunate in finding a witness who had an interesting—and chilling—story to tell them. She was slender and pretty, but shaken when she learned that a woman had been stabbed to death on the trail.

"This weird guy started following me," she began with a tremble in her voice. "I tried to avoid him, but he caught up with me on the trail to the beach. He told me that he was a photographer for *Playboy,* and he offered me fifty dollars to pose for him in the nude. He sure didn't look like any photographer for *Playboy,* and I didn't see a camera, either. I told him to just go away."

The woman looked down, biting her lip to keep from crying. She told them that she was feeling both frightened and guilty. "Just after that, another woman came along the trail. I'm afraid it might have been the woman who died. It *must* have been her—and he just stared at her, and then he turned around, and started following her."

"What did he look like?" the Clallam County officers asked.

"Big. He was really big—probably over six feet, and kind of blubbery around the middle. Not real clean. He was wearing a purple shirt, and a cowboy hat, a dark hat. He gave me the creeps."

The young woman told them she had hurried away, grateful to be free of the stranger. She hadn't thought that anything was wrong because she had heard nothing. Certainly, there had been no screams, no cries for help at all.

"If I'd stayed, maybe I could have helped her," she said somberly. "Maybe the two of us could have stopped him."

"No. Maybe both of you would have been killed," a

deputy said quietly. "You couldn't have known what he was going to do."

The witness said that the man on the trail had appeared to be in his late thirties or early forties.

"You ever see him before?"

She shook her head. "Never—not until he came up to me on the trail."

The deputies talked to other hikers, who gathered in quiet clusters in a clearing. Several of them remembered seeing a man who matched the first witness's description. Two hikers had met him on the trail, but he had been in a great hurry, plunging past them. "He had dark red stains on his purple shirt," a man said. "It looked as if he'd been picking berries, and wiped his hands on his shirt, at least at first. I realize now that wasn't what it was."

Park Rangers Gordon Boyd and Steve Underwood and Deputy Michael Lenihan headed down a trail that wound toward the beach. They came upon a husky man wearing a black cowboy hat, and a purple shirt. The shirt was soaking wet, and it clung to his beefy chest. But it didn't have any stains on it at all. It was obvious to the investigators that the man had just washed it in the ocean.

They ordered the man to lean against a rock while they searched him. Lenihan pulled a hunting knife out of his belt and several lengths of rope from his pockets. The big man refused to answer any of their questions. He would only give his name: Dale C. Harrison, thirty-seven, from Othello, Washington. Othello is a farming community in eastern Washington, a ferry ride, a mountain pass and hundreds of miles away from Cape Alava. He refused to say why he was in the park.

They arrested Dale Harrison on suspicion of murder,

handcuffed him and placed him in the back of a ranger's car. Because Jane Costantino had been stabbed to death in a national park, her murder was a federal crime.

The FBI would continue the investigation. FBI Special Agent Paul Mack fed the name Dale C. Harrison into the computers to see if he was wanted. Surprisingly, he was not currently on any wanted lists, but he did have a record. His rap sheet showed a number of arrests for sex-related crimes dating back almost two decades. He had been convicted in 1962 of sexual molestation against two young girls. He had used a knife in that incident. He had served two years on yet another molestation charge and had been paroled from prison in 1965.

Yet Dale Harrison had apparently lived a "normal" life, too. In the fifteen years since he had been released from prison, he had married and fathered two children. He worked as a forklift operator and as laborer, and had a good employment record. Apparently, his predatory sexual fantasies had only been banked—until they erupted on a sunny day in July.

And Harrison had to have been a man consumed by lust and rage. The initial report from the Medical Examiner said that Jane Costantino had been stabbed six times in the chest with "hard, vicious thrusts." The knife had pierced so deeply that the Medical Examiner believed Jane's killer had to be a man of more than usual strength.

Dale Harrison fit that description. They believed he was the person who had shattered the forty-two years of serenity in the park. Forty-two years and never a murder.

The investigators doubted that Jane had known her killer. She was, almost certainly, a chance victim. Harrison had approached the other woman first. He hadn't known her and he hadn't known Jane either. When the first woman he accosted told him to "get lost," he had turned around and seen Jane Costantino coming down the trail. When the agents and deputies checked on Jane's background, they learned about her quest to ride a bike coast to coast. She had come so close to completing her journey. Just another fifth of a mile and she and her bike would have reached the ocean.

Instead, Jane had the tragic misfortune to cross paths with the man who pretended to be a *Playboy* photographer. She wouldn't have believed that ruse for a minute. But a woman who had worked for years as a cocktail waitress would have become very adept at turning away men without offending them. Jane Costantino could think on her feet. She wasn't a woman to panic and run. She would have tried to reason with an attacker—if he gave her a chance to do so. Why then had Jane Costantino been killed? Her clothing hadn't been disarranged at all, so a sexual attack hadn't even been begun. Had Jane said something to the man who approached her that had enraged him? It was possible that she had inadvertently made a remark that triggered terrible violence.

It looked more likely that Dale Harrison had been looking for a woman to kill. He had done it swiftly and violently. And silently. There was a great deal of both circumstantial and physical evidence that linked Harrison to the inexplicable murder of a stranger. His hunting knife matched exactly the wound measurements taken at Jane Costantino's autopsy.

Tests of his wet purple shirt showed that the ocean had failed to wash away traces of human blood. The shirt fibers still held enough blood to test, and the blood matched Jane's genotype.

A man whose appearance was as striking as Dale Harrison's was not easily forgotten. Several people who had been in the park picked him from both a mugshot lay-down, and from a line-up, positive that he was the same man they had seen on the beach trail. The first woman he accosted had no doubt at all that Harrison was the man who followed Jane Costantino as she hurried toward the ocean.

Dale Harrison was arraigned and held in lieu of $100,000 bail. When agents questioned him, he was adamant that he knew nothing at all about the murder of Jane Costantino. But then, faced with the hard evidence against him, he changed his story. *He* wasn't the person who had killed her, he said confidentially. But he admitted that he had been a witness to her stab-bing.

The suspect said that he had looked on helplessly as another man, a stranger to him, had grabbed his knife and plunged it into the woman with the bicycle.

The special agents glanced at each other. If ever they had heard a weak explanation, this was it. Here was a husky forklift operator, a man who should have been a formidable opponent. Why hadn't *he* jumped to Jane's defense? And even if he had been afraid to help her, how could he have turned his back on her as she lay bleeding to death? He could have at least gone for help.

They asked him what had happened to the "mysteri-ous stranger." It was Harrison himself who was found with a knife, the bloodied shirt, and the rope.

Dale Harrison insisted that he had run away because he was terrified of being falsely accused of murder. Yes, he admitted, he had a record for sex crimes, and that was what scared him.

"Who would have believed me—once they knew about my record?"

Who indeed? The investigators stared back at him. His story made no sense at all. They wondered if he was going for a split personality defense. *It wasn't me; it was this guy who invades my body . . .*

While Dale Harrison awaited trial for murder, he continued to insist that he was innocent. The investigators and special agents continued to check into his background, sure that they still didn't know the entire story. They believed that Harrison had gone into the national park with a cruel mission in mind; he seemed to have no other reason for being there.

At length, they made contact with a man who said he was one of Harrison's closest friends. Boyd Blaunt* nodded uncomfortably as they explained what they were looking for. Had Harrison ever talked about his former crimes? Had he ever spoken of something that might explain his vicious attack on a woman he had never seen before?

Boyd Blaunt said that he had. "He's had some kind of fantasy—or obsession maybe you'd call it—for about a year and a half."

There was another side to Dale Harrison, the hardworking, devoted family man—information that hardly surprised the FBI agents who had tried to categorize their suspect. Blaunt said that Dale had fashioned a very intricate and deadly fantasy. Once he first told Blaunt about it, Dale had brought it up many times—at least a dozen times, detailing every aspect of it to his friend.

"I didn't take him seriously at first," Blaunt said. Harrison's plan was just too kinky and far out for anyone to really mean it. He had been turned on by the idea of finding a girl all alone in an isolated forest. Away from everybody else, he figured she would be helpless, and Harrison would have a rope handy to tie her up. Then, at his leisure, he would make a sex slave of her. His discipline and bondage fantasy included beating the captive woman with a belt.

The knife was part of it too, according to Blaunt. Dale Harrison said he would use a knife to force his victim to submit to "acts of degradation and rape."

Boyd Blaunt said that Harrison had even gone so far as to urge him to join in the plan to find and attack a woman. "But I always refused. It was only after that girl died that I realized how serious he was."

Blaunt's information on Harrison's compulsion was an exact blueprint of what had occurred on July 23. At least up to a point. But Jane Costantino had not been raped. Even alone in the forest, she wouldn't have been helpless; she would have fought back when she realized that he was determined to tie her up. That must have shocked Dale Harrison, the investigators thought.

Instead of being passive and frightened, Jane would have argued and struggled with her captor. Panicked, full of rage and frustration, all of his planned fantasy in disarray, Dale Harrison had stabbed her with the knife that was supposed to be used only as a threatening tool. If she had submitted to the fantasy, would she have lived? No one will ever know.

There are no hard and fast rules on how to react to a rapist. Some will be scared off if a woman fights back and some will be enraged. Some will listen to quiet reasoning or to hard luck stories. More are turned off by women who vomit or claim to have AIDS, but there are no guarantees. Jane Costantino fell into a fatal synchronicity of time and place. She had the terrible luck to be on the same path that Dale Harrison was when he was acting out his fantasy.

Harrison went on trial in U.S. District Court in November 1980 for the stabbing death of Jane Costantino and a jury found him guilty. His defense team attempted to bring in a motion that would mitigate his sentence because he was mentally ill. According to defense attorney Dan Dubitsky, psychologists had indicated that ". . . something is there, but they can't put their fingers on it."

Assistant U.S. Attorney James Flush was adamant that Judge Donald Voorhees should not consider Harrison's allegedly "exemplary life between 1965 and 1980 as an indication that he might be safe to be free. Either he has been very careful in committing crimes since 1965 or this is something that can occur [again] after a long period of time."

On December 5, Judge Donald Voorhees denied the defense motion for a psychiatric study that might have allowed Harrison a chance for early parole, and sentenced him to life in prison.

Judge Voorhees spoke very firmly as he meted out Harrison's life sentence, "In the light of his past history and this heinous crime . . . I am sentencing him to life imprisonment."

Jane Costantino's friends and relatives gathered at her funeral services for a last good-bye. An uncle from Long Island talked about her family's continuing concern over the chances Jane had taken. "Naturally we worried about her, but you can't dwell on those things. But we never thought of murder. Maybe being hurt in an accident, but not murder."

Nor, quite probably, did Jane herself. She lived her short life to the fullest. And like Amelia Earhart, she took soaring chances and reaped many wonderful rewards before her life ended early; just as she had known it would.

Ruby, Don't Take Your Love to Town

Death is unexpected for most murder victims, a small blessing, indeed. But at least they lived their lives without the sure knowledge that an angry executioner was waiting just around a corner. For one lovely young woman, her early death was as inevitable as the waning of the moon. She knew, but neither she nor any of her friends could stop it. She even knew who her killer would be, but that didn't help her either.

It's impossible to say just when the seeds of violence that threatened to destroy her were sown. The rage in her killer may have been a direct result of the war in Vietnam. Or it may have been a small kernel of hostility that had grown in him since he was a child.

Their story began as a love story, but it ended full of murderous hate and jealousy.

Eloise Amelia "Amy" Packard* was only six-teen when she met the man she would one day marry. The fine bone structure of her face and her ebony hair had come from her Indian heritage, and her perfect complexion from her Irish relatives. The tall redheaded young man from Oklahoma couldn't take his eyes off her when they met for the first time in 1962.

Amy worked as a mother's helper for a family in Olympia—the capital city of Washington State—and they loved her like their own. But she wanted to be with Eric Shaw* and they knew that it wouldn't be long before they were going to be looking for someone else to help with their children. They advised Amy to wait until she was eighteen, and she did, although it was difficult. It appeared to be the culmination of a perfect romance when Amy and Eric Shaw were married in January 1964, in Olympia. Amy was then eighteen and Eric almost twenty-one.

The future seemed all charted out for the couple, but then the Vietnam War intervened and Eric was drafted. He was inducted into the Army on December 5, 1966. He went off to basic training, and Amy stayed behind. She was enormously pregnant with their first child, and frightened to travel to a strange Army town where she didn't know anybody. Eric seemed to understand her need to stay in Olympia. Their little girl, Rose*, was born in 1967.

With her husband headed toward the Far East, Amy was having a very difficult time. For some reason, Eric had never signed the papers that would qualify her to receive dependent's benefits, and she had barely enough to live on. She wrote to him again and again asking him to sign the papers but he never seemed to get around to it. In the meantime, she lived on their savings. Her friends were worried when they realized that Amy had actually lost weight because she had run out of food. In desperation, Amy finally wrote to Eric's commanding officer to ask about her benefits.

It was possible that Eric never got Amy's letters, and Amy hoped that was true; she didn't like to think that it was out-of-sight–out-of-mind as far as she was concerned. She had agonized about writing to his C.O., but she was desperate. Then she worried that her husband might be angry when he found out she had gone over his head.

Eric was very much occupied at the time fighting a war. The Army suited him. By March 20, 1968, he had risen to Specialist 4th Class in Company B, 1st Battalion. He was an expert in light weapons, something he realized wouldn't be of much use in the civilian world. But he knew he could use the G.I. Bill when he needed it to go to college. The world outside Vietnam seemed as distant as another planet.

Amy waited for him to come home and busied herself taking care of their little girl. And once she began to receive her dependent's allotment check, her life became much easier.

Eric did come home, far sooner than they had hoped, but under tragic circumstances. The six-foot, one-inch, 170-pound soldier had seen duty all over the north part of Vietnam and he had almost begun to believe he was invincible. But one moonless night, as he was walking guard duty near the Cambodian border, a sniper with a Russian AK-47 fixed Eric in his gunsight. The blast hit him in the right shoulder, traversed his chest, and exited near his stomach. And it severed his spinal cord.

From that moment on, Eric Shaw was a paraplegic, his spinal cord severed at thoracic level three. He still had some strength in his arms and upper body, but his legs began to wither and they would never support him again. He was sent home to Madigan Army Hospital in Tacoma to heal and to begin rehab.

Eric was awarded a Bronze Star, an Army Commendation Medal, Vietnamese Service Medal, Republic of Vietnam Campaign Medal, National Defense Service Medal and a Combat Infantryman's Medal. And he would be eligible for extensive educational, housing, and living expense benefits. But, before he was thirty, he was profoundly disabled.

Amy and Eric were together again, even though he offered her a divorce. She shook her head in disbelief. She had loved him when she married him, and she still loved him. She told him she would stick with him. Eric had not lost his ability to engage the physical side of their relationship, and Amy became pregnant for the second time. This time they had a son.

With Eric's benefits, both he and Amy enrolled in Bellevue Community College east of Seattle. It looked for a time as though they really *could* pick up the pieces of their lives and start over.

But things were never the same again. The first over-powering romantic love they had shared was gone. According to those who knew Eric well, he had always found men superior to females. Women were second-class citizens to him. And that included his wife. His confinement to a wheelchair seemed to make him even more adamant about male superiority.

Eric considered jealousy a weakness, and he often said that women were far more jealous than men ever were—always snooping and asking questions. He liked to come and go without explaining himself. The marriage began to crack around its edges, minute flaws that were scarcely noticeable but which weakened the structure nonetheless.

Eric Shaw was a bitter man, railing against the cruel fate that had taken away the power in his legs. He began to flout the law in small ways; it was his way of proving he was still a man, perhaps. He bought a new, hand-controlled car and had it fitted with a muffler that roared, the loud pipes audible for blocks. He was stopped by the local police, who gave him a warning ticket. But Eric confided to his friends that he didn't worry about the police: "They have no facilities to take care of me," he said. "So I can do whatever I want."

As a mature woman, Amy was more beautiful than she had been at sixteen. She was caught up with her marriage, her two children, and her school work and she had neither the time nor the inclination to flirt with other men. But Eric didn't believe her. Jealousy, the very emotion that he derided, became the central focus of his life. He had a favorite song—"Ruby, Don't Take Your Love To Town." The lyrics seemed to fit his life: a Vietnam veteran chained to a wheelchair complaining that his legs were "bent and paralyzed" while he begged his wife not to go to town without him.

The "Ruby" of that song popular in the seventies had "wants and needs," and her agonized husband sang of getting his gun and putting her "in the ground."

The irony of it was that Amy still loved Eric. It was *he* who was destroying their marriage with accusations and bitter complaints. She didn't have a boyfriend; she'd never had any man but him, but he had changed. She had long since forgiven him for leaving her alone without money for food, but it was hard to forgive him for taunting her with vicious remarks about her character. Eric seemed to believe that the whole world was against him, and at the same time, that the world owed him a living. He felt he no longer had to obey the rules that everyone else did.

Amy Shaw didn't talk to her friends about her problems, but they could see the strain on her face. She occasionally visited the family where she had been the mother's helper so long ago. Without her saying a word, they could see that she was troubled.

Eric didn't want to work, even though there were many jobs he was still qualified for. The government would send him to college for years; he could have a profession. But he chose to sit home and weep in his beer. Nothing Amy did seemed to be right. And Eric began to call her "Ruby" instead of Amy.

Sometime after Easter of 1972, Amy Shaw told her friends that she was going to divorce Eric, but she wouldn't say why. She didn't want to be disloyal to him or say anything bad about him. She felt guilty enough that she couldn't stay with him. That spring, she and the children moved out.

Although he had complained about her constantly and made fun of her when they were together, Eric would not let Amy go. In July, he called her relatives and threatened them. "You'd better find Amy and get her over to my house or you'll be sorry—"

Frightened by his vehemence, they did as he asked. But they had no idea what he was going to do; they thought that he was just going to plead with Amy to come back to him. Amy's family watched in horror as Eric wheeled over to a nightstand in the master bedroom and pulled out a .38 revolver.

He pointed it at Amy, and said he was tired of supporting her and paying for her car if she wasn't going to live with him. "This gun is always loaded," he said quietly, "and I have nothing to lose."

Finally, they were able to persuade him to hand over the gun. Still, Eric Shaw's hatred of Amy seemed to permeate everything he did. Over and over again, he threatened to shoot her. He told anyone who would listen that he would kill her before he'd ever let her have custody of the children. They suspected he didn't really want the responsibility of the children, but he used them to get back at Amy.

Once, Eric told his friends that he was going to hire someone to kill a man he thought Amy was seeing.

Eric Shaw was far from being a pitiful, loveless man. He had already met another woman, Mariel*, who was also a paraplegic. She had lost the use of her legs when she was injured in an automobile accident. She was a lovely young woman who quickly fell in love with Eric, who when he wanted to be, could be completely charming.

* * *

Amy and Eric's divorce was final in July 1973. Amy won custody of their two children, but Eric had visitation rights. Eric wasted no time in remarrying; he and Mariel married just days after his divorce was final. He claimed to be euphorically happy in this new marriage, and he and Mariel lived in a $50,000 house and had an income of almost $1,400 each month from veterans' benefits and Social Security. Today, in Seattle, that would mean living in a $250,000 house and having close to $5,000 a month, tax-free.

But even while he lived with Mariel, Eric Shaw could not forget Amy. He let her know often that he would never forgive her for whatever sins he imagined she had committed. He was a man obsessed. He carried his .38 with him all the time and he made sure Amy knew it.

Amy Shaw was trying to make a new life for herself and the children. She enrolled in a library science course at Highline Community College in Des Moines, Washington, so that she could support them. The small girl and boy would continue to receive the Social Security allotted to the children of those disabled in the service of their country. But those benefits were only $260 a month, and not enough to keep a household going.

Amy had gone hungry before when Eric failed to list her as a dependent, but she would not allow her children to be deprived. She tried to get the court-ordered support that Eric was supposed to pay, but he withheld it. On one occasion, she went so far as to have him jailed for non-support and he spent a week in the King County Jail. This only enraged him.

Amy tried to honor the visitation rights Eric had with the children, but he devised new ways to torment her. She always sent the youngsters to visit wearing clean clothes and she sent extra clothes along. Eric began to keep that clothing, forcing her to buy them new outfits all the time. On her limited budget, she couldn't afford that. She begged him to bring their things back, but he kept the clothes until they were outgrown.

In desperation, Amy asked her attorney to write to Eric and say that he would either have to bring the clothing back or provide clothing for them himself.

It was an age-old dilemma in divorce where children were concerned. The children still loved their father, and Amy didn't want to deprive them of his company. On the other hand, she became afraid to have him come to pick them up. His hatred of her was almost palpable and she didn't know what he might do when he saw her. Finally, she asked a friend to walk the children out to Eric's car on visitation weekends.

It worked for a while, and then Eric backed his vehicle into Amy's girlfriend one day. He claimed that his grip had slipped off the hand controls, but it was frightening. When he pulled his .38 from the holster and pointed it at the woman on the next visit, there was no way to explain that away. As much as she wanted to help Amy, her friend was now too afraid of Eric.

Things got worse; Amy was living a scary "Gaslight" existence, wondering what Eric would do next. Rather than forgetting about her and turning to his new wife, he seemed to grow more obsessed. He began a subtle war of nerves. When she unpacked the children's bag, she would find that Eric had pulled up flowers and sent the dead vegetation home to her.

"Daddy said those were a present for you," her seven-year-old daughter said, innocently.

Even worse, he frightened the children by telling

them, "I wish your mother was dead; I wish she was never even alive."

She tried to tell him that he was doing damage to their children, and he only smiled.

When she picked up the mail, she found pictures of herself—only Eric had cut off her head in all the photographs.

At some point, Amy Shaw faced an awful truth. She lived with the sure knowledge that Eric meant to kill her. She couldn't have him arrested; she learned that the police couldn't arrest a man for something he *intended* to do. And he had a legal permit to carry a gun.

In the end, even though she had friends, Amy was all alone with two small children, the oldest only seven. Her son was barely past toddler stage. Without realizing it, she had begun to expect less and less of life. Her world had grown incredibly small. She no longer dreamed of marrying again or of having a career. She could not remember a time when she could walk outside free of fear. All she wanted, hoped for, and prayed for now was the opportunity to take care of her children.

She considered moving far away where Eric couldn't find her. But her family, her friends, her college, her entire support system was in the Seattle-Olympia area. She didn't know how she could manage all alone. And aside from her gnawing fear of Eric, she had made a little life in Des Moines. The Driftwood Apartments where they lived were attractive and the neighbors were friendly. Both she and the kids were only a few blocks from their respective schools. There was a beach half a mile away and parks where the children could play.

Amy decided that she couldn't hide forever; if Eric

meant to kill her, she knew he would find her someday. She decided to stay and face the problem head-on. She went to school, came home, and watched from behind the window blinds as the night grew dark outside. She worried most about what would happen to her children if she should die—both immediately, and over the years ahead. Who would take care of them?

Finally, although she hated doing it, Amy told her seven-year-old daughter, "If Daddy ever shoots me, I want you to go to the telephone and dial "0" and tell the operator to call the police."

Amy Shaw lived that way for a year; sometimes she was more afraid than others. But she was never not afraid. It was, sadly, the fear that plagues thousands of tormented women across America.

On the morning of September 21, 1974, Amy expected Eric to pick up their children. And he was supposed to bring clothing for them to wear; she had just bought them new school clothes, and she simply couldn't afford to lose any more. She was determined to make sure he had kept his part of the agreement before she let the kids outside.

The little girl was up first that morning and woke Amy, who said, "Come on, kids. Let's go and have breakfast." She fixed them toast and Cheerios. It was a Saturday morning like any other Saturday morning, but Amy was a little more frightened than usual. There was no one to walk the children out to the car, and she knew she had to talk to Eric about the clothes.

Amy cautioned the youngsters to stay in the house until she had picked up the clothes he was supposed to bring. "Don't come out until I come for you," she said, "because Daddy might take you away in your home clothes if you come out."

If Eric hadn't brought the clothes, Amy had decided she wasn't going to let the kids go. She couldn't take any more of his mean little games. She fully intended to turn around, go back to the house, and call the police.

She'd told her friends what she was going to do. She told them not to worry about her, but she asked her closest friend, "Call me at nine-thirty, would you, just to be sure everything's all right?"

There were more than two dozen apartments in the Driftwood complex. It was a little after eight-thirty on a sunny weekend morning and almost all the residents were home. Some of them saw the white Ford drive into the carport area. A tall red-haired man sat behind the wheel, and a pretty young woman sat beside him. They looked as if they were ready for a pleasant weekend. In fact, they looked so ordinary that they scarcely merited a second glance.

Those neighbors who lived close to the carport heard a man shout "It's all over!" Others would recall that they had heard a string of obscenities. Only a few heard the woman's voice cry out, "My God! Leave me alone!"

It was a little early in the morning for a family fight, but not unheard of. But then they realized that this was far more serious than a domestic squabble. The air crackled with a sound that resembled a string of firecrackers exploding.

A woman who ran to her open window and looked down saw the still form in the carport. It was a slender woman with long black hair, and she lay face down with her legs close together and one arm tucked under her, as if she hadn't had time to even break her fall. She wore white shorts and a brown blouse, and a scarlet pool was already beginning to stain the concrete beneath her.

Two of the apartment residents were registered nurses and they raced now, still wearing robes, with curlers in their hair, to help the woman. One bent to turn the woman over and she saw the awful damage to her face. Nevertheless, she began the "kiss of life"—mouth-to-mouth resuscitation—while the second straddled the woman's unconscious body and began to pump her chest.

Someone brought a blanket and tucked it around the injured woman. The nurses knew that she probably wasn't going to make it, but no one wanted to acknowledge that yet. She was so young.

No one saw the little face watching from a nearby window or realized the child there had disappeared. A moment later, an operator heard a small voice asking for the police. "My daddy shot my mommy," she said. Gently, the operator questioned the little girl, learned her name and her address, and nodded to another operator to go ahead and call the Des Moines police. When she turned back to the child on the line, there was only a dial tone. Someone in the Driftwood Apartments had already called for an aid car. The fire department automatically alerted the Des Moines police that there had been a shooting.

Robert Fox happened to be patrolling only seconds away from the Driftwood Apartments, and he spotted the white Ford with what appeared to be two adults and two children inside pulling out. He turned on his blue lights, and the car slowed and stopped.

It was a potentially explosive situation for a policeman. He knew there had been a shooting, but no more than that. There were children inside the car, and he dared not fire himself. Fox activated the outside mike and shouted, "Come out with your hands in front of you!"

The driver's door didn't open, and Fox realized that the man in the car was shouting something back. Fox could not make out what he was saying. Then the woman in the passenger seat called from her window, "He can't get out of the car—he's a paraplegic!"

A split second later, she reached down to the seat and tossed something out onto the pavement. It was a revolver. As it hit the street, the cylinder popped out and Fox was close enough to see that it still held three live rounds of ammunition.

His first concern was still the youngsters, and he held his hand out to them and said, "Come on, kids."

They ran to him, and the little girl then made what was probably the most poignant res gestae (spontaneous) statement Fox had ever heard, "My daddy shot my mommy in the head. I tried to make him stop—but he wouldn't. My daddy killed my mommy. My mommy told me that if daddy ever shot her, we were supposed to go live with my aunt. Will you make sure we get to live with my aunt?"

She was such a little kid, Fox thought—not more than six or seven. She should never have had to witness what she had obviously just seen. He sheltered the kids in his arms and led them to the back seat of a patrol car. The little boy didn't seem to understand what was happening, but Fox feared the girl would never forget it.

Although it had been only a few minutes since the shooting, the scene on the Kent–Des Moines Road was alive with squad cars, both from the city of Des Moines and from the King County Police. Detective Sergeant Marty Pratt (soon to be the Chief of Police) joined them a few minutes before nine. He helped the woman companion of the gunman into his car. She, too, was a paraplegic. The .38 was locked in the trunk of a county car while the investigators made sure that the shooter didn't have more weapons.

In the seventies, Des Moines was a city of just over 4,000 people and had not had a homicide in many years. Like many small departments in the county, the local police operated on a reciprocal program with King County Police. They now requested help from that department's homicide unit. Detective Sergeant Len Randall and Detective Rolf Grunden joined the Des Moines police and King County patrolmen in trying to sort out just what had happened.

The victim had been rushed to the emergency room of Highline Hospital in nearby Burien, and Randall and Des Moines Sergeant Ken Schnorr saw that the crime scene was secured and left deputies guarding all that was left of it—a huge pool of coagulating blood, a stained blanket, and numerous bullet casings. Then the two sergeants drove to Burien Hospital to see about the condition of the victim.

They knew her name because neighbors had identified her as twenty-eight-year-old Amy Shaw. But that was all they knew about her world, her life or why the red-haired man had shot her.

And they would not learn the truth from Amy; although the paramedics had used heroic procedures on the break-neck run to the hospital and the ER doctors had worked frantically over her, Amy was pronounced dead at 9:40 A.M. There was no way she could have lived no matter how much medical treatment she received. Eight .38 caliber bullets had crashed into her body. All of her wounds were to the left side of her body, as if she had turned, prepared to run, after she saw the gun in the shooter's hand.

Bullets had pierced Amy's left lower jaw, breast, lung, ear, and thigh. Ironically, the bullet that penetrated her shoulder had gone on to sever her spinal cord at the same level where Eric's had been cut six years before in Vietnam. She might have survived those bullets, but not the one that entered her skull and coursed through her brain. Doctors and cops alike shook their heads. Amy Shaw's killer had had to *reload* his gun to cause so much carnage.

Eric Shaw and his second wife, Mariel, were transported to the Des Moines police station to be interviewed separately. Detectives used the wheelchair in their car to move Mariel, and improvised with an office chair with wheels and padded arms, maneuvering it carefully as they brought Shaw himself in.

Mariel Shaw was understandably distressed, but she fought to control her emotions as she tried to reconstruct what had happened.

"We'd gone over to pick up Eric's children," she said softly. "And then Eric and Amy were having an argument—I think about their clothes."

Eric had turned to her and asked her to hand him a sack of clothes they had brought with them. She reached down and picked up the bag from the floor. Only then, as he took it from her hand, had she seen the glint of the gun beneath the bag.

The pale woman in front of them looked anguished as she remembered the shooting. She said Amy Shaw had still been walking toward the car when the shots began. Her husband had fired all the bullets and then reloaded. "I tried to stop him but he's too strong," she said.

She had had no idea how deep her new husband's hatred for his ex-wife ran, no idea that he had brought a loaded gun with him. She was willing to give a verbal statement to the Des Moines detectives, but she was reluctant to sign a written statement until she had talked to an attorney.

In sharp contrast to his bride, Eric Shaw did not appear shaken by the tragedy. When Detective Rolf Grunden approached him with a swab that would show if he had gunpowder residue on his hands, Shaw quickly held up his left hand. "You might as well only take this one," he drawled. "That's the only one that did it."

Detective Jerry Burger faced the man who had just shot his ex-wife eight times. He asked Shaw if he was comfortable.

"As comfortable as I can get," Shaw answered, pointing to his crippled legs with a massively muscled arm.

"You've served time in the military?" Burger asked, trying to find some possible explanation for the carnage he'd just witnessed.

"Yeah . . . I was all over Nam. That's where I got greased," he answered, touching his shoulder and lazily tracing the path of the bullet which had paralyzed him. "Can I have a glass of water?"

When Burger returned with it, he was shocked to hear Shaw whistling cheerfully. Eric Shaw declined to make any statements at all without the presence of his attorney. When he was informed of his rights under Miranda for the third time, he waved his hand, "I know about all that good stuff—I took business law at Bellevue Community College."

As unbelievable as it seemed, Eric Shaw appeared very pleased with himself that the woman he'd once been married to, the mother of his children, was dead. His children were now, for all intents and purposes, orphans, but that wasn't bothering him. Nor was he concerned about Mariel, who sat weeping in another interview room.

The investigators didn't know yet just how much of the shooting—if any—the children had witnessed, and they were reluctant to question them so soon after their mother's death. A policewoman came into the station to comfort them until they could be removed to a receiving home to wait for their aunt to arrive.

Eric Shaw had claimed that the police could never touch him because they had no facilities to care for him, but he was wrong. He was booked into the King County jail, and the investigation continued. Des Moines had only eight policemen at the time, and they would all be busy for days trying to sort out what had happened and interviewing the dozens of witnesses who had seen Amy Shaw fall in a blaze of gunfire. There was no paucity of evidence and witnesses' statements in the Amy Shaw case.

Many of Amy's neighbors in the Driftwood Apartments gave statements. They had seen Amy Shaw, clad in a brown blouse and white shorts, as she walked out to the white Ford. They had seen the gun in the driver's hand, heard him shout obscenities at her as he continued to fire even after she had fallen. And sadly, they had seen the small girl witness the whole thing, heard her screaming for the shooter to stop.

Rolf Grunden processed the white Ford, and found a nearly-full box of .38 special ammunition in the front seat. Des Moines detectives searched Amy's apartment and found the chilling photographs that had once been cheerful family scenes—only Amy Shaw's head had been snipped from each picture, as if she were already dead in Shaw's mind.

Detective Burger faced the task of interviewing the young daughter of the victim. In any testimony given by a child, it is necessary to establish that the youngster understands the difference between reality and fantasy. Carefully, the Des Moines detective gave the little girl some examples of truth and lies and she nodded wisely, showing him that she did, indeed, know the difference.

"Can you tell me what you remember about the morning when your mother got hurt?"

She knew that there had been trouble between her parents because her dad was keeping all their clothes. "My mom told us to stay in the apartment until she got us clothes to put on from dad. My mom walked out and said, 'Where are their clothes?'

"And he said, 'What do you mean? What clothes?' and then BANG! BANG! BANG! And Mariel was crying and telling him to quit. When I came out, he was still shooting her a couple more times and I tried to get him to stop but he wouldn't."

The little girl said that her father had never moved from his seat in the car while he shot her mother. When the loud BANGS! finally stopped, she had done exactly what her mother had asked her to do. She had turned around and gone into the house and dialed "0" and asked for the police.

"She told me if she ever got killed, she would go up to heaven—and she told me to call the police."

Then she had taken her little brother by the hand and led him outside. Her father had told them to get into the car. "I didn't tell my dad that I called the police because he really would have gone [far away] and then you guys would have never found me. That's what I thought, anyway, so I didn't let him know."

If Bob Fox hadn't been almost in front of the Driftwood Apartments, Burger realized, the tragedy might have been compounded. The little girl said they had been so glad to see the policeman, and as soon as he had said, "Come on, kids," they had scrambled out of the car to the safety of his car.

Eric Shaw was charged with murder in the first degree. His attorneys argued that his health would be threatened if he were forced to remain in jail, because there weren't proper facilities to care for him. They almost pulled off that argument and one Superior Court judge wrote an order that would allow Shaw to go to his specially equipped home. However, that was quickly rescinded when prosecutors argued that he was too dangerous to be allowed his freedom pending trial. Besides, it would have cost the county $150 a day to guard him.

In January 1975, Shaw changed his plea to guilty of second-degree murder. On February 21, 1975, he was sentenced to twenty-five years in the state penitentiary. He was paroled to supervision in Arizona in 1987, and was released from supervision in July of 1993. He was fifty years old. To put the woman he called "Ruby" in the ground, Eric Shaw gave up a promising new marriage, a lifetime of financial security, and an education that could have led to a meaningful career.

Worst of all, he robbed Amy of her life, and he robbed his children of their mother.

That Was No Lady

I once went to the most peculiar murder trial I'd ever experienced. The defendant in the second degree murder trial in Judge Donald Horowitz's courtroom didn't create the usual courtroom disruptions; there wasn't any swearing or shouting or wrestling with courtroom deputies. The pretty woman at the defense table was actually a perfectly mannered lady. Jackie was quite demure, turning only occasionally to greet friends in the spectator section. She smiled sweetly at a couple who had brought a change of clothes for the next day's session. It was important to her to look her best each day of her trial, and she never wanted to be seen in the same outfit two days in a row.

I remember how Jackie nodded happily when she saw the lime green pantsuit on the padded hanger. She was obviously something of a clothes horse, although her taste ran to the slightly bizarre. On this day, she wore a pair of tight pink slacks, a figure-revealing green sweater, and high-heeled pumps. Her hair was teased into a huge bouffant with youthful pigtails, and her makeup had been expertly applied—base, eyeshadow *and liner, false eyelashes, and her full lips were deep red.*

It might have been any trial where an attractive female sat in the defendant's chair, only there was a vast difference. Jackie wasn't a woman at all. She was a twenty-four-year-old transvestite prostitute. It would have been hard for a casual observer to tell; the defendant mimicked women so well that he would have fooled anyone.

Jackie's attorney had made a motion asking that his client be allowed to wear women's clothing and a wig during the testimony and that he be referred to as "Ms." After pondering this request, Judge Horowitz granted the motion.

While some of the circumstances of this trial had a humorous side, there was sadness too. The victim had died, the prosecution said, because the defendant had fooled him with "her" disguise, and because he had confronted her. There was nothing funny about the end of their story.

The two principals in this violent drama that would come to a fatal conclusion on a stormy February night in 1976 could not have been more different. The chance that they would one day meet was as remote as a head-on collision on a lonely road.

Jonathan Lewis "Jackie" Emerson* was born on October 16, 1951, in Yakima, Washington, right at the peak of the apple harvest. The central Washington city has exactly the right climate for apples, peaches, pears, cherries and plums, and the hills of Yakima County are dotted with fruit trees as far as the eye can see. Both of Jonathan's parents were hard workers, which was fortunate because he joined a family that already had six children.

Jonathan never really had time to know two of his sisters; one died within three days of her birth of pneumonia and another—Rose—succumbed to spinal meningitis when she was three years old. His older sisters thought their baby brother looked like Rose, and they started dressing him up in girls' clothes, trying, perhaps, in their innocent way, to bring back the sister they had lost. He was so young that he wouldn't remember that, but his mother told him about it.

The dress-up games may well have been for a different reason. For as long as Jonathan could remember, he had been far more comfortable playing with dolls than he ever was with a toy truck or a BB gun. He didn't have much male influence around the house; his father worked all the time, and even when he was home, Jonathan remembered that "he was so busy he didn't know what was going on around him."

Once his father found him playing with dolls, and Jonathan froze, waiting for an explosion. At some level, he knew that his father would disapprove. "But all he did was tell me to put them away. And the next time he caught me, he didn't say a word."

When Jonathan received masculine toys like footballs and guns, he gave them to his brother. He had absolutely no interest in playing sports, or in watching sporting events on television. He had a fight with his brother once, who had tried to force him into a football game.

His mother seemed to find no fault with the way Jonathan was; she kept him very close to her and was somewhat overprotective. She had lost her two little girls and she wasn't taking any chances with Jonathan. She called him "Jackie," and he felt that she always thought of him as a daughter rather than a son.

The first memory "Jackie" Emerson had of his sisters dressing him in female clothing was one Halloween night when he was six. The frilly dress and wig was supposed to be only a costume, but he loved it. He felt right in those clothes.

Mrs. Emerson worked at a hospital in Yakima and wasn't home much more than her husband was. They both had to work overtime to support their family. Jackie seemed content enough and she never had any problems with him. Unlike his lost sisters, he was healthy and easy to raise. His mother's extended family and the neighbors accepted him easily as a different sort of child. He played with his cousins who treated him as they would a girl, and the older folks in the neighborhood always referred to him as "a pretty boy."

As Jackie neared puberty, he saw his father even less; his parents' marriage was strained and his father began dating other women. "I'm glad he was gone," he would remember. "I'm glad he didn't interfere with my life, and make me be something that I couldn't be."

But someone else *did* interfere with Jackie Emerson. When he was twelve, one of his father's male friends sexually abused him. In pain and shock, he cried to himself—but he never told his father. Perhaps he kept the secret because he had felt some sexual release. "He kept leading me on, and I wanted to . . .

"After this, doors started opening. I realized what I was; this is what I wanted. That man brought me out. The only guilty feelings I had were that I had to *hide* my feelings."

Jackie would never be much bothered by guilt; he took what he wanted. When he was thirteen, he was arrested for shoplifting. He was not prosecuted. A few months later, he was arrested for assault. He was puzzled by that; he had "only been throwing rocks at a bum near the railroad tracks." He was not prosecuted. When he was about fourteen, he was arrested for auto theft. His father wouldn't let him have the family car for a prom at school, so he "took someone else's." Jackie was sent to the Youth Center for a week or two, and then to an outpatient program.

Sometime during his adolescence, Jackie Emerson

came to see himself as a woman. He identified with his grandmother more than any person in his life. She had been the closest person to him, and she was always there while his parents worked. During psychological testing, he actually drew himself as a female, as this was his inner picture of himself.

His mother, who had thought it was "cute" to have a passively sweet little boy, was horrified to find that her sixteen-year-old son was still dressing in women's clothes. Since she had encouraged his wearing little girls' dresses when he was eight or nine, it seems odd that she was so surprised to find he had never stopped.

"Jackie could never accept himself as a male," his aunt once said. "He was high-strung, and he's still argumentative sometimes because he feels people won't accept him. He's insecure too," she added.

Jackie Emerson never managed to graduate from high school; he was always running away from home. Some of his relatives were sure he was working as a homosexual prostitute, although his mother would never accept that. Eventually, he started working on his GED (General Equivalency Diploma) and told his friends and family that he was going to save up for surgery so he could become a real woman. Until then, he said, he planned to study to be a beautician.

Jackie Emerson was slender and doe-eyed, far more feminine than masculine. His mother finally threw her hands up and conceded that Jackie was more her daughter than her son. A formal picture of the family taken in the early seventies included Jackie in full female regalia.

Even so, Jackie's sexual identification warred with his strict Baptist upbringing. "I was scared that I would go to hell if I got my sex changed in an operation," he recalled once. But he read the Bible until he found a passage that he felt was meant for him. "God does not expect flesh in heaven," he explained. "He expects your soul."

Had Jackie Emerson lived within the strict parameters of the Bible quotations he found, tragedy might have been averted. But Jackie had a heedless, wild streak, and a kind of ruthless pride that would get him into trouble time and again.

Jackie's rap sheet as an adult began in 1970, and he had arrests all up and down the West Coast: "Offering and Agreeing," "Resisting Arrest," "Gross Indecency," "Hitchhiking," "Prostitution," "Obstruction of Public Thoroughfare," "Larceny Shoplifting," "Grand Larceny," "Resisting, Offering and Agreeing." Some of his arrests were for parking tickets and for having no driver's license, but most were connected to prostitution and stealing. Usually, he walked away clean or had to pay a small fine. Jackie Emerson had long since learned that he could do just about anything he wanted and get away with it. He rarely told the truth about anything, and soon began to believe his own self-serving version of events.

On February 23, 1974, Jackie Emerson approached a man who was visiting Seattle in his motor home. Jackie looked very pretty that night and it's unlikely that the "John" had any idea that he had made a date with a man. Jackie suggested that the man park his motor home under the freeway where they "wouldn't be disturbed." When they were settled, Jackie poured himself a drink and suggested that the man take a shower to freshen up. He pretended to be looking in the other direction when his customer placed his wallet under a seat cushion, but he could see everything beneath his lowered false eyelashes.

An embarrassed "John" went to the police. "I hired this girl for, ahh—certain sexual privileges. I was washing up, and I heard the door slam," he said. "When I looked, that girl—Jackie—was gone, along with $200 in cash, and a check for $783.49."

Jackie was arrested and convicted—and sentenced to three years' probation. He was not the "ideal probationer," according to his probation officer. He failed to report time and again, and bench warrants were issued. He forged his sister's name on her income tax refund check, cashed it, and kept the money. On July 21, 1975, his probation was revoked and he was given a suspended sentence of fifteen years on the condition that he serve three months in the King County Jail.

Twenty-one-year-old Brad Lee Bass was completely masculine. Born in the mid-fifties to a California family, he, too, had once been a sensitive child as Jackie Emerson was described, but Brad's sensitivity was about the feelings of other people and not directed toward his own desires. Brad never forgot a birthday or a holiday that meant something to someone else, and he always showed up with a card or a present on time, even if he had to walk miles to deliver it in person. He dragged home stray cats and dogs, grinning and saying, "Look what I found." But Brad was also the kind of kid who played all-star Little League baseball and junior high basketball.

Brad had a brother, Dalton*, who was a year older than he and an avid scholar, but he himself was a somewhat lackadaisical student. He loved to read, however, and would spend hours with a book—but you couldn't *tell* him to do it. He tired of the restrictions of organized education after his junior year in high school and dropped out.

When his parents divorced in 1966, Brad Bass's father had gained custody of his sons and took over their care, settling with them in California. Neither of them gave him any trouble, particularly not Brad. Within a year or so, Brad Bass grew to be a muscular six feet, three inches and 195 pounds.

Disappointed when Brad dropped out of high school, his dad was pleased and relieved when Brad immediately enrolled in evening classes in a junior college. Brad received his high school degree there, and went on to a four-year college. But he didn't graduate, the way his brother Dalton had. His interests lay elsewhere.

Brad had always been fascinated with the intricacies of mechanics, and he bought himself a 1957 Chevrolet pickup truck in a sad state of repair. The teenager didn't know anything about machines but he read manuals, talked to mechanics, and, all on his own, he replaced the engine, overhauled the transmission, clutch, differential and brakes. When that was finished, he reupholstered the interior and finally painted the whole truck, making it a work of art.

At twenty, Brad Bass was a powerful man who swam, jogged, and lifted weights. In 1975, he moved to Renton, Washington, from his father's home in California, and he and Dalton shared an apartment. Brad found work as an apprentice shipfitter, and he and his brother returned to their lifetime relationship as best friends. It happens that way with brothers sometimes, and theirs became an incredibly strong bond.

They weren't alike, except for their common background. While Dalton Bass was completely comfortable in social situations and dated frequently, Brad was still shy around women. He was ill at ease socially. He was a loner and an observer, but not a joiner. He had a low-key sense of humor and, when he felt comfortable, he could be hilarious. He had lots of friends at work.

By the mid-seventies, Brad Bass had become a very handsome man, tall and muscular. He had recently grown a mustache which suited him, but he remained reluctant to approach women.

He explained to Dalton that he couldn't bring himself to go up to girls on beaches or in taverns and just ask them out. He froze at the thought of it. Ironically, there were undoubtedly a hundred girls in the Seattle area who would have been delighted to date the good-looking shipfitter, but he lacked the courage to ask them.

And so occasionally, Brad Bass had gone to prostitutes. He could be sure that they wouldn't turn away when he talked to them. Later, Dalton estimated that Brad might have sought out a prostitute about every two months, and Brad had told him he'd only been with the ladies of the downtown Seattle streets three times. He was not the first young man to seek out such company, and he surely will not be the last. Despite his imposing build, Brad, was somewhat naive and inclined to believe the best about people. He thought the women really liked him.

"Jackie" Emerson had yet to get his GED, and he bemoaned that fact. "I have a natural ability in hair, makeup, and clothing design," he bragged. "The only thing that keeps me from it is I need a GED. When I set a goal, I stick to it."

But Jackie had not stuck to any educational goals at

all. He was more interested in changing his gender at all cost. He had had many chances to work toward his GED, and he hadn't taken them. He had his head in the clouds about being a wealthy designer and he couldn't lower himself to get a high school certificate. First, he would have his surgery and that would make him a complete woman. *Then* he would become famous doing what he liked. But Jackie's dreams had no grounding at all in reality.

Although he worked as an aide at a Seattle nursing home, he wasn't paid nearly enough to afford an operation to change the mistake he felt nature had made. He was not a valued employee—not even in a job he felt was beneath him. "Her quality of work and attitude are poor," a supervisor wrote on Jackie's evaluation. The nursing home managers recalled that she bristled at any "constructive criticism" and resented having to show her identification that gave her true name and Social Security number. But they didn't know Jackie's deepest secret. Since he had been hired as a female, his reticence was understandable.

Jackie had long since left Yakima behind, working briefly in Seattle, and traveling on to Los Angeles, where he had no work—not officially, at least. "Jackie" was working as a prostitute in the guise of a woman. He found a doctor there who gave him female hormonal therapy with prescriptions for 100 milligrams of stilbestrol. In 1974, he visited Tiajuana, Mexico, where he received silicone enlargements of his "breasts." He paid three hundred dollars for three treatments, but only took the first one. All he got for his money was one injection that settled into a hard lump within a day or so. That frightened him, and he didn't go back.

Moving back to Seattle, Jackie Emerson again started stilbestrol therapy, but he felt cheated. "That doctor was watering the pills down," he complained.

Jackie not only had a problem with his female hormone therapy, he also had a problem with drugs. By 1974, he was hooked on heroin. He was "strung-out" for a year, and needed sixty to seventy dollars a day to take care of his habit. He had tried amphetamines and barbiturates, but they never had the power over him that heroin did. He also used marijuana and alcohol, although Jackie didn't feel those were a serious complication in his already murky life.

Jackie Emerson did not consider himself a homosexual; he continued to insist that he was a woman in the wrong body. He applied for public assistance—and received support—as "Miss Emerson." Jackie, who had a rap sheet as long as his arm, was a highly skilled con man. Welfare workers didn't know about his criminal activities; they saw only a confused and tearful boy/girl who didn't seem able to face life or employment because of her unfortunate sexual situation. The State of Washington paid for extensive dental work for Jackie, and for an operation that removed an undescended testicle. "It is hoped that this corrective surgery will aid in the rehabilitation for Miss Emerson. She seemed hopeful and optimistic," a naive caseworker noted in 1974.

However, Jackie could not see "herself" in a job until she had undergone a complete sex change operation. "I can't get a job," he lamented. "I can't pass the physical."

Jackie Emerson told a psychiatrist about his sad life, apparently unable to see that he had any responsibility at all for the troubles he had encountered. Emerson's only income for four years had been through prostitution and welfare, and he had been jailed thirty or forty times in California, the last time for robbery.

If Jackie had bewilderment over his gender, his confusion was nothing compared to that of the doctors and social workers he encountered; they never could decide whether to call him "he" or "she," and his voluminous file was filled with studies that called him both.

"Diagnostically," one psychiatrist wrote, "she is best categorized under the heading 302.3 [in the *Diagnostic Statistical Manual*—the psychiatrist's bible], *Transvestitism*. She also has some hysterical features in her makeup, tends to rationalize her behavior, to be quite gullible and somewhat given to fantasy. There is a fairly substantial antisocial element in her makeup. She tends to overly emphasize her need for surgery as a prelude to undertaking self-support . . . Her current employability is very much to be questioned, on the basis of her emotional stability, her history of prostitution, and her transvestite situation. Some counseling would seem appropriate for her to assist her in a more realistic appraisal of the opportunities open to her and how to make the best use of her resources."

This psychiatrist had chosen to identify Jackie Emerson as "she," and clearly he/she did have a sexual identity problem. But so had—and *have*—myriad others who had not turned to crime for support or to pay for a hoped-for operation.

Jackie Emerson was five feet, ten inches tall, and weighed 145 pounds. He had a fury in him, waiting to be unleashed if anyone questioned his persona or threatened him. The pretty face with the big eyes and the soft skin were a remarkable mask, a mask that made him more dangerous because he was not what he seemed to be at all.

February 13, 1976—Friday the 13th—turned out to be an incredibly unlucky day for Brad Bass. He certainly had no reason to be worried about his physical safety when he stepped into an all-night restaurant for a bite to eat and a cup of coffee. He was big enough and strong enough to take care of himself.

Larry's Take 5 at 601 Pike Street was deep in the heart of the downtown section of Seattle. It was up and running twenty-two hours a day, with a cocktail lounge and a restaurant. It was also in the middle of the "stroll" in Seattle; Pike Street was prostitution territory, although those who sold sex for a price were sorely besieged by the Seattle Police Department's vice squad. Pimps turned their women out along Pike Street and sat back in their zebra-upholstered Cadillacs to wait for their money. The hapless girls got arrested often and, when their faces became too familiar to the vice detectives, they were moved around the circuit to Portland or San Francisco and replaced with new faces. They were as expendable as women could be, trapped by circumstances and the lack of enough money to escape.

The pimps seemed to go on forever; it took the testimony of two prostitutes to nail a pimp, and the women were afraid of a beating with a hot coathanger—or worse. It wasn't easy to find two women brave enough to turn on the men who controlled them.

Most of the prostitutes who worked the Pike Street stroll were no threat to their customers beyond the possibility of a sexually transmitted disease, and the seventies was an era when AIDS and even the herpes virus were unknown to the public. However, some of the prostitutes who approached men were not what they seemed to be, but it would have taken a physician to know it.

Larry's Take 5 drew business from straight customers, cruising women of the night, and, inevitably, from the vice squad. The restaurant's policy was to serve everyone who was behaving himself, and things were relatively calm on Thursday night, February 12. Ike Stone was the chef. The grills and ovens were in the front of the restaurant and had an excellent view of the place through the opening where orders were picked up. He could see both the booths and the front door. Ike had seen the flotsam and jetsam of life come and go through the doors of the Take 5 for a year, and nothing surprised him much anymore. On Thursday night/Friday morning he was working the graveyard shift.

Sometime around two-thirty A.M. on that Friday the 13th, an attractive and slender black woman walked up to the counter and, in a husky voice, ordered a grilled tuna fish and cheese sandwich and french fries to go. She wore a green pantsuit and her hair was teased in a bouffant style. Stone watched idly over the serving counter as the woman walked to the booths directly opposite him. She talked for a while with a man who appeared to be in his sixties. The man laughed and shook his head. Stone couldn't hear the conversation but he had a pretty good idea what it was about.

Curious, the chef kept watching as she moved to a booth where a young man sat alone. The man looked up, grinned at the woman, and Ike saw that they seemed to be getting along well, as he turned away to put the woman's order in a bag.

When she came to pick up her tuna melt and fries, the tall young fellow was with her. They were chatting easily, although Ike couldn't tell if they were old friends or new acquaintances. They walked out the door together and Ike Stone dismissed them from his mind. He was looking forward to the two-hour break the Take 5 employees got when the restaurant closed for cleaning up before the breakfast rush.

Stone worked in a kitchen that had a solid wall on the west side. The noise of the jukebox, the hum of voices from the restaurant patrons, and the clang of pots and pans overwhelmed any street noise. So Stone neither saw nor heard what was happening outside. But he *could* see the enraged woman who ran into the Take 5 a few moments later. It was the patron in the green pantsuit who'd ordered the tuna and cheese to go. She was holding what appeared to be a black wig at arm's length and screaming, "Look what he did to me!" at the top of her lungs.

Ike looked twice. Without her wig, it was apparent now that the woman wasn't what she had seemed to be; usually Ike could spot one of the numerous transvestites who frequented the Pike Street stroll, but this one had fooled him completely.

Before Ike could stop him, the man in drag reached into a tray of silverware kept near the first booth and grabbed what looked to Stone like a knife. In an instant, the cook was around the serving barrier and wrestling the weapon away from the maddened man, kicking it with his foot so that it slid away from him. Thwarted, the man in the green pantsuit turned and ran back outside.

Curious, Ike Stone stepped outside to see what was going on. He could see that a crowd had gathered around someone on the sidewalk. When he pushed his way in, Stone recognized the young man who had left the restaurant with the transvestite. The youth appeared to be seized by convulsions. Stone could see no wounds, but he knew the kid was in trouble. He turned and went to the phone next to the cash register and dialed 911. He requested a Medic One aid car, on the double.

It was only a few minutes before paramedics from the Seattle Fire Department responded, followed by Seattle Police patrol officers K. Christophersen and P. McCloud. A call of a fight or a "man down" on Pike Street was hardly unusual. The tall husky youth was semiconscious now, and he appeared to be cyanotic, his face suffused with a gray-purple tinge. He seemed to have suffered a grand mal epileptic seizure, from the descriptions of the bystanders. If that was the case, he should have begun to come around by now, but he seemed to be getting worse.

As the paramedics checked him carefully, they found a very small lateral wound in his right upper chest. It was almost bloodless, and didn't appear to be serious. They began immediate efforts to combat shock and the nameless young man was transported to the emergency room at Harborview Hospital, only a few blocks away.

Harborview Hospital (the King County Medical Center) is used to dealing with patients with major trauma and its physicians and staff are probably the best in the county in dealing with the results of violence and accidents. If a patient could be saved, they would do it. They had a chance with this patient, it seemed; his admission came well within the parameters of the "Golden Hour" before shock can begin to shut down the body's functions forever.

"John Doe" was admitted with a systolic blood pressure of fifty, and a diastolic so low that it was off the scale of the sphygmomanometer. His pulse rate was fifty-six beats a minute and dropping rapidly. He could still speak, and he asked weakly where he was, and what had happened to him. ER physicians couldn't answer his second question. They had hoped *he* could tell *them.* When they asked for his name, he was able to gasp, "Brad Bass."

The only wound he had was the tiny transverse cut in his upper chest, and it wasn't bleeding—at least externally. The first danger in a knife wound is exsanguination—death by loss of blood. And often that bleeding is internal. Life slips away silently as the lungs or abdominal cavity fill with blood. Some victims can suffer massive stab wounds and bleed enough externally that it appears as if every drop of blood in their bodies has seeped out, and still survive. Others, like Brad Bass, can die from one innocuous-looking shallow thrust.

Something was terribly wrong with Brad Bass, and he was rushed into surgery. Once the trauma surgeon had opened his chest, he could see that Bass had sustained a one-inch wide stab wound that had penetrated two and a half to three inches through his chest wall. But, in doing so, it had nicked the right auricular appendage of the heart and the aorta—the large artery that carries blood to all parts of the body. A silent, often-fatal medical situation called "cardiac tamponade" had resulted. The pericardial sac that encases the heart had begun to fill up with blood. The sac that usually protects the heart was rapidly crushing it. Each time Brad Bass's heart contracted, more blood filled the sac surrounding it, compressing the heart so tightly that less and less blood could be pumped to the extremities of his body. Despite the surgeon's efforts, his blood pressure continued to drop.

The surgeon mended the damage done by the tip of a thin blade to the heart and aorta, but it was too late. Brad had begun to die.

It is essential to look at all the ramifications of Brad Bass's demise to understand what legal death is. The human body does not die all at once. Rather, it dies in stages. When there is a lack of oxygen and nutrients, death occurs first in the most fragile cells. The brain cells are the most sensitive of all to lack of oxygen and may die in a matter of minutes while skin and bone cells can continue to "live" for weeks after brain, heart, and lung death.

It was still Friday, February 13. As dawn broke only hours after he had walked out of Larry's Take 5, Brad Bass, until this day a perfect physical specimen, lay motionless. The cells of his brain had flickered out like light bulbs cut off from electricity, and they would never live again. He was *legally* alive, but not in the sense of his having any meaningful life. But he was not yet officially a homicide statistic.

The detectives assigned to the Seattle Police Homicide Unit arrived at work at 7:45 A.M. Detective Sergeant Jerry Yates talked to the head nurse in the emergency room at Harborview. She told him that the victim of the street stabbing of the night before was "very bad"—worse than critical, if possible. He had been admitted with ten dollars and change in his pockets. They had found no wallet and no I.D. "He was able to give us his name," she said. "But that's all. We have no way of knowing if he has any relatives or friends in Seattle."

When Yates heard that the victim's prognosis was almost nil, he realized that he and his men would have to treat this as a probable murder case.

Information gathered by patrol officers at the site of the stabbing had been sketchy; habitués of the nether world along Pike Street were not traditionally known to confide in the police. The only information that had survived the chaos of the scene was that the victim had been involved in a scuffle with a tall, sexy, black woman. Some said the glamorous figure was most certainly a female; others questioned that.

The "woman" had left the scene in a dirty, dark, old car—possibly a Chevrolet—which had held several occupants of undetermined sex.

Jerry Yates asked the hospital to place a hold on the victim's clothing and to call if, by some miracle, the youth regained consciousness. Solving a homicide that was not even a homicide yet, a case with so many conflicting witness statements at that, didn't seem likely.

Dalton Bass was worried. Brad had been gone all of Thursday night and still wasn't home by Friday night and that wasn't like him. He would never have stayed away all night without calling. The brothers had talked on the phone Thursday and Brad said then that he was going to try to cash his paycheck Thursday night. He had been temporarily laid off from his shipfitting job but his last paycheck was for over $200.

Dalton called the Seattle police after he'd checked all of his and Brad's friends. They told Dalton that a Brad Bass had been injured in a street fight and was in the hospital. Shaking his head in disbelief, Dalton Bass was horrified when he reached Harborview to find Brad in a deep coma. He asked where Brad had been hurt and was given the address of the Take 5. As far as he knew, Brad had never patronized the restaurant; he certainly had never mentioned it.

When Dalton Bass asked the detectives where Brad's truck was, they said they hadn't known he even had one. Everyone had assumed he was on foot the night he was stabbed. Dalton drove to the Take 5 and looked for his brother's prized truck. He found it quickly; it was still parked a few paces away from the restaurant.

Dalton knew that Brad seldom carried a wallet, but he thought that he would have had his payroll money with him. Searching the truck, he found approximately $280 hidden in the tape deck.

Dalton called their father, who flew immediately to Seattle. The elder Bass found his son comatose, kept alive only by life support machines. The tracings of the EEG were almost flat, indicating that his brain was barely active. He was told that Brad had almost no chance to survive, and that, if he did, he would live in a state of vegetation. If there was to be any turning point, it would surely come within the next few days.

Brad Bass had chosen to will his kidneys and eyes after death so that they might save another's life and sight. He was only twenty-three; he could not have known how soon his legacy would be used. On Friday, February 20, one week after he was stabbed, Bass's brain waves were completely flat. His father asked physicians to remove him from the respirator that made it look as if his chest rose and fell through some conscious effort on his part. It was an agonizing decision for any parent. If Brad could breathe on his own, even if he never regained consciousness, his father would have taken care of him forever. But it was a travesty of life to keep the bloated body of a once vital young man alive by mechanical means.

The breathing machine was turned off. Sometimes miracles happen and clinically dead patients *do* breathe on their own. Brad Bass did not. For two and a half minutes, the doctors, nurses, and his father hoped for some sign of life, but there was none. At that point, with the physicians' support, Brad Bass's father decided to fulfill Brad's wish to donate his kidneys and eyes to someone else.

The life support systems were reconnected, but this time it was only to keep these vital organs alive until donors could be prepared for surgery.

On Saturday, February 21, Brad Bass's kidneys were removed. Two people would live because of him, but Brad himself was pronounced dead at 2 P.M. Dr. Donald Nakonechny, Deputy King County Medical Examiner, began the postmortem almost at once. To Nakonechny, there was no question that Brad's brain was "grossly dead," and had been for some time. It had softened and swollen as the brain will after death, until it extruded through skull openings and the spinal cord. His cause of death was listed as "anoxic encephalopathy—softening of the brain due to lack of oxygen, secondary to piercing of the right auricular appendage."

Now it was up to Seattle Homicide detectives to bring in a killer. Most of the information they were receiving had filtered down from the street people through the beat cops. Detective Benny DePalmo got a tip from one of the street officers that the "woman" with the knife was Jacqueline Emerson. DePalmo ran the name through Seattle Police records and found that there was a *Jonathan* "Jackie" Lewis Emerson, twenty-four, whose occupation was listed as a female impersonator. But there was no current address for Emerson, who had a rather lengthy rap sheet for various charges, many of them soliciting for prostitution.

But Emerson was only one of the names rumored to be the person who'd stabbed Brad Bass. Vice Detectives Bill Karban and John Boren had heard other rumors. One was that the night bartender of a well-known gay restaurant and lounge had been in the crowd around Bass. The bartender had named another transvestite hooker.

Primary responsibility for finding Brad Bass's killer was assigned to Detectives Ted Fonis and Dick Sanford. They began a tour of several gay gathering places, carrying a laydown montage of suspects' mugs. Jonathan Emerson was number four. Many of those they questioned seemed to recognize Emerson but they were evasive and wouldn't admit knowing him. If they did recognize him, they said they had no idea where he was at present.

The detectives went to the club where the bartender, who was supposedly an eyewitness to Brad's stabbing, worked and learned that he had suddenly taken a trip East. But other witnesses were in town and the detectives were soon flooded with informants. On February 24, one called to give them the name of Sonny Jimson*, who was claiming he had seen the stabbing. Fonis and Sanford found Sonny, a tall, lean, transvestite with bright orange hair. He told them he'd seen the killer. "It was 'Large Tillie' Schwenk*," he said firmly.

Large Tilly, he said, worked as a transvestite hooker and hung around a waterfront tavern. However, Sonny was not as forthcoming when Fonis and Sanford arranged for him to take a polygraph examination. He looked very nervous and admitted he'd made up the whole thing. "I told my sugar daddy that I was there because I was really someplace I shouldn't have been and I was afraid he'd find out I cheated on him."

Just on the off chance that Sonny had been telling the truth the first time around, Sanford and Fonis went to the Seashell Tavern and asked for "Large Tillie." The bartender said he'd never heard of a "Large Tillie" or of Sonny Jimson. He did identify the mug of Emerson as a transvestite he knew as Jackie, and he promised to call them if he saw Emerson again.

DePalmo interviewed the dishwasher of the Take 5 who had been on duty when the attack took place. He had observed "Jackie" and Brad Bass, and recalled that they had been friendly until they got out on the sidewalk in front of the restaurant. Then a scuffle had started. "It was the 'woman' who was kicking and punching," the dishwasher said. "The tall guy in the brown shirt was just trying to avoid her blows—but he wasn't fighting back.

"Finally, he grabbed at 'her' to stop her, I guess, and her wig got torn off."

The "woman" had run into the Take 5, screaming she was going to get a knife. When she came out empty-handed, a car had driven around the corner, evidently full of people she knew. She had yelled that she needed a knife and apparently someone in the car had handed one to her. "I didn't see her stab him," the witness said, "I looked away for just a second. When I looked back, the guy was looking down at himself and then he held out his hands toward the "woman" as if he was begging her to stop . . ."

While the witness watched, the person in the green pantsuit had hopped into the car and sped off. Everything had happened so fast. The young man had collapsed to the sidewalk and gone into convulsions, but the witness didn't know that Brad Bass had been stabbed. Something was wrong with him, so he had called to Ike Stone to get an aid car.

He was certain of one thing, however. The person the victim was fighting with wasn't a woman; he was a male in drag. The dishwasher was positive he would recognize him if he saw him again. The man who'd stabbed Bass had had a distinctive broken tooth. When he saw that, he would know.

It wasn't difficult to figure out what had happened. Brad Bass had thought that Jackie Emerson was a woman when she came up to his booth. In the dim lights of the restaurant, Jackie had looked very feminine. But in the bright street lights at the corner of Pike and 6th, he would have realized that Jackie was a male and backed away. Jackie Emerson had become enraged and started kicking and beating Brad. And Brad could not bring himself to strike a "lady," even when he knew she wasn't a female. He'd backed away and just stood there until Jackie got too rough. Finally, he pushed at "her" and dislodged her wig.

But this had only served to make Emerson more furious, and he'd borrowed a knife from the passing car when he couldn't get one inside. No more than two or three minutes had passed during the confrontation, but Brad Bass had been terribly wounded by one snakelike thrust of a filleting knife. Because there had been no blood loss, precious time was lost—time that might have saved Brad's life.

On February 25, the detectives were handed the name of another eyewitness to the assault. She was a twenty-year-old girl who made a rather precarious living by her wits. Her nickname was "Chi-Chi," but her real name was Barbara Palliser*. She reportedly worked as a cocktail waitress. Fonis and Sanford went to the club where she worked only to find that "Chi-Chi" had not shown up for work in three weeks. The manager gave them her last address. They found a listing for B. Palliser in the lobby of a run-down apartment house. She opened the door of her apartment only a crack, and wouldn't let the detectives in until they pushed their cards under the door.

"I saw it," she finally admitted. "I saw that guy get stabbed. I've been afraid to go to work ever since." Tearfully, she agreed to go to the homicide offices to make a statement.

"I went to the Take 5 at 2 A.M. to meet a friend," Barbara Palliser recalled. "I waited twenty minutes and she didn't show so I went to walk around and look for her. I still didn't find her, and I went back to the Take 5. I was standing just inside the front door when I saw a white male in his twenties and a black female impersonator just outside. It looked like he grabbed at her wig and pulled it off. 'She' grabbed it back and started swearing. They exchanged words, and 'she' threw her purse at someone and asked them to hold it. Then 'she' started fighting with him. The onlookers tried to tell them to take it easy. They calmed down and she took her purse back. Then the male grabbed her wig again, and the fight started again. She went inside to get a weapon. Then this car drove up. It looked like there were two black males and one black female—I'm not sure if she was a woman or not—inside. The two men tried to get this 'Jackie' in the car but she was really mad and stepped back and started fighting again. The man just kind of reached out toward her, and then he fell down. The car drove away fast with 'her' in it."

The girl known as "Chi-Chi" quickly selected the mug shot of Jonathan Emerson as the "woman" who had stabbed Brad Bass. She had no doubt at all that she was right.

Jonathan Emerson, aka "Jackie" Collins, aka Jacqueline Collins, aka "Jackie" Blackshire had been picked by too many witnesses not to believe that he was the killer of Brad Bass. The King County Prosecutor's Office filed second-degree murder charges against him on February 26, 1976.

But the charges were filed in absentia. "Jackie" Emerson had gone underground. A flyer describing the five-foot eight-inch, now 160-pound fugitive was sent to California, Oregon and British Columbia as well as Washington State. Jackie's disguises were perfect, and it was hard to tell *who* he would be next. The bulletin warned that Emerson would probably be dressed as a woman, wearing a wig, false eyelashes and makeup. "Suspect has needle tracks on both arms."

Every Seattle Police patrolman had been apprised of the urgency in locating "Jackie" Emerson at line-up briefings. The homicide detectives believed if he was still operating in Seattle, he would be spotted sooner or later—even if he didn't have a permanent address. It was ten minutes to three A.M. on March 7 when two first-watch patrolmen observed a woman walking in the 1400 block of E. Yesler Street, not far from police headquarters. She drew their attention because she was very tall and had exceptionally broad shoulders for a woman. She wore a tight green sweater, slacks, and a blue coat. As they studied her more closely they agreed that her billowing hair could only be a wig.

They pulled out the wanted bulletin on Jackie Emerson, and studied it with a flashlight.

"It's Jackie . . . No doubt about it."

Jonathan "Jackie" Emerson was arrested and advised of his rights before being transported to jail and booked. He refused to make any statements to detectives without the presence of his lawyer.

With Emerson safely in jail, detectives located the driver of the car who had picked Jackie up at the stabbing scene. The driver admitted that it was his knife that was used to kill Bass. He said he had met Jackie that morning, and he, too, had thought that he was a woman. He said the knife had been in his jacket pocket when he drove up but he denied giving it to Jackie. When he jumped into the car after the attack, the driver said he realized that it *was* his knife, and it had blood on it. He was lying. Witnesses saw him toss it to Jackie.

When Jonathan Emerson went on trial for the murder of Brad Bass, it took a while to get a jury. Prospective jurors viewed the defendant, who sat demurely beside "her" lawyer, as they were asked if they had prejudices or convictions that would make them unable to render a fair verdict. Many did. By Monday morning, May 24, 1976, four women and eight men and an alternate juror had been seated and the testimony began.

Senior Trial Deputy Jon Noll spoke for the prosecution, outlining an incredibly senseless and vicious crime and Brad Bass's state of living death. There would be an agonizing question—a question that brought to mind the Karen Ann Quinlan case. The defense would certainly question whether twenty-one-year-old Brad Lee Bass had died as a result of an attack by the defendant, or because life support systems had been turned off.

The first witness for the prosecution was Brad Bass's father, a man still wracked with grief over the inexplicable tragedy that had befallen his son. The agony of parents who have lost their children in a homicide is painful to observe, yet it is often necessary for them to go through the final ordeal of recalling their child's life for a jury.

"Jackie" Emerson sat impassively at his trial as the prosecution presented its case. His whole posture was feminine and demure. He tiptoed daintily along on his three-inch high-heeled sandals during morning and afternoon breaks, seemingly oblivious to the stares he drew from startled onlookers. Occasionally, he patted his luxuriant wig with his painted nails or nodded to his friends in the gallery.

During the extensive newspaper coverage of his trial, the two major Seattle papers could not agree on how to refer to him. One called him "him" and "he." The other referred to him as "her" and "she."

Wes Hohlbein, a prominent criminal defense attorney, did not deny that Jackie had stabbed Brad Bass, but suggested he had done so only because he had been in fear of his life. Jackie took the stand in his own defense and explained his lifestyle to the jury.

He said that he had been raised as a female child and had worn girls' clothes since the age of six. "All through life it has caused me difficulties but I can't be no other way," he explained.

As he had done for so many psychologists and psychiatrists, he detailed his plans for a sex change, and said he was taking female hormone treatments that made him feel more like a woman.

Emerson said he had lived in Seattle for about eight years, and had worked as a nurses' aide during part of that time, but admitted under cross-examination that he had been arrested "a lot of times" for prostitution and also had convictions for grand larceny and shoplifting.

Regarding the morning of Friday, February 13, Emerson testified that he had stopped at Larry's Take 5 at three A.M. to get food to take home and had met Brad Bass there for the first time. He said Bass had offered him $50 for an act of prostitution. He insisted that he never told Bass he was not a woman, and didn't know why Bass became angry at him. He said that, when they got outside, Brad accused him of stealing money from him in the past.

Jackie fluttered his eyelashes at the jury as he said he had only been trying to avoid trouble and that Brad Bass had pulled off his wig, kicked him in the groin, and threatened him with a knife. He said he'd gone back into the Take 5 to try to get a knife or some weapon to protect himself but the cook stopped him. He returned to the fight, and twisted the knife out of Bass's hand and "stuck it to him."

"I was scared," he testified huskily. "I was trying to defend myself. He was big. I was smaller than I am now," Emerson confided.

Jackie's testimony left gaping holes in the truth. His story that Brad Bass carried a knife differed from every other eyewitness's testimony, and from the testimony of Brad's father and brother, who had testified that Brad had never carried a knife in his life. And it differed a great deal from testimony that Brad Bass had tried to avoid a fight, had been reluctant to strike out at the enraged transvestite who was flailing at him.

It was very clear to those in the gallery that Jackie, a veteran of many mean streets and an expert at con games, had met a young man who was entirely out of his element. Only twenty-one, Brad Bass hadn't even been experienced enough to recognize who Jackie Emerson really was, or the danger he was courting unaware. When he *did* recognize that Jackie wasn't a woman at all, he had been disgusted and embarrassed and he'd wanted out. But Jackie wasn't willing to shrug his shoulders and let it go. He had gone into a screaming, kicking tizzy. He had been "insulted" and he wanted revenge. Tragically, he got it.

The jury spent fifteen hours in deliberation pondering the case. When they returned with their verdict, it was clear they hadn't believed Jackie's version of what had happened that Friday the 13th. They found him guilty. As the jury was polled, three of the four women jurors brushed tears away. Later, one of them burst into uncontrolled sobs in the corridor outside the courtroom.

Beyond the guilty second-degree murder finding, the jury found Jackie Emerson guilty of using a deadly weapon in the commission of his crime. In Washington State, that meant a mandatory five-year sentence in addition to the sentence meted out for the murder charge.

The question naturally arose: where was Jackie Emerson going to be incarcerated? In a men's prison or in Purdy, the Washington State facility for women? Jackie was neither fish nor fowl and a real puzzle for the Washington State Department of Corrections. Chuck Wright,

District Administrator for that department, was the man who had to deal with this hot-potato decision.

Wright gathered all of Jackie's records and studied the psychological profiles done earlier. He shook his head at the number of offenses and at the attempts to categorize a difficult subject. He could see the potential for problems. Jackie still had a complete complement of male equipment. How could he be put into a woman's prison? On the other hand, could Wright recommend that Jackie be sent to a male prison—where he might well cause a riot?

After talking to Jackie himself and recognizing the sociopathic traits he had seen over and over again in prisoners referred to him, Chuck Wright turned to forensic psychiatrists and psychologists for help in his decision. Jackie was a transvestite, certainly, but he was first and foremost a murderer—or murderess—depending on your viewpoint, and Wright wasn't taking any chances. He read Jackie's statement to the court about Brad Bass's murder many times, frowning at the lack of any compassion or insight there. "I'm sorry Bradley had to die," Jackie had written, "but he became a threat to me when he pulled a knife on me and attempted to kill me. I also suffered cuts and whip lashes [*sic*] from this on my hand. I don't feel guilty, but hate that my hand had to put a misorable [*sic*] man out of his missories [*sic*]."

One psychologist wrote after his examination of the peculiar prisoner, "Emerson fully identifies himself as a female . . . *Outline of Psychiatry* defines transsexualism as a deviancy where the person is physically normal but has a total aversion to his [or her] biological sex that dates from early childhood. Emerson began cross-dressing as a female at the age of six."

After reviewing Jackie's long psychological and criminal history, the doctor concluded, "Although well controlled most of the time, this individual is unable to tolerate frustration with respect to his sexual identity and has shown the propensity to react to the frustration with physical aggression . . . A history of deviancy such as evidenced by this individual would virtually preclude a sex change operation. For society's protection, commitment of Emerson to . . . the Mental Health Unit at Monroe for further observation and evaluation regarding placement [is indicated]."

A highly respected forensic psychiatrist talked to Jackie Emerson next. Even he had to remind himself that it was not a woman he was evaluating, but a man. "This individual appeared to be quite convincingly feminine. Had I no information about his identity prior to the interview, my first impression probably would have been that this individual was a woman. Upon entering the examination room at the jail, he appeared to be somewhat flirtatious and attracted comments and glances from other inmates. His skin appeared to be smooth and relatively free of hair. The more subtle mannerisms during the interview were convincingly feminine. There was no evidence of severe anxiety or depression. There was surprisingly minimal fear regarding the ultimate disposition, although he was quite persuasive in presenting himself as a female and requesting the women's prison."

The psychiatrist had to decide whether Jackie suffered from primary transsexualism or merely a variant of the disorder. If the first was considered, Jackie's active sex life as a *homosexual* made it doubtful. The doctor was more inclined to believe that Jackie had a secondary transsexual reaction. That is, that he was a homosexual with a long-standing cross-dressing fetish. There was no evidence that showed Jackie had any endocrine dysfunction. He was more likely to be a passive-role homosexual.

Such delineations might seem to be nit-picking. But they were vital when it came to selecting a prison for the man with the long eyelashes and sweet smile.

Jackie had been dumped by his male lover two years before Brad Bass was murdered, and the examining psychiatrist was convinced that his demands for a sex change operation had sprung from that rejection. "I think this is more of a transsexual reaction to severe rejection in a homosexual relationship," he wrote. "This reaction is chronic, severe, and needs to be observed under psychiatric supervision to determine where the client eventually stabilizes. For this reason, I recommend that [he] be observed for an extended period of time in the mental health unit at Monroe Reformatory."

He went on to surmise that—if Jackie turned out to be a true transsexual—he probably should be transferred to the women's prison at Purdy. If Jackie proved to be only a man in women's clothing, he probably should be kept in segregation at a male prison. "In no case," the psychiatrist wrote, "should this individual be integrated into the general population of either Purdy or the male institutions."

Whatever else Jackie Emerson might prove to be, he was clearly a man completely devoid of empathy or conscience. He had taken what he wanted all of his life, and Wright doubted that he would change. Armed with the suggestions of experts in deviant sexual behavior, Chuck Wright made his recommendation on July 14, 1976: "It is our recommendation that Mr. Jonathan Emerson be sentenced to the Department of Social and Health Services, and before he receives a specific institution, that he be evaluated at Monroe's Mental Health Unit."

Wright's counsel was sound. But apparently no one listened to him. In less than two years, Jackie Emerson was a fixture in the Washington State Penitentiary in Walla Walla, the state's largest prison for men. Although he could not wear his wigs and dresses in Walla Walla, Jackie managed to maintain his feminine persona with makeup, a velvet cap and sheer tank tops. He found a "husband," and the two shared a cell. One of about a dozen transvestites in Walla Walla, Jackie was the most popular, and charged other inmates $30 for his "favors." He had one protector after another, but, if he found himself in a tight situation, he used his own fists and muscles to fight back.

He no longer desired surgery, saying, "If God truly wanted me to be a female, he would have given me all the female equipment. I know I can be happy and loved without a sex change."

Jackie Emerson's sentence was akin to the old fable of Br'er Rabbit, who begged Farmer Brown not to "throw me in that cabbage patch," which was, of course, *exactly* where he wanted to be.

Jackie served a long sentence in Walla Walla, and returned to western Washington when he was paroled. Today, he is an aging prostitute, nearly fifty years old, who continues to get into penny-ante scrapes with the law. Nothing has really changed in Jackie's life, and the memory of a young man named Brad Bass is buried so deep in his consciousness that he scarcely recalls the rainy night in February twenty-three years ago.

Brad Bass would have been forty-four years old today. He left only a few bequests, but they still exist. The most important were the perfect kidneys and eyes he donated to help people he never knew. His father kept his 1957 Chevrolet pickup, testimony to the fact that Brad could do anything once he made up his mind to do it. What Brad might have accomplished with the rest of his life will never be known. He was fooled by an expert at disguise and he paid for it with his life.

The Killer Who Talked Too Much

"Show me a homicide where we don't pick up any meaningful physical evidence and I'll show you a 'loser,'" the Seattle police detective said vehemently. "It doesn't matter how much circumstantial evidence we have, or what our gut feelings are, or even how much probable cause we have to arrest. You still have to show a jury something they can see."

Although I have written articles and books about well over a thousand true crime cases, I have seen only a very few convictions on circumstantial evidence, and I know that detective was right. Homicide investigation has become a science involving physics, chemistry and ballistics, lie detector tests, computers, DNA, electronics and even laser beams. The world of television attorneys and their amazing courtroom coincidences is only fiction, after all. In real life, it's more difficult.

One classic example of the need for physical evidence in proving a murderer guilty occurred in the courtroom of King County Superior Court Judge Stanley C. Soderland during a four-week trial in October 1976. Have a seat in the front row of the jury and weigh the evidence in this incredible case. What would you have decided?

One of the most disheartening cases Seattle homicide detectives ever faced began on Wednesday morning, June 2, 1976. True, there were moments when everything seemed to be going their way, but their successes were soon blunted. In the end, they would win only a *half* a victory, but it was enough to lock up a murderer who was infinitely dangerous to beautiful dark-haired young women.

Marcia Perkins lived in a unit on one of the upper floors of an apartment house on East Madison Street in Seattle, close to the funky and exciting Broadway District and Seattle University, and near what was known as "Pill Hill," where many of the city's hospitals were located. Marcia was twenty-four, beautiful and raven-haired. She was slender and tall, and she looked a lot like Cher with her waist-length hair and miniskirts, so much so that she got a lot of double takes—which amused her.

Marcia was a nurse at the University of Washington Hospital; she was estranged from her husband and in the process of beginning a new life. For the moment, her husband had temporary custody of their children and she was on very good terms with him. It wasn't a bitter separation at all. In fact, they often dated. They had discovered that they got along better when they dated than they ever had when they were married.

Marcia had married very young, and, now, she didn't limit her dating to her estranged husband. She had other friends, but she was in no particular hurry to get a divorce or to marry again. She was enjoying some of the freedom she'd missed as a teenager. She suspected that she might end up back with her husband, but first she needed some time to breathe.

Marcia's husband attempted to reach her by phone many times over the Memorial Day weekend of May 29–30. At first, he'd gotten nothing but a busy signal; later, the phone had rung and rung and no one had answered. He hadn't been particularly concerned because Marcia had told him she might take a trip over the holiday, but by Wednesday morning he still hadn't found her home. He knew that she was supposed to be back in Seattle on Tuesday for her job at the hospital. He was beginning to feel a niggle of concern.

And so, on that Wednesday, he went to the apartment building where she lived before he headed to his own job. It was 7:30 in the morning when he knocked on the door of the manager's apartment. "I'm worried about Marcia," he said, trying not to be an alarmist. "I haven't been able to reach her—I'm a little afraid she might be sick, or—"

The manager nodded, and reached for his passkey. Marcia was a pretty predictable lady, and it *was* strange that she wasn't answering her phone. They knocked first, but got no answer. Still, they could hear a radio or television playing somewhere beyond the door. The manager put the key in the lock and turned it.

When the door swung open, and they stepped a few feet inside, they could see why Marcia hadn't answered her phone. She lay spread-eagled between the kitchen and living room of her usually neat apartment. There was no question at all that she was dead. The shocked men quickly backed out and ran to call Seattle police.

The two patrol officers who responded confirmed that Marcia was dead—and that it looked as if she had been for several days, lying alone in the hot apartment. Along with their sergeant, the officers secured the premises with yellow crime scene tape, and stood by until detectives from the Homicide Unit arrived at 8:30.

Detective Sergeant Don Cameron's crew—specifically Detectives Duane Homan and Benny DePalmo—were next up on call. They would do the crime scene search, a task that always took many hours as they gathered every possible bit of evidence they could find and photographed the scene. Ideally, they hoped to get to the scene of a murder as quickly as possible; time was their enemy. And, this time, they were running behind.

There was the faint odor of a death too long undiscovered in the apartment. Marcia Perkins lay just inside the entrance, her legs spread wide in the classic position of a rape victim. She wore only a short blue terry cloth robe and a bra, and both had been pushed up to her shoulders. Rigor mortis, the rigidity that comes soon after death, had come and departed, a natural process that took several days. They noted that there also was considerable skin slippage on the victim's body because decomposition had begun.

Marcia had suffered a beating, although she had obviously put up a terrific fight against her attacker. Dark purple abrasions marred her face, throat and left knee.

There were definite indications that she'd died of strangulation—manual strangulation—at the hands of a powerful killer. Her eyes showed the burst blood vessels (petechiae) that are characteristic of death from strangulation.

A pair of blue bikini panties lay crumpled in a nearby doorway, and oddly, a pair of women's shoes with both straps broken—as if the wearer had been lifted forcibly out of them—rested close to the panties.

The motive for Marcia Perkins's murder was apparent; she had clearly been the victim of a violent sexual attack. It would take an autopsy and laboratory tests to say whether rape had been committed.

There were signs in the apartment that seemed to say that Marcia had known her killer and had admitted him willingly to her home. Two cups with a teaspoon of instant coffee powder in them sat on the kitchen counter, and there was a pan of water on the stove, although the burner beneath was turned off. A partial bottle of rum sat on the counter. Since the kitchen was otherwise immaculate, it appeared that Marcia had been in the process of serving refreshments when someone had come up behind her, seized her boldly, and literally yanked her out of her shoes as the attack began.

Her killer had to have been a man possessed of tremendous strength. And cunning. The three homicide detectives noted that someone had made a concentrated effort to wipe away all traces of himself from the premises. There were no fingerprints on any of the smooth surfaces which ordinarily would be expected to reveal latent prints. Everything had been laboriously wiped clean. The killer had even swept up long strands of the victim's black hair into a dustpan, although he hadn't thrown them away. Maybe he'd realized there was nothing incriminating about the hair of a person who lived in this apartment. He had yanked the phone cord from the wall, although the phone was already off the hook.

All the drapes were tightly shut, closing the apartment off from the world outside, and the radio still played—loud enough to cover sounds in the apartment, but not loud enough to draw complaints from other tenants. It looked as if the killer had wanted to move around his victim's home unseen and unheard.

A woman's purse—probably Marcia's—had been dumped on the floor. There was no wallet or money inside. For some obscure reason, the bedding from the victim's bed was tangled on the living room floor. A steam iron and an empty Miller's beer can were caught inside the bedding.

Benny DePalmo checked the only bathroom, and found the sink spotless, with bottles of perfume undisturbed on its ledge. But he *did* find a man's ring on the counter behind the sink. That seemed strange; if the killer had gone to such efforts to wipe his presence away, why would he leave such a distinctive ring behind?

With so many questions, one thing was clear: Marcia Perkins had to have been been killed by someone she knew and trusted. The apartment house had an excellent security system. Marcia would have had to buzz open a downstairs lock to let anyone come up to her floor. Then, she had to let a visitor into the locked apartment itself. She was in her robe, and she had been preparing to serve coffee when she was attacked. A complete stranger wouldn't have been so obsessive in wiping away his fingerprints. The killer must have had reason to believe he would be questioned and printed, and so he had tried to make certain he couldn't be placed in her apartment near the time of her death.

But the investigators didn't know enough about Marcia Perkins at this point to speculate who that might have been. Her estranged husband was outside with the apartment manager, and he seemed to be genuinely grieving. Who else was there in Marcia's life whom she trusted enough to let into her apartment?

Duane Homan and Benny DePalmo attended the postmortem examination of Marcia Perkins. Their original supposition that she had died by manual strangulation had been correct: the cricoid cartilage was fractured and there were hemorrhages in the strap muscles on either side of her neck. There were no ligature marks that would have been left by a rope or noose, but there were bruises where fingers and thumbs had exerted intense pressure.

In addition, there were many, many scratches and lacerations on Marcia's body; she had fought her killer like a tiger. But she had lost. She *had* been brutally raped and sodomized, and there were tears and contusions in her genital organs. Purple teeth marks encircled her right nipple. Her killer had been a man of great strength and, certainly, possessed with terrible anger.

The medical examiner pointed to the right portion of the victim's forehead and explained, "This wound was administered with a blunt instrument. This was a stunning wound, but there is no fracture."

The two detectives headed out to interview Marcia's neighbors. Whoever had killed her had a running start. Even the time of death was not a certainty at this point, although it had been at least three days earlier. Along with Detectives Bill Baughman and George Marberg, they began a canvass of the apartment house where Marcia Perkins had lived and its twin adjacent building.

Some people seem to remember every strange noise or out-of-place person in their neighborhoods; others apparently go through life wearing earplugs and blinders. The quartet of investigators hoped to find the former.

The building next to Marcia's was occupied by patients or families of patients receiving cancer treatment at the nearby Fred Hutchinson Cancer Clinic. Because that was why they were in Seattle, many of the occupants were away from their apartments most of the daytime hours, and the detectives would have to check back several times to make contact with them. Also, a lot of people had taken advantage of the three-day holiday weekend and left town for Memorial Day.

But there *were* some illuminating statements coming from the victim's neighbors. The manager of Marcia's building remembered now that someone had buzzed his intercom between four and six o'clock on Saturday morning, May 29. "It woke me up," he said. "I answered and I talked to a man who sounded drunk. He asked for Marcia and I told him he'd made a mistake and to buzz the correct apartment."

The manager had been annoyed enough to stay on the intercom to listen in on the ensuing conversation, and he heard the man talking to Marcia. He was pleading very insistently to come in. "He was saying, 'Please, little sister, let me in.' "

"Did she buzz him up?" Bill Baughman asked.

"Not at first—but she finally agreed to unlock the door when the guy kept begging."

He had apparently stumbled up to her apartment. That is, the manager had heard some faltering steps clumping up the stairway, but he hadn't looked out to see who the man was.

The manager's apartment was just across the hall from Marcia's quarters, and he could have peeked out the door, but he wasn't that curious; he was sleepy and went back to bed. However, he told Marberg and Baughman that the occupants of the building next door would have been in a better spot to hear what went on in Marcia's apartment. "Their windows face the same breezeway as Marcia's. It's almost like being in the same room in the summer when the windows are open . . ."

And that proved to be true. One of the residents in the next-door building told the detectives she had heard a woman's voice in a "loud argument" about 6 A.M. "There were doors slamming and banging, all right," she recalled. "It went on for about three minutes." But she hadn't gone to the window and looked over into Marcia's apartment. This was a live-and-let-live neighborhood where people didn't poke their noses into their neighbors' business.

Still, one of the women who lived in Marcia's apartment house had also been been awakened on the morning of the 29th by someone at the intercom just outside the front door. It was practically under her bedroom window. She told the detectives that the man had first said he was the police. "But then he laughed, and I heard him say that he was Marcia's brother. I could hear him talking first to the manager and then to Marcia."

As it happened, a number of people who lived in the apartment buildings had seen a stranger about midnight on Friday night. One occupant recalled seeing a stocky man in a blue denim jacket and cap at the entrance to the building where Marcia lived. "He was pushing all the buttons trying to get in, but it looked to me as though nobody was buzzing him up."

The apartment manager said that Marcia Perkins had a number of visitors—men she dated or knew as friends, and a woman with three children who seemed to be a good friend. He thought Marcia was dating a quiet, well-mannered man on a regular basis, although he had not seen him at the apartment in the past week. He was not aware of any trouble between Marcia and her boyfriend, or anyone else for that matter. She was a good tenant.

On June 3, Detectives Benny DePalmo and Duane Homan got two interesting bits of information. The victim's grieving estranged husband called to report something that seemed a little strange to him. A man named Melvin Jones had dropped in on him at ten o'clock the previous night to discuss Marcia's murder. Jones had fervently denied any involvement in the pretty nurse's death. In fact, it seemed to her husband that he was almost protesting too much. He went to great pains to explain that he hadn't seen Marcia since Thursday, May 27, when he'd stopped by to pick up a stereo set that belonged to him. "He told me he hadn't stayed longer than fifteen minutes," the widower said. "He insisted on leaving me his phone number—just in case I needed him for anything."

Marcia's husband was quite sure that Melvin wasn't Marcia's boyfriend, at least not anyone she would have dated steadily. Rather, he thought he was a friend of Marcia's sister who had moved to Montana. He described Melvin as being a husky man, broad-shouldered and thick in the chest. He didn't know where he worked—or *if* he worked, for that matter.

On the heels of that interview, the apartment manager called detectives to say that a man had been by asking for Marcia. This struck him as eerie since her body had been removed the previous day, and she'd been dead for five. He told the man that Marcia had been murdered, and the man had left, driving a two-tone green General Motors car. Oddly, he hadn't seemed devastated or even shocked by the news. "I got the license number," the manager said, and handed over a scribbled note.

Homan and DePalmo quickly ran the plate numbers through the WASIC computer and found the car registered to a Ralph Ditty* with an address on Thirty-first Avenue in Seattle. More interesting was the fact that Ralph Ditty was a relative of Melvin Jones, and Jones lived at the same address. If Melvin Jones had known that Marcia was dead at 10 P.M. on June 2, then why was his relative looking for her on June 3? Maybe he'd come by to check because he didn't believe Melvin when he told him.

Melvin Jones came into the Homicide Unit later that day. He was a huge, muscular man, but he had a very young face, handsome and soft. He seemed earnest when he said he'd be glad to give a statement about his friendship with Marcia Perkins. He said that he had lived with Marcia and her sister from the previous October until February. But he pointed out that it was her sister—not Marcia—with whom he'd been romantically involved. When her sister decided to move to Montana, Marcia took an apartment by herself. He stressed that his breakup with the sister was friendly, and that he and Marcia were buddies, still. He had no idea who might have wanted to harm her.

Jones said he last had seen the victim on May 26—a day earlier than he had told her husband—when he went to her apartment to retrieve a stereo set which belonged to him. He said he had learned of her murder on June 2 when her sister called him from Montana to tell him. He said he didn't know anything about his own cousin's visit to the apartment house. "He wouldn't have had a reason to go over there asking questions," Melvin said, puzzled.

The investigators studied Melvin Jones. He was a big man, six feet three or more, and he easily topped 230 pounds. He was a good-looking man, with an easy-going manner despite the tragedy to his friend. When they commented on his size, he smiled and said he'd been working out with the Seattle Seahawks during spring training for the professional football team, although he wasn't yet officially on the squad. "Needed a tackling dummy, I guess," he said.

Although they didn't say it out loud, the homicide detectives were both thinking the same thing: a man that big and powerful could easily have subdued Marcia Perkins and crushed her throat. He could have lifted her right out of her shoes with one hand. But that wasn't enough to arrest him. There were thousands of other big, strong men in Seattle.

A look at Melvin Jones's rap sheet, however, did little to quell their gut feelings. Melvin had been convicted of Indecent Liberties in 1969 and sentenced to the state prison at Monroe for six years. That might well mean he was still obsessed with violent sex. On the other hand, it also could explain why he might be apprehensive about being accused of Marcia's murder. He had served his time for the first offense, and so far he was clean.

But Melvin Jones seemed to have a problem with alcohol. The day after his interview with the police, he called Marcia's husband, and he was obviously drunk. "He told me that he wasn't the one who killed Marcia," her husband told the detectives. "And he said he didn't want anyone to hang the rap on him."

Since no one was trying to hang a rap on him at the moment, the investigators thought Melvin was getting awfully skittish—especially for an innocent man. But they weren't going to get any help from the man's ring found on the sink in Marcia's bathroom. "It's mine," her husband said. "I left it there a long time ago. Just forgot to get it back."

That made sense, considering that the sink bore no traces of blood either in the bowl or the trap; the killer would surely have had to clean up after the murder, but he hadn't done it there.

On June 5, DePalmo and Homan talked to Melvin's cousin and asked him how he had happened to be asking for Marcia. He told them that he had been to her apartment house about midnight on Saturday night, but that no one would buzz the door to let him in. Then he'd called her repeatedly, but the phone was always busy. He had gone so far as to call the operator—who had told him that Marcia's phone was off the hook. He had worried about it sporadically, until he finally went back on June 3 and learned from the manager in the apartment house that Marcia had been murdered.

Asked if he were in the habit of seeing Marcia often, Ditty said he wasn't. "I guess I hadn't seen her for about two months. I just suddenly thought of her and dropped by at midnight."

Now they either had one man who had been back

twice on one night to try to get into Marcia Perkins's apartment, or two *different* men who had called on her between midnight and six A.M. on the Friday night/Saturday morning she had probably been murdered. Marcia was alive between four and six; the manager had listened in to the intercom and heard her voice. Ralph Ditty, Melvin Jones's cousin, seemed sincere and volunteered to take a lie detector test if the detectives wanted him to do so. They did, and made an appointment with him for just that.

They also had an estranged husband who seemed remarkably understanding about his legal wife's boyfriends, but he seemed to be in genuine mourning and he was very open with the detectives. But most of all, he had a solid alibi for the early morning hours of May 29. He had been home taking care of their children. He told them what he had been able to put together about Marcia's last "steady" boyfriend, whose name was Chuck Lyons.* He said that Lyons didn't drink at all. He was a teetotaler whose main interest—beyond Marcia— was in cars. In fact, Lyons owned four, one a black Lincoln. Marcia had been fond of Lyons, according to her husband, but she had vacillated about her future with the car buff. "She thought he had no plans and no purpose in life," her husband said, "and they didn't have much in common. Marcia worked hard but she liked to party." He described Lyons as being too much of a straight arrow for Marcia, even though he was very attracted to her.

But still, questions arose. If Chuck Lyons thought so much of Marcia, why hadn't he come around to see her? Why hadn't he gone to her funeral? That didn't make sense. The woman had been dead for a week, and no one knew if Lyons even knew it.

None of the people the Seattle detectives talked to knew where Chuck Lyons lived, although the detectives were told that one of his relatives was supposed to own a barber shop on Rainier Avenue South. Homan and DePalmo went there and found the shop closed. Marcia's husband was at a loss to help the investigators until he remembered a letter that Marcia had written to him. "You know," he said, "she talked about Lyons in that letter, and she said that she and Lyons would like to have a baby boy and name him 'Beaufort Charles Lyons, Jr.' "

While the name "Chuck Lyons" had sparked no information on the police computers, the name "Beaufort Charles Lyons" did. Homan and DePalmo found a man by that name who owned a classic 1962 black Lincoln, among other cars, and worked at a Seattle marina. The detective partners walked along the bobbing docks of the marina until they found Chuck Lyons's boss.

"Chuck was off over the three-day weekend, starting the 29th," the man said. "But he came back to work on June 1st, and he's been here regular ever since." Lyons was not, however, working the present shift, so they asked that he call police headquarters when he appeared.

When "Chuck" Lyons showed up for work, he called DePalmo immediately, his voice edgy, having gotten a message from the Homicide Unit. He clearly had no idea why they were calling him. When Benny DePalmo told him that Marcia was dead, he gasped, "Oh no!" and seemed to be stunned. He asked how she had died and, when he was told that she had been murdered, he said he would be in to talk to detectives right away.

This was the fourth male who had been closely linked to Marcia Perkins—her ex-husband, Melvin, Melvin's cousin—and now, Chuck Lyons. All of them sounded seriously upset and shocked. Chuck was as good as his word and walked into the fifth floor Homicide Unit within half an hour. To the trained eye of the detectives, he seemed to be barely fighting back tears.

"I haven't seen Marcia since about 9 P.M. on the Wednesday before Memorial Day," he said softly. "I didn't even try to call her over the weekend because she said she'd probably be going to Montana to see her sister. Then when I tried to call on Tuesday and Wednesday [June first and second], the phone just kept ringing on and on. I figured she was still in Montana or on the way back."

"You didn't read about it in the paper?" Homan asked him.

"Nope. Haven't read the paper, or even caught the TV news, I guess. All this time, she's been dead—I didn't go to her funeral. I didn't even know she was dead," he said brokenly.

They talked to Chuck Lyons about people in Marcia Perkins's life. He said he knew Melvin Jones, but only as an acquaintance. He remembered, however, that Melvin had already picked up his stereo set by Wednesday night, May 26. He wouldn't have been coming by to get it on the Friday before Memorial Day, since he didn't have any other belongings at Marcia's.

Some homicide cases have too few suspects, and this one was floundering because there were so *many* suspects. Still another one surfaced when an attorney friend told Duane Homan that Marcia Perkins had been the object of another man's obsession. Marcia worked at the University of Washington Hospital, and there had been a patient there who was convinced that he was having an affair with her. He talked on and on about Marcia. The patient, who was a prisoner at the Monroe Reformatory, was in the hospital because he'd been stabbed in the back in a prison fight. He was partially paralyzed.

"He's a little weird," the lawyer said, "and this affair was all in his head, but I thought you ought to know."

It wasn't out of the realm of possibilities that a man, slightly deranged, should have been in love with his beautiful nurse. Stalkers have hounded women literally to their deaths because of imagined romantic connections. Had the prisoner somehow found where Marcia lived and gone to her apartment, begged to be let in, and then turned violent when she offered him no more than a cup of coffee? It sounded plausible until Homan and DePalmo found that the prisoner had been back in the reformatory by the Memorial Day weekend, and every minute there was accounted for.

Marcia's sister, who had flown to Seattle for her funeral, had the most vital information. She told the detectives about her relationship with Melvin Jones. He had once been her boyfriend, and the three of them—herself, Melvin, and Marcia—had indeed lived together. "He used to call Marcia 'Sister Dear,' and I know he'd been coming around to see her," she said. "When I talked to her by phone from Montana on Wednesday night [May 26] she said, 'That damn Melvin is here again.' I told her just not to let him in, and we continued to talk."

Marcia had apparently been having trouble with Melvin Jones. She told her sister that he'd come by her apartment four days earlier at three in the morning. "She said he was really drunk and he was pressing the call buttons to her apartment. She didn't let him in because he sounded so drunk."

"What does Melvin drink?" Benny DePalmo asked.

"Bacardi rum and Miller beer. He does weird things when he's drunk."

"Was he involved with Marcia?"

She shook her head. "No. *No.* He never had a physical relationship with Marcia. He always considered her his 'sister.' "

Sister was the word they were looking for. Melvin Jones was emerging as the investigators' best suspect. The man who had buzzed Marcia's apartment the morning she was killed had referred to her as "Little Sister." And the liquor found at the crime scene was a bottle of Bacardi rum and a can of Miller High Life beer. The detectives knew now that Melvin had tried before to gain entrance to Marcia's apartment during the wee hours of the morning when he was drunk. It seemed now that she had probably given in to his pleas—and with tragic consequences—on May 29. The only thing they really needed now was some direct physical evidence that would tie Jones to the murder scene.

If only the apartment manager had opened his door that morning to get a look at the man who stumbled toward Marcia's door. But he hadn't—and it looked as though the only eyewitness was dead.

Benny DePalmo learned one more thing about the unknown killer when he talked with officials at the telephone company. Marcia's phone had been busy when friends called during the first hours after her murder. That would have happened if it were simply off the hook. But he had witnesses who said it had rung normally later that morning and no one answered. Phone technicians said that could only have occurred if the cord was yanked from the phone itself or from the wall. Obviously, someone either had waited for hours beside Marcia's dead body and yanked the wire as he left, or returned later to do it. DePalmo suspected that someone had returned to her apartment to clean it up several hours after the murder.

But now Melvin Jones suddenly became elusive. He could not be found for further questioning. Days later, when the investigators finally located him, he was even more confident and self-assured than he had been when he talked to them the first time. He explained that he had spent the evening of May 28 (Friday) at a party at the University of Washington with a friend and the friend's girlfriend, a pretty American Indian girl named Jeanie Easley. He had drunk a great deal of rum, he said, and returned home long after midnight.

"Ralph woke me up," he said. "He wanted to know Marcia's telephone number." Melvin said he would be happy to take a polygraph test to verify his movements at the time Marcia was murdered. Ralph Ditty took the polygraph test first, on June 14. He passed, although he appeared nervous on questions having to do with any possible guilt on the part of Melvin Jones. Detectives thought perhaps Melvin had told Ralph that Marcia was dead and Ralph had gone to her apartment on Saturday night and again the following Wednesday to assure himself that Marcia's murder was not an alcoholic dream on Melvin's part.

Jones himself had so little response to the lie detector leads that they might as well have been hooked up to a hollow log. All the polygrapher got were horizontal lines across the tracing paper. Melvin apologized. Without thinking, he had taken a drug to ease the pain of his bad back. That explained it. The drug he'd taken would effectively blunt responses enough to render polygraph readings useless.

Melvin denied that he'd ever had sex with Marcia or that he'd killed her. He did admit going to her apartment before six o'clock on the morning of May 29 after leaving Jeanie Easley's apartment, but he said Marcia wouldn't let him in, so he'd gone home. With every questioning session, his answers changed slightly, but he was adamant that he would never hurt a hair on Marcia Perkins's head.

The friend who had gone to the dorm party with Melvin and his date, Jeanie, verified that Melvin had spent the entire evening with them at the party, and that Jones had left them sometime very, very early in the morning of May 29. Melvin had been so intoxicated that he'd passed out in Jeanie's apartment. "Jeanie and I had to prod Melvin to get him to wake up and ready to leave her place," he said.

By this time Duane Homan and Benny DePalmo had worked eighteen-hour days on the homicide investigation for two weeks, and all they had been able to do was eliminate one suspect after another. Most of the also-rans had started out looking promising. They had a gut feeling about Melvin Jones, but they had not one shred of physical evidence placing him at the scene of Marcia Perkins's death. It was not from lack of trying, or skill: the detective partners had an enviable reputation as meticulous crime scene investigators, but someone had been clever enough to erase the very things they needed for an arrest.

Six days later, Seattle homicide detectives were called out on another sexually motivated murder. The name of the victim would shock even them.

At 4:33 P.M. on Tuesday, June 22, a worried woman had knocked on the door of her daughter's apartment on

Bellevue Avenue East. She hadn't heard from her since the weekend, which was unusual. Her twenty-one-year-old daughter was employed at the Seattle Indian Center as an Emergency Assistance adviser but, when her mother had called her there earlier, she learned that her daughter hadn't come to work that morning, nor had she called to say she was sick. The young woman was a very dependable employee who never failed to report in before.

Her daughter's name was Jeanie Easley.

When no one responded to her knocks, Jeanie's mother looked toward the front windows. She saw that the drapes on Jeanie's apartment were still drawn. Jeanie only kept her drapes closed at night. She pounded again on the door, but no one answered. Always careful about invading her daughter's privacy, her concern now overrode any hesitancy to intrude. She tried the door and found to her surprise that it wasn't locked. She walked into the foyer.

A horrendous sight greeted her, something no mother should ever have to see. Jeanie lay spread-eagled in the living room which was littered by the debris and the dirt from crushed and broken plants and pots. It looked as if a tremendous struggle had taken place. A mammoth split-leaf philodendron barely covered the girl's near-naked body. Without any real hope, her mother felt for a pulse and found none; the skin on Jeanie's wrist was cold to her touch. Her mother knew she had been dead for a long time. She walked leadenly to the phone.

Detective Sergeant Jerry Yates and Detectives Baughman and Marberg sped at once to the scene, a scene that would prove to be sadly familiar to them.

The lovely Indian girl was nude except for a pink

bathrobe and a torn bra pushed up around her neck. Her apartment was in utter chaos: clothing had been dumped on the floor, food was mixed in with the garments, drawers stood open, and Indian jewelry and crafts were scattered around in piles. It was as if someone had torn through the apartment looking for treasure, heedless of the disorder he created as he raged. Even as the detectives surveyed the damage, a radio still played loudly and jarringly. The scene was very like that in Marcia Perkins's apartment twenty days earlier.

Jeanie Easley had had a lovely face and figure; now her skin was marred by bruises and scratches and there were vicious marks around her neck where her robe's belt had been tightened. Despite the disarray in Jeanie's apartment, it was apparent that the place had been kept spotlessly clean. There was no dust, kitchen appliances gleamed and all the white walls were sparkling—except for the east wall where the detectives saw two discernible hand prints. A palm print to a homicide detective is like a glint of gold to a Forty-Niner; Tim Taylor, a forensic technician from the Latent Prints Section, took careful precautions to preserve the two hand marks that seemed so out of place on the clean wall.

Jeanie Easley had either been about to eat or to serve someone else when she was killed; two cooked hamburger patties rested in their congealed grease on a plate on the kitchen counter.

While Billy Baughman sketched the apartment, George Marberg took dozens of photographs. Then Jeanie Easley's hands were encased in plastic to protect any evidence that might still cling beneath her fingernails, and her body was removed by King County deputy medical examiners to await autopsy.

They saved the dirt from the uprooted plants, too; there was a good chance some of it still clung to the killer's clothes or shoes.

The similarities between the murder of Jeanie Easley and that of Marcia Perkins fairly shouted for attention: both victims were young, attractive women, both had worn robes that were pulled up around their shoulders, both had been strangled and beaten, and both women had been left staged in the classic rape position of widespread legs. Each of the women had been left close to the front door of her apartment, and both of the apartments had been ransacked and the victims' wallets stolen.

Also telling was the indication that Marcia Perkins and Jeanie Easley had been preparing food or coffee for a guest: two cups with instant coffee for Marcia, and the two hamburger patties for Jeanie. They had lived in close proximity to one another, their drapes had been drawn, and in each case the radio had been left on at high volume.

Melvin Jones had known both young women. It was more than a grotesque coincidence that Jeanie, the second murder victim, had been Melvin's alibi for the night Marcia was killed. It was Jeanie's apartment where Melvin was seen last—inebriated and drowsy—after the party at the University of Washington on the final night of Marcia's life.

The viciousness of the attack on Jeanie Easley was noted during the autopsy on her body. She was slender, five feet, six inches, and weighed 125 pounds, but someone far stronger than she had beaten her so severely that a dental bridge was lodged far down in her throat. Like Marcia, Jeanie had been raped and sodomized.

Jeanie Easley's death was a great loss to her family and friends. They described her as a tireless worker for good, a young woman obsessed with bettering the life of her people. Beyond her work in the Emergency Assistance Program at the Indian Center, she had made weekly trips to the Monroe Reformatory to try to help Indian prisoners prepare themselves for the world outside when they were paroled. Her apartment reflected her pride in her heritage and her desire to overcome the oppression that Indians sometimes encountered. Posters, calendars and pictures of Indian leaders decorated her walls; one reading "The Earth and Myself Are of One Mind" depicted an heroic ancestor.

Jeanie had had a green thumb, too, and her apartment had been full of plants. It was ironic that her killer should have chosen to drape her body with the plant of which she'd been proudest. It was a new acquisition, according to her mother, who had given her the split-leaf philodendron a week before—on June 15.

Her mother told detectives that she had seen Jeanie last on Sunday, June 20, when she had driven her daughter home after a visit, a regular weekend routine. Her boyfriend, Linc Kitsap*, told Detectives Ted Fonis and Dick Sanford (who had taken over primary responsibility for the Easley case) that he last saw Jeanie on Monday night at five o'clock when he'd driven her home from work. As he dropped her off, he'd noticed a tall man who looked to be about twenty-five to thirty waiting near the front of her building. Jeanie had not spoken to the man, or even acted as if she knew him. She had just gone quickly into her apartment.

Kitsap said Jeanie had no enemies. The whole concept seemed alien when he thought of Jeanie; everybody loved her. She was a very careful woman, he said, and she'd always kept her doors locked. "She wouldn't let anyone in unless she checked to see who it was first," he said quietly.

"You have a key to her apartment?" Sanford asked.

The young man shook his head. "Her mother's the only one who has a duplicate key."

Everyone from Jeanie's boyfriend to her landlord attested to her meticulous housekeeping. "She was the type who picked up an ashtray as soon as you finished a cigarette and took it to the kitchen and washed it," Kitsap recalled. The detectives asked him what the apartment had looked like the last time he had been inside—on Sunday morning.

"Were the walls clean?"

"Always."

"You didn't see any hand prints on the walls?"

He looked surprised. Hand prints? He was sure he would have recalled if there had been any hand prints on the wall then. "Jeanie wouldn't have allowed it," he said. "There was nothing on that wall but a mirror, two posters, a macrame hanging—no stains of any kind."

As they had in the Perkins case, the Seattle police investigators began a canvass of neighbors. A man in the apartment directly above Jeanie's quarters told Sanford that something roused him from his sleep very early in the morning of June 22. Between 1:20 to 1:30 A.M., two short screams for help had burst through his dreams. "I thought they'd come from the street, but when I looked out my window, I didn't see anyone out there. I listened, but everything was quiet, and I finally went back to bed."

The couple who shared an adjoining wall with Jeanie's

apartment had heard nothing at all during the night of June 21–22.

Two young men came forward and told the police that they had spent several hours visiting with Jeanie on Monday night, June 21. It was the first day of summer, and the longest day of the year and, in Seattle, that meant it was light until well past ten. Lots of people in the Broadway and University districts were out that Monday night, visiting.

Detective Dick Reed interviewed the men who volunteered the information about being with Jeanie on Monday night. They told Reed that they had dropped in around 7:30 and had stayed until 10:30 or 11. Jeanie was busy around her apartment, talking to them while she cleaned. She told them she planned to leave on her vacation in a few days, and wanted to leave her place clean so it would be nice to come back to. She had also confided in them about a man she was "afraid" of. He wasn't a complete stranger, she said, but she didn't know his name.

"She said, 'I told him not to come back again,' " the men told Reed, but she hadn't gone into any more detail than that. No one had knocked on her door while they were there and Jeanie had no phone, so there were no calls.

A coworker at the Indian Center came up with a suspect's name and a possible motive. He said that Jeanie had been instrumental in catching and convicting an obscene phone caller who had plagued the Center in January and February of 1976. He explained, "Jeanie kept the guy on the line for half an hour and he was trapped. She testified in court against him."

The investigators checked and found that the man had

been convicted of making obscene calls on the basis of Jeanie's testimony, but he was reported to have left the Seattle area.

All of the detectives involved in the two murder investigations met to discuss the many commonalities in the two cases, *and* the fact that Melvin Jones's name kept surfacing in each. Both Jeanie and Marcia had had very full social lives and many admirers, but at length, the investigators had eliminated every possible suspect *except* the husky ex-convict.

Jeanie Easley's friend, the man who had brought Melvin along to the dorm party on May 28, was interviewed again. Although he worked with Melvin at an upholstery company, he said they had met originally at the Monroe Reformatory. They asked him about Melvin's mood during the first part of June, and the man recalled that Melvin had been at work regularly the week after Marcia Perkins died. "He mentioned once that he had to take a polygraph because he had some friend who died," the man said. "But it didn't seem like he was upset about it or anything."

"Melvin ever talk about wanting to date Jeanie, or about going to see her after you all went to the party together?" Sanford asked.

"No, not that I can remember. He never said anything about her after that night."

While the circumstantial evidence was pointing more and more at Melvin Jones, technicians and criminalists at the Washington State Crime Lab were evaluating evidence. There was nothing from Marcia Perkins's apartment. The scene had just been too clean. But the investigators were excited when Tim Taylor called with the news that he had "made" Melvin Jones's palm prints.

"Those are his prints on the wall of Jeanie Easley's apartment."

It was enough probable cause for an arrest.

Ten minutes later, Duane Homan and Benny DePalmo pulled up in front of the home where Melvin Jones lived with relatives. He was outside working on his car, and he squinted at them as he wiped grease from his hands. He agreed to accompany the detectives to headquarters, but he did not seem unduly alarmed. When informed of his rights and told they wanted to discuss the case with him, Jones asked, *"Which* case?"

"Marcia Perkins. What about that party you went to on the 28th?" De Palmo asked.

Jones seemed to relax even more, as he told them about going to the party with Jeanie Easley and her friend, and then going back to Jeanie's place, "You know, the one—the girl—that got did in," he added. For the first time, Melvin looked away from DePalmo and Homan.

"How did you find out about that?" Homan asked.

"One of my cousins read about it in the paper and told me."

Melvin Jones suddenly realized that he had become a suspect in both murders, and he sat in his chair a little less easily. When Benny DePalmo reminded him that he'd often referred to Marcia Perkins as "Sister" and "Little Sister," he acknowledged that was true, but he became very nervous when he was told that the building manager and other witnesses had heard the last visitor to see her alive use those words over the intercom. He continued to deny that he had any involvement with Marcia's death, even though he seemed at the point of tears.

"We made your print on Jeanie Easley's wall," DePalmo said quietly.

And now, the hulking man suddenly broke into real sobs, but he insisted he had no guilty knowledge in either case. "I already told you I was in her apartment once," he said. "I already told you I went to Jeanie's place that once."

"Where were you on June 21st?" Homan asked.

Jones said that he'd gone to Moses Lake with his girlfriend on a fishing trip over the weekend of June 19 and 20. "We must have got back about a quarter after four on Monday afternoon. I dropped off some of my relatives, and then I went to my friends' house to give them some fish. They weren't home—so I went to some other friend's house."

Melvin had the time period carefully accounted for. He said he'd stayed at his friend's for about two hours. Then he'd picked up his girlfriend and driven her to the house where she babysat.

"I had some sherry," he continued, "and arrived home about one to one-fifteen A.M. I went to bed. I haven't seen Jeanie since the night of May 28th and 29th."

Melvin's relatives had already told the detectives that he got home at 2 A.M. on June 21.

"We know you got home about an hour later than that," Homan said. "And Jeanie's boyfriend picked out your mug shot from a lay-down. He says you're the man he saw hanging around Jeanie's apartment about five on that Monday afternoon."

It was odd to see a man big enough to scrimmage with the Seattle Seahawks and walk away without a scratch reduced to tears, but something was scaring Melvin Jones. He didn't have an answer to Homan's comments; he only cried harder.

Homan and DePalmo backed off and allowed their suspect time to calm down. When Melvin stopped sobbing, they asked him to go over his recall of the vital Sunday and Monday again. But his responses were exactly the same. He could not have been the one who killed Jeanie Easley; he was fishing or with his friends and family the whole time.

Benny DePalmo asked him if he remembered Jeanie Easley's apartment well enough to draw a sketch of it that would show how she had arranged her furniture. It appeared that the questions would stop for a while, and Melvin was almost relieved to pick up a pencil and the pad of paper. He proved to be quite adept at drawing, and he slid his rendition of the apartment toward the detectives.

They saw that he had placed every piece of furniture, every appliance properly. That surprised them since both Melvin and Jeanie's friend said that he was "passing out" drunk when he was in Jeanie's apartment on May 28.

But Melvin made one fatal error in his floor plan.

He had drawn in the split-leaf philodendron in its pot and a second large plant. Neither of those plants had been in Jeanie's apartment until June 15. If Melvin had never had gone back to see Jeanie in her apartment after May 28, how could he know about those two new plants her mother had given her only a week before she died?

When Homan told Melvin that the two plants had been recent gifts to Jeanie, he stonewalled, insisting that they had been there before. Only they hadn't been; Jeanie's mother was positive of that.

Melvin Jones was placed under arrest for suspicion of both homicides and booked into the King County Jail.

On June 24, detectives armed with a search warrant removed plaid pants, a green T-shirt and a pair of tennis shoes from Melvin Jones's bedroom. They noted that there were multicolored fibers still clinging to the treads of the shoes.

Chesterine Cwiklik is a criminalist whose speciality is hairs and fibers. With a spinarette to draw those fibers into the thinnest possible thread and scanning electron microscopes, there is little that Chesterine cannot determine about their origin. In the crime lab, she compared known samples of fibers from the murder scenes to those found on Melvin's shoes. She was able to match fibers from the living room and kitchen carpets in Jeanie Easley's apartment microscopically to the filaments that Melvin had carried away on his shoes. Chesterine also found that fibers in the weave of his plaid pants were identical to those retrieved from Jeanie's living room rug.

Every criminal takes something of the crime scene away with him—no matter how minute, just as every criminal leaves something of himself at the crime scene—no matter how minute. It is the oldest axiom of crime scene investigation, but not one that most killers think about. Melvin Jones had taken a plethora of infinitesimal bits of his victim's home away from her murder scene without knowing it.

Even the soil from Jeanie's beloved plants had lodged in his shoes. Dirt may look like only dirt, but the components there, too, can be matched to one source.

Melvin Jones was in a panic, but he continued to insist that he was innocent. Now, he switched to another story of where he had been the night Jeanie Easley died. Taking the lesser of two felonies, he recalled that he had been out stealing tires on June 21–22.

He took another lie-detector test, and polygraphist Norman Matzke reported that he had given deceptive responses on several questions. The pens had moved in wide arcs on the questions, "Did you kill Jeanie Easley?" "Did you have intercourse with her?" and "Was she alive the last time you saw her?"

Matzke reported, "His responses went right off the page. He blew ink all over the walls."

Although the similarities between the murder scenes of Marcia Perkins and Jeanie Easley were numerous, there was a basic difference, and that was essential. There was direct physical evidence in the latter case, but in Marcia's murder, there was only circumstantial evidence. In Jeanie's murder, the homicide detectives were able to take two palm print matches, a half dozen minute rug fibers, and a bit of potting soil to the King County Prosecutor's office. In a court of law, the differences were magnified a thousand-fold. The jury could *see* the defendant's connection to Jeanie's apartment, even if they had to see it through a magnifying glass. With Marcia, they had to weigh a preponderance of circumstantial evidence.

During Melvin Jones's month-long trial, Senior Deputy Prosecutor Roy Howson gave the jury a crash course in understanding hair and fiber evidence and on the makeup of potting soil. He outlined the multiple connections between Marcia Perkins and Melvin Jones, and the similarities between the two women's murders. Juxtaposed that way, the commonalities in the M.O. used in the murders was like something from a serial killer's game plan. But no one could tell how the jurors were thinking. They listened to all the evidence and all the arguments intently. On October 26, almost exactly five months after Marcia Perkins's murder, four since Jeanie Easley's, they retired to ponder their verdicts.

The principals in the case didn't have to wait long. After five hours, the jurors signaled that they had agreed on a verdict. When they returned to the courtroom, the foreman announced that they had found Melvin E. Jones guilty of first degree murder in the death of Jeanie Easley. But they had found him not guilty in the death of Marcia Perkins.

Later, jurors said that they could not come back with a guilty verdict in Marcia's case because of the lack of physical evidence in her apartment. Although the Seattle detective team was disappointed in the second verdict, they weren't surprised; they knew all too well the weight a tiny bit of direct physical evidence can carry.

Melvin Jones hadn't yet reached his twenty-sixth birthday, but he already had one prison sentence and a parole violation behind him. Now, his hopes to play professional football were gone. He was sentenced to life in prison for Jeanie Easley's murder. He is currently incarcerated in the Washington State Reformatory in Monroe. His maximum sentence is still life, but his early release date is June 5, 2000.

Marcia Perkins's patients missed her for a long time, and those who knew Jeanie Easley know that her death took away a woman who would have been a strong positive force in the Indian Nation. Neither of them knew the danger that waited outside their apartment door long after midnight on a fragrant spring night.